*Imagine That*

# *Imagine That*

## Developing Critical Thinking and Critical Viewing Through Children's Literature

### *David M. Considine*
### *Gail E. Haley*
### *Lyn Ellen Lacy*

1994

**TEACHER IDEAS PRESS**
**A Division of**
**Libraries Unlimited, Inc.**
**Englewood, Colorado**

Copyright © 1994 David M. Considine, Gail E. Haley, Lyn Ellen Lacy
All Rights Reserved
Printed in the United States of America

No part of this publication may be reproduced, stored in a retrieval system, or transmitted, in any form or by any means, electronic, mechanical, photocopying, recording, or otherwise, without the prior written permission of the publisher. An exception is made for individual library media specialists and teachers, who may make copies of activity sheets for classroom use in a single school. Other portions of the book (up to 15 pages) may be copied for in-service programs or other educational programs in a single school.

TEACHER IDEAS PRESS
A Division of Libraries Unlimited, Inc.
P.O. Box 6633
Englewood, CO 80155-6633
1-800-237-6124

---

**Library of Congress Cataloging-in-Publication Data**

Considine, David M., 1950-
   Imagine that : developing critical thinking and critical viewing
through children's literature / David M. Considine, Gail E. Haley,
Lyn Ellen Lacy.
    xx, 207 p.  22x28 cm.
   Includes bibliographical references and index.
   ISBN 1-56308-145-8
   1. Children's literature--History and criticism.  2. Children's
literature--Illustrations.  3. Critical thinking.  4. Art
appreciation.  I. Haley, Gail E.  II. Lacy, Lyn Ellen.  III. Title.
PN1009.A1C647  1994
302.23'2--dc20                                                  94-20259
                                                                     CIP

Considine/Haley/Lacy, *Imagine That: Developing Critical Thinking and Critical Viewing Through Children's Literature*

Errata Sheet, page 163

Note: Thanks and appreciation is extended to Beverly Slapin and Doris Seale for the inspiration for the ideas on this page. Their model and ideas were adapted from: Beverly Slapin and Doris Seale, eds. *Through Indian Eyes: The Native Experience in Books for Children.* Philadelphia, PA: New Society Publishers, 1992.

*In memory of my teacher, Charles Smith. [GEH]*

*For my mother, who introduced me to Noddy and the Folk of the Far Away Tree and let me dream. [DMC]*

*For Dave Gatewood and grandbaby Jasmine, who have so many wonderful books ahead to share. [LEL]*

> Pictures invite the eye not to rush along, but to rest a while and dwell with them in enjoyment of their revelation.
>
> —Joseph Campbell, *The Mythic Image* (1974)

# Contents

**Acknowledgments** ........................................... xi

**Preface** .................................................. xiii
   Organization and Objectives of This Book ................... xv
      Chapters 1–2 ........................................... xv
      Chapters 3–7 .......................................... xvi
      Chapter 8 ............................................ xvii
   References ................................................ xix

**1 Information and Imagery: Expanding the Use of the Picture Book** ....... 1
   The Picture Book Paradox ................................... 1
   Ignorance of Imagery ....................................... 5
   Beyond "Kiddy Lit" ......................................... 8
   Stories That Tell; Stories That Sell ........................ 12
   References ................................................ 15
   Other Reading ............................................. 20

**2 Pictures and Pedagogy** ...................................... 21
   Imagery and Instruction ................................... 21
   Visual Literacy ........................................... 23
   Learning from Visuals: What the Research Shows ............ 25
   How Children See Pictures: Preferences and Processes ...... 28
   References ................................................ 34
   Other Reading ............................................. 38

**3 The Look of a Book** ........................................ 41
   Toward Critical Thinking Skills ........................... 41
   Format and Features of Picture Books: A Framework for Analysis:
      Activities and Strategies ............................. 44
      The Cover ............................................. 45
      Endpapers ............................................. 46
      Front Matter .......................................... 48
      Author/Artist Notes ................................... 48
      Type .................................................. 49
      Shape ................................................. 50
      Gutter ................................................ 51
   References ................................................ 53

## 4 Design, Composition, and Visual Language ... 59
- Training the Eye to See ... 59
- The "5P" Approach to Analyzing Pictures: Strategies and Activities ... 61
  - Element 1: Posture ... 61
  - Element 2: Point of View ... 65
  - Element 3: Position ... 69
  - Element 4: Proportion ... 70
  - Element 5: Props ... 72
- Panels, Pages, Spreads, and Vignettes ... 74
- On the Border ... 77
- References ... 79

## 5 Illustrating As Art: Media, Method, and Message ... 85
- Introduction ... 85
- Art and Multicultural Education ... 89
- Styles, Media, and Techniques ... 91
  - Collage ... 94
  - Linoleum Cut ... 95
  - Painting ... 95
  - Papercut ... 95
  - Pencil ... 95
  - Woodcut ... 95
  - Wood Engraving ... 96
  - Scratchboard ... 96
- "And the Winner Is ...": Awards for Illustrating ... 98
  - Caldecott Medal Winners Since 1960: Artistic Medium ... 99
- Strategies and Activities ... 101
- References ... 102
  - Children's Literature Archives ... 106

## 6 Playing with Pictures: Nontraditional Picture Books ... 107
- Introduction ... 107
- Criteria for Form and Content ... 110
- Playing with Dimensions and Movement ... 111
- The Golden Age of Mechanical Books and Contemporary Classics ... 112
- A Quick Glance at Lift-the-Flap Books ... 114
- Partial Pages and Panoramas ... 115
- Strategies and Activities ... 116
- Nonlinear Storytelling ... 116
  - Strategies and Activities ... 117
- Wordless Picture Books ... 118
  - Strategies and Activities: Playing with Ideas from David Wiesner ... 119
- References ... 120

## 7 Painting with Words: Writing with Pictures . . . . . . . . . . . . . . . . . . . . . . . . 123
Introduction . . . . . . . . . . . . . . . . . . . . . . . . . . . . . . . . . . . . . . . . . . . . . . . 123
    Strategies and Activities . . . . . . . . . . . . . . . . . . . . . . . . . . . . . . . . 131
The Write Stuff . . . . . . . . . . . . . . . . . . . . . . . . . . . . . . . . . . . . . . . . . . . 133
Planning an Author/Artist Visit: Guidelines by Gail E. Haley . . . . . . . . . . 136
References . . . . . . . . . . . . . . . . . . . . . . . . . . . . . . . . . . . . . . . . . . . . . . . 140

## 8 Windows on the World: Picture Books as Social Construction and Representation . . . . . . . . . . . . . . . . . . . . . . . . . . . . . . . . . . . . . . . . . 145
Demographics Is Destiny . . . . . . . . . . . . . . . . . . . . . . . . . . . . . . . . . . . . 145
Pictures of Pluralism . . . . . . . . . . . . . . . . . . . . . . . . . . . . . . . . . . . . . . . 148
Gender Fair? . . . . . . . . . . . . . . . . . . . . . . . . . . . . . . . . . . . . . . . . . . . . . 153
Starting Safely . . . . . . . . . . . . . . . . . . . . . . . . . . . . . . . . . . . . . . . . . . . 156
    Appalachian Stereotypes: Hillbillies, Coal Miners, and Moonshiners . . . . . . 157
    Animal Stereotypes, or Who's Afraid of the Big Bad Wolf? . . . . . . . . . . . 159
"Isms" and Attitudes That Diminish Us All: Strategies and Frameworks . . . . . 160
PWADs and PWANDs: Who Were the "Different" People? . . . . . . . . . . . . 162
Outsiders Looking In . . . . . . . . . . . . . . . . . . . . . . . . . . . . . . . . . . . . . . 164
A Rich Resource: Selected Caldecott Award Winners and Honor Books . . . . . 166
    Caldecott "Who, What, Why, and How" Stories from Africa . . . . . . . . . 167
    Caldecotts About Long-Ago China . . . . . . . . . . . . . . . . . . . . . . . . . . 168
    Caldecott Folklore from Eastern Europe . . . . . . . . . . . . . . . . . . . . . . 168
    Heroes and Heroines in Caldecotts About France . . . . . . . . . . . . . . . 169
    Caldecott Classics About Great Britain . . . . . . . . . . . . . . . . . . . . . . 170
    Ancient Wisdom in a Caldecott Tale from India . . . . . . . . . . . . . . . . 171
    Homecomings in Caldecotts About Japan . . . . . . . . . . . . . . . . . . . . 171
    Breaking Down Hispanic Stereotypes in a Caldecott About Mexico . . . . . 172
    Synthesized Legends in Caldecotts About Native North America . . . . . . 172
    Contemporary American Children in the Caldecotts . . . . . . . . . . . . . 173
Case Studies in Social Construction . . . . . . . . . . . . . . . . . . . . . . . . . . . 175
    Sports Mascots and Picture Books . . . . . . . . . . . . . . . . . . . . . . . . . 176
    Unlearning Stereotypes: Case Study on Images of Native Americans . . . . 178
Positive Trends and Titles . . . . . . . . . . . . . . . . . . . . . . . . . . . . . . . . . . 181
Strategies and Learning . . . . . . . . . . . . . . . . . . . . . . . . . . . . . . . . . . . . 183
References . . . . . . . . . . . . . . . . . . . . . . . . . . . . . . . . . . . . . . . . . . . . . . . 184

**Index** . . . . . . . . . . . . . . . . . . . . . . . . . . . . . . . . . . . . . . . . . . . . . . . . . . 197

**About the Authors** . . . . . . . . . . . . . . . . . . . . . . . . . . . . . . . . . . . . . . . . 207

# Acknowledgments

For their assistance in photographic reproductions used in this book, we would like to thank Jeff Fletcher, Bob McFarland, and Lee White from the Media Studies program at Appalachian State University. Many thanks for patience, endurance, and cooperation through all the revisions and rewrites are also due to Melissa Cook, whose work was invaluable in the preparation of this manuscript.

## *About the Art*

When we began organizing the visual materials for this book, we knew we would rely heavily on the art of Gail Haley. As a Caldecott and a Greenaway medal winner, there were obviously aesthetic reasons for this choice, including that her work demonstrates proficiency in a number of different techniques. We also, however, wanted to include a number of pieces of art from other illustrators who have made or continue to make important contributions in children's literature. Commercial constraints have limited the number of pieces that we have been able to include. In seeking permission to use art, we were surprised to find that the fees quoted ranged anywhere from a very reasonable $100 per picture, to quite prohibitive amounts in excess of $500 per picture. In some cases, permission also required that we give layout and caption approval to an individual artist, which we found unacceptable. We are aware of a number of books dealing with children's literature, including children's picture books, that do not contain any illustrations to help readers understand the concepts discussed in the text. One can only imagine that prohibitive prices prevented the use of artwork in such books. We believe it is in the interest of the publishing industry, authors, and artists to provide teachers and librarians with materials to facilitate the understanding of children's literature. We encourage the industry to make this art available for such educational purposes at a reasonable cost. For those who have done that and assisted in the development of this book, we thank you.

# Preface

*More Than a Thousand Words*

> "Let there be a wider examination of picture books of all types, past and present."
> —Marcia Brown, *Lotus Seeds* (1986)

This book had its genesis almost a decade ago when the three of us attended a conference of the International Visual Literacy Association in Madison, Wisconsin. At the time, one of us had just completed work on a study of the art and design of children's books (Lacy 1986). Another of us had recently published an analysis of the image of adolescents in American motion pictures (Considine 1985). The author/illustrator among us had just completed the first of what was to be a series of children's books based on the traditional Appalachian Jack Tales (Haley 1986).

The interdisciplinary nature of the program addressed all forms of visual communication from computer graphics to the design and analysis of children's picture books. This literary link was further strengthened by the presence of Morton Schindel from Weston Woods Studio, long known and respected for the development of quality audiovisual programs based on award-winning children's literature

The theme of that Madison conference was "Visible and Viable: The Role of Images in Instruction and Communication." As an academic, an author/illustrator, and a library media specialist, three of us together were struck by the growing presence of visual modes of communication in our own lives and the need to help children understand, appreciate, and use the codes and conventions of this visual language.

In the time that has elapsed since then, we have been afforded, almost on a daily basis, ample evidence of the old adage "a picture is worth a thousand words." The proliferation of cable, distance learning, computers, telecommunications, video games, and hypermedia rush us headlong toward the so-called information superhighway. Other than the speed of these technological developments, one key element connecting them all is the increasingly pictorial or iconic nature of these information forms. These visual messages require new definitions of literacy, definitions with wider meanings to the concepts of reading and writing. In the case of the computer, for example, a screen is not a printed page and, despite its appearance, a computer is not a typewriter. Striking a keyboard and entering words that appear on a screen cannot pass as an acceptable definition of computer literacy. To effectively communicate with a computer, some understanding of its language is necessary. Successful computer literacy implies more than screen display, it requires screen design. For this to occur, key variables such as scrolling, density of text, letter size, and the form and function of graphics must be understood and integrated.

Despite the relatively high visibility of computers in our classrooms, media centers, offices, and industries, the real day-to-day business of communication in this country still occurs in our living rooms as we immerse ourselves in the glow and flow of the visual messages assailing us from the omnipresent television. In the last decade, as a result of the growth of cable and satellite, these messages have changed quantitatively and qualitatively. Our children today are exposed to more media messages than any other groups of young people in the history of the world. What those messages say to them and how they say it has come to be of increasing concern to parents and educators all over the country as we face the pictorial proliferation, the ever-expanding electronic envelope, the cabled cocoon in which our children are increasingly raised. From the toxic levels of visual violence on our television screens, to the images implanted in impressionable minds by the words of gangsta rap, our children and adolescents are being reared on a steady diet of iconic information that is capable of affecting their world-view, as well as their self-image and self-esteem.

Nor are we as adults immune to the seductive appeal, the friendly persuasion of these pervasive media messages that surround us. For despite our diplomas and degrees, most of us have been educated in a system that privileged print and provided us with little or no understanding of the visual modes of communication that now dominate our society (Samuels and Samuels 1975). On a day-to-day basis, our own world-view, our own understanding of the key issues and problems facing our nation and our world, is mediated by television and the mass media. In 1993, the complex issues of NAFTA (North American Free Trade Agreement) were reduced to a televised shoot-out and sparring match between Vice President Gore and Ross Perot on *Larry King Live*. The struggle for health care reform has been dominated by bickering between the White House and the insurance industry over the scare tactics of the so-called "Harry and Louise" commercials. Democracy and the entire concept of responsible citizenship are threatened when complex issues and serious examination of these issues is reduced to what the *Washington Post* called "the slogans and sound bites that make up too much of the political dialogue in the country" (Broder 1994, 4). Beyond the domestic scene, American foreign policy and public perception of that policy is also increasingly shaped and influenced by visuals. President Bush took American troops into Somalia largely as a result of the persistent televised images of starving children. The American public, politicians, and press called on President Clinton to withdraw from Somalia in 1993 after seeing pictures of Michael Duran and other U.S. troops being brutalized and degraded.

In February 1994, following CNN's televised images of the bombing of Sarajevo, NATO, the United States, and the United Nations quickly responded. In an extraordinarily candid interview, Madeline Albright, Washington's ambassador to the United Nations, said, "there is no question that television has become the 16th member of the Security Council" (CNN 1994). But these images, no matter how moving, are only part of the picture; a selected and edited version of reality driven like most television by emotional appeals rather than the analytical, logical, and reasoned process necessary to formulate policy. The result is "a powerful, at times destabilizing impact of television news on the making of foreign policy" (Hoagland 1994, 28). More importantly, however, is the central problem that occurs because "industrial democracies involve themselves abroad only when crisis hits the television screen and forces them to engage" (Hoagland 1994, 28).

Although the complexities of foreign policy may seem a long way removed from the quiet contemplation of a children's picture book, we believe these books and the visual language they use can serve as media literacy primers, building bridges to the electronic, rapid-paced visual messages that come to us from our television and movie screens. In fact, many creators of children's books consistently make the connection to other visual media. Fred Marcellino, a Caldecott honor winner said: "I was faced with creating characters and bringing them to life. It was so much fun, like making a movie—dressing them and posing them and moving them around" (1991, 1).

Though some may question the need to read media, believing perhaps that "what you see is what you get" or "the camera never lies," new technologies underline the fact that in this day and age there is "more to it than meets the eye." A recent newspaper photograph, for example, depicted President Clinton and the First Lady standing on the White House lawn, greeting Elvis Presley. Developments such as digital imaging now "make deceptions much easier and faster to accomplish—and much harder if not impossible to detect. We are approaching the point at which most of the images that we see in our daily lives, and that form our understanding of the world, will have been digitally recorded, transmitted and processed" (Sawyer 1994, 38).

In response to the changing nature of communication and the growing reliance on visual technologies, school systems around the country have begun to develop curricula and courses to foster the competencies necessary to become pictorially proficient and media literate. In the Minneapolis Public Schools for example, the student progress report includes an evaluation section for teachers to indicate that the student "uses critical viewing skills for television and other media" (1993). In Oregon, students are expected to be able to communicate "through reading, writing, speaking and listening, as well as through the integrated use of visual forms" (Oregon State Board of Education 1993). Perhaps the most advanced and sophisticated rationale for these visual skills of comprehension and communication is the argument articulated by North Carolina's Department of Public Instruction. The Communication Skills document of the Basic Education Plan states: "In a visually oriented world, the skills of viewing have assumed greater importance. Visual shape actions, promote thoughts and occasionally warp meaning. Students must be made aware of these influences" (1985, 29). The state's K-12 Information Skills curriculum says that, "the sheer mass of information and variety of media formats challenges every learner to filter, interpret, accept, and/or discard information and media messages" (1992, 11). Both documents provide a holistic approach to visual communication, encouraging the analysis and creation of diverse media formats including picture books, photographs, advertisements, motion pictures, and television.

It is in this context and against this background that we have written *Imagine That*. The book is intended to provide an argument for incorporating more visual teaching and learning strategies into education, while also demonstrating frameworks, activities, and techniques to facilitate the way students and teachers look at and think about children's picture books. Far from being developed in the ivory towers of academia, these techniques and approaches have been validated in our own classrooms and in the Visual Information Education Workshops (VIEWs) that we have conducted over many years with teachers, librarians, and media specialists throughout the country. What has been evident in these sessions is that once teachers and students have been given conceptual frameworks for looking at specific picture books, they become capable, in fact excited, about transferring these frameworks applying them to books of their own choosing, which they now see with new eyes. Once they begin to ask not just "What is this story about?" but "How is this story told?" students and teachers are capable of reading picture books on a higher level. As a result, they derive a richer awareness and appreciation of the dual nature of these creations; the unique balance between image and text as carriers and conveyors of the narrative.

## Organization and Objectives of This Book

### Chapters 1-2

Despite the prevalence of an increasing number of visual messages in our lives, "our formal schooling has been almost entirely a matter of words" (Bassett 1969, viii). In *Seeing With the Mind's Eye* (Samuels and Samuels 1975), the authors argued that visualization in their own lives had been "avoided by the standard educational process" and they noted that "man has long been in conflict between the power his visual images have over him and the control he can exert over his environment through the spoken word" (p. xi). It is not simply a matter of more and more media messages influencing our young people, it is also a question of the way in which the messages influence them. While education has typically worked with words and the cognitive domain, "the world of commerce has proved more amenable to visual appeal . . . and these media now play a large part in shaping the public mind" (Bassett 1969, viii) Hence, while our children live in a world of visual communication with powerful affective appeal and persuasion, their formal schooling does little to help them recognize or read the messages that surround them. As such, they are schooled in two different classrooms, two different cultures, and two radically different curricula. Today, in the midst of the communication revolution, progressive educators throughout the country are beginning to recognize this and to call on universities and teachers to respond. Theodore Sizer is one of the most respected voices in the school reform/restructuring movement. He recently said, "Television has become the biggest school system, the principal shaper of culture. Willy nilly, television is powerfully influencing the young on what it is to be American" (Sizer 1992, 24). In the first two chapters of this book, we argue that the visual language of the children's picture book offers a bridge to the more sophisticated electronic messages of the mass media. Because these books are already in our classrooms and collections, they offer us a significant media literacy primer at no financial cost. With the appropriate perspective and process, these products can increase their utility with children beyond K-6, who may be familiar with the stories but not with the visual language or the role it plays in telling these tales.

## Aims

- To document the research evidence related to the role visual materials and strategies can play in the teaching and learning processes.

- To articulate the need for greater incorporation of these materials and techniques into teacher training.

- To demonstrate the relationship between the visual language of the children's picture book and electronic media like the motion picture, advertising, and television.

- To explore the attitudes successful authors and illustrators have about visual communication.

- To articulate an expanded and holistic approach to the literacies with particular emphasis on the common skills required to process picture books and mass media messages.

## *Chapters 3–7*

The majority of this book consists of a series of chapters used to explore the unique language of picture books, including the artistic technique or medium, the relationship between image and text, and the design, composition, and organization of the book as an artifact. Formal features of picture books such as front matter, endpapers, and the gutter are discussed with numerous examples and a variety of activities and tasks that children can engage in individually or as part of cooperative learning. The unique characteristics and attributes of the rule-breakers—those delightful but often difficult to handle and store "popup" books and movable books are also explored. These chapters also emphasize a framework, the so-called "5 P" approach for analyzing illustrations. Once again, the language of the children's picture book is related to the mass media, frequently through the words and experiences of the artists who have created these books. Though we recognize that many people tend to regard books as inherently good and television and the mass media as inherently bad, we attempt to place emphasis not on the product, but on the common process of the skills necessary to read the stories television and the mass media tell. This argument is perhaps best presented by Mem Fox, who said: "Television and books have one thing in common; it's what the child gets out of them that matters. Reading is not inherently good. Television is not inherently bad. What counts is the pleasure, the experiences, the relaxation, the growth in understanding, the satisfaction of need in each medium" (1993 103). By helping children to recognize the language of picture books, we believe teachers will stimulate their interest and curiosity, providing them with the cognitive capacity to explore these books on a more sophisticated level, enriching their understanding, enjoyment, and appreciation.

### Aims

- To demonstrate the way in which the content of the picture book is related to its formal elements, such as shape, cover, front matter, and endpapers.

- To demonstrate a variety of different media formats used by contemporary illustrators including papercut, linoleum cut, scratchboard, and woodcut, connecting artistic techniques to the mood, period, culture, or setting of the story.

- To provide a conceptual framework for reading various elements used in illustrations, such as posture, point of view, props, and position.

- To show how these elements are also present in motion pictures and other electronic media.

- To explore the relationship between words and pictures as carriers of the narrative in a variety of children's books.

- To provide a series of activities and strategies teachers can use to help children understand the form and content of picture books.

## *Chapter 8*

While the vast majority of this book studies the artistic and literary elements of picture books, analyzing the way words and images tell stories, in the final chapter we turn our attention to multicultural education and the more controversial question of whose stories are told and sold. Though questions of ideology in children's literature have often been ignored, the increasingly pluralistic nature of American society, and the role of picture books as a window on the world, make it necessary that educators now ask: "whose window, whose world?" Anyone questioning the need for multicultural children's literature need only look at the composition of our classrooms and the changing demographics of American society. More importantly, they need only look at the growing evidence of racism, intolerance, and prejudice in our society. A 1994 study by Louis Harris noted somewhat ominously, for example, that "the persistence of negative stereotypes and inter-group hostility implies that the further splintering of America into bickering ethnic and religious groups is a very real danger" (Morin 1994, 37).

Our classrooms and the materials we select for them can help students recognize what they have in common while they respect and celebrate their differences and diversity. But there is ample evidence that curricula content and the textbooks and materials that have supported that curricula have not always presented a balanced or accurate view. "These materials project images of society, as well as of other aspects of culture such as what constitutes good literature, legitimate political activity and so on" (Sleeter and Grant 1991, 79). One of the most respected voices in American education, Michael Apple has argued: "It is naive to think of the school curriculum as neutral knowledge. Rather what counts as legitimate knowledge is the result of complex power relations and struggles among identifiable class, race, gender and religious groups" (1993, 46).

Multicultural education is, to a very real degree, an attempt to respond to this imbalance. What it represents is institutional responsiveness to the changing character and compositions of our schools and society. "Culture evolves; it is dynamic. Such is the definition of ethnogenesis.

American culture, like any other, is not what it was nor what it will be. As a reflection of society, schools should be places where a match can be made between the student and his world" (Rosenman 1989, 86). If mishandled, multicultural education becomes a matter of guilt, accusation, defensiveness, finger-pointing, and endless variations of the blame game. Recent developments in children's literature make it a potentially powerful ally to promote multicultural education in such a way that children recognize and value the characteristics and contributions of the diverse racial and ethnic groups that compose American society. One need look no further than *Grandfather's Journey* (Say 1993), the most recent recipient of the Caldecott medal, to locate a teaching tool to help children value and understand the experiences of those who came to America from distant shores. Motion pictures, too, have begun to address this subject, and recent films like *The Joy Luck Club* (1993) and *Mississippi Masala* (1992) have begun to give greater visibility to many of the American minorities too often absent from the nation's screens.

In preparing this chapter, we have attempted to address the context in which children's literature can respond to the issues of multicultural education. This includes a special section using Caldecott medal books to explore multicultural stories. We have also recognized the concern and uncertainty some educators may have about these issues, particularly when matters like stereotyping can sometimes lead to conflict. As such, we have developed a unit for those who want to defuse this issue, starting safely by exploring stereotypes of animals like wolves and bears. This section offers an opportunity to note the relationship between the perceptions these images have created and the ecological and environmental consequences that have followed as a result of these perceptions.

## Aims

- To demonstrate the relationship between multicultural children's literature and the changing composition of the American population.

- To identify quality picture books that teachers can use to promote awareness of and respect for diverse cultures.

- To identify strategies and activities that teachers can use to help children critically analyze and evaluate cultural representations in picture books.

- To address the issue of gender representations in children's books and to connect these concerns to gender issues in American society.

- To provide an in-depth case study of the depiction of Native Americans in picture books.

The approaches we have suggested throughout this book are clearly capable of promoting higher-order thinking skills providing students with the concepts and frameworks they need to analyze and evaluate the form and content of picture books. As such, these critical frameworks greatly expand the life of these books, increasing their relevance and utility not only to the upper levels of the elementary school but well into the middle-school years. Children can learn to use these picture books to group, to classify, to discover relationships between parts and wholes, between form and content. They can be taught to compare and contrast the construction and representation of minorities in picture books and the mass media with the real-life situations and circumstances of these groups. They can bring a holistic perspective to children's literature, providing opportunities to learn to read pictures as well as words, ideology as well as narrative. Finally, we hope teachers and children will more fully recognize the nature of the children's book as a product of both art and industry. As such, picture books are not only cooperative ventures, the product of the authors' and artists' visions and voices, but also of the unseen forces of the industry: the editors, art directors, book designers, and marketers. In an era when education is faced with limited budgets and scarce resources, we believe that children's books can greatly expand their presence in our classrooms and their contribution to learning if we begin to look at them in new ways. Writing in *The Open Eye in Learning,* Richard Bassett put it succinctly when he said, "the words' imagination, foresight, scope and a host of others all bear witness to the fact that a good look at a thing is a condition of understanding it" (Bassett 1969, vii). Let the looking begin!

# References

Albright, Madeline. (1994). Interview. CNN, 13 February.

Apple, Michael. (1993). *Official Knowledge: Democratic Education in a Conservative Age.* New York: Routledge, Chapman and Hall.

Bassett, Richard. (1969). *The Open Eye in Learning: The Role of Art in General Education.* Cambridge: MIT Press.

Broder, David. (1994). Debating Issues for a Change. *The Washington Post Weekly Edition,* 14-20 March, 4.

Considine, David M. (1985). *The Cinema of Adolescence.* Jefferson, NC: McFarland.

Fox, Mem. (1993). *Radical Reflections: Passionate Opinions on Teaching, Learning and Living.* San Diego, CA: Harcourt Brace Jovanovich.

Haley, Gail E. (1986). *Jack and the Bean Tree.* New York: Crown.

Hoagland, Jim. (1994). Don't Blame CNN. *Washington Post Weekly Edition,* 7-13 March, 28.

Lacy, Lyn Ellen. (1986). *The Art and Design of Children's Picture Books.* Chicago, IL: American Library Association.

Marcellino, Fred. (1991). *Caldecott and Newbery News,* July: 1.

Minneapolis Public Schools. (1993). *Student Progress Report.* Minneapolis, MN: Minneapolis Department of Public Instruction.

Morin, Richard. (1994). Those Who Live in a House Divided Against Itself. *Washington Post Weekly Edition,* 7-13 March, 37.

North Carolina Department of Public Instruction. (1985). *Teacher Handbook: Communication Skills.* Raleigh, NC: Author.

———. (1992). *Standard Course of Study: Information Skills K-12.* Raleigh, NC: Author.

Oregon State Board of Education. (1993). *Working Designs for Change.* Salem, OR: Author.

Rosenman, Alba. (1989). The Value of Multicultural Curricula. In *Taking Sides: Clashing Views on Controversial Educational Issues,* edited by James Null. Guilford, CT: Dushkin.

Samuels, Mike, and Nancy Samuels. (1975). *Seeing With the Mind's Eye: The History, Techniques and Uses of Visualization.* New York: Random House.

Sawyer, Kathy (1994). Down to a Photo Refinish. *Washington Post Weekly Edition*, February 28-March 6: 38.

Say, Allen. (1993). *Grandfather's Journey.* Boston: Houghton Mifflin.

Sizer, Theodore. (1992). School Reform: What's Missing? *World Monitor* 5 (11): 20–27.

Sleeter, Christine, and Carl Grant. (1991). Race, Class, Gender and Disability in Current Textbooks. In *The Politics of the Textbook*, edited by Michael Apple. New York: Routledge, Chapman and Hall.

# Chapter 1

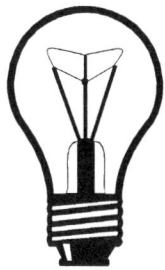

# Information and Imagery: Expanding the Use of the Picture Book

> More often than not, the things we need are already there; all we have to do is make use of them.
> —*The Tao of Pooh*, Benjamin Hoff, (1982)

## The Picture Book Paradox

The illustrated children's book is a potentially powerful teaching tool to foster critical viewing and thinking skills. Such books link the high-technology world of the electronic environment and the so-called information revolution to the low-tech world of the picture book, through the common denominator of the visual messages contained in these programs, products, and publications.

Despite the opportunity afforded by this resource that is readily available in our libraries, media centers, and classrooms, the true potential of the picture book as a teaching tool is seldom recognized. A typical library-science degree exposes students to only one or two courses dealing with children's or young adult literature. These courses, and the textbooks that support them, place heavy emphasis on the literary aspects of children's books (genre, plot, character, theme), to the detriment of the visuals that constitute half the books. In addition, it is not uncommon for these courses also to include a consideration of audiovisual materials for children, thus creating an even more crowded curriculum that leaves little time for serious analysis of the visual components of picture books. This hemispheric bias to the left-brained world of the linear, logical, literary, and print mode is equally prevalent in teacher training. Exposure to the picture book in undergraduate teacher preparation, although occasionally occurring in a separate course in Children's Literature, is more typically subsumed in another course in Language Arts, Reading, English, or a related discipline. Such courses seldom offer substantive consideration of the form, content, composition, or design of the illustrations in picture books.

Ironically, the failure to help teachers and librarians to recognize and use the power of pictures comes as information in our society is increasingly produced in iconic, nonprint form. In February 1992, for example, *U.S. News and World Report* noted this trend, observing that, "America thinks it is a meritocracy, but in fact, it has become a mediacracy.... Mediacracy is not ruled by the media but by those who know how to manipulate symbols, information and the media" (Wolcott 1992, 6). Responding to the growing presence and power of pictures in American society, prestigious universities and foundations have begun to focus attention on the need to integrate media literacy into the curriculum, following the example set by Australia, England, and Canada. These developments were clearly evident during 1992, when the Annenberg School of Communication hosted several think-tanks on media literacy, and the Aspen Institute, supported by the Carnegie Foundation, convened the National Leadership Conference on Media Literacy. One development of particular interest to those who work with children was the Catholic initiative under the heading "Who Tells the Stories?" Developed by the National Catholic Education Association and the Center for Media and Values, the project recognized the role of the electronic media as modern storytellers and argued for "reclaiming the story-telling and value-assigning roles that media, especially television, have taken over from families, schools and religion" (Wessell 1992, 1). Such a goal may be phrased more combatively than necessary, but it does at least address the relationship between picture and print by recognizing the presence of new forms of storytelling in our culture.

The integration of media literacy into the curriculum as an information skill, should logically embrace the children's picture book as an early primer in visual communication and a window on the world capable of socializing children into the values and attitudes of society. Although some purists regard children's books as a literary respite from the onslaught of mass media and pop culture, in reality children's picture books utilize much of the visual language employed in film, television, and other visual art forms. Many of today's leading illustrators have backgrounds in these fields and clearly acknowledge the relationship between picture books and mass media. Jerry Pinkney, for example, worked in advertising, and Alice Provensen and Martin Provensen worked as illustrators for Disney. In his biography of Arnold Lobel, George Shannon says, "[F]rom his childhood he saw story, film and theater as one.... [B]oth clearly resemble the dual world of word and image found in picture books" (1989, 14-15). Gail Haley sees a clear relationship between puppetry and picture books: "Both are direct descendants of storytelling, in which all visuals were created internally by the imagination of the audience. The iconography and economy of suggestion in both fields are similar—designed to create the greatest experiential participation by audience or reader. A good illustration is a frame through which the viewer moves, carrying action forward in his or her own mind" (1992b, 11). Don Wood said that the picture book is "as close to drama or a thirty-two page movie as it is to either literature or art" (1986, 556). Charles Mikolaycak also clearly acknowledged the role mass media played in his own childhood and his own imagination: "Movies intrigued me as a child... they stimulated a curiosity in me about ways of life different from my own. I could observe details about clothing, faces and house furniture through movies" (1986, 168).

Teaching children to recognize and read the language of picture books therefore introduces them to a significant and strategic process, preparing them to interpret the wider world of iconic information that characterizes the information age. This link has been made easier in recent years, as an increasing number of authors and illustrators have placed greater emphasis on the ability of form and content to stimulate the minds and imaginations of young readers and viewers. What better way to introduce children to critical viewing skills, and the concept of multiple perspectives or points of view, than to engage them in an exploration of *The True Story of the Three Little Pigs* (Scieszka and Smith 1989)? Young readers and not so young readers alike delight in discovering that they must relinquish some of their assumptions and beliefs. Now, they discover, they must rethink their opinions based upon new evidence. As the book begins, A. Wolf, the hero-narrator, informs the reader, "Everybody knows the story of *The Three Little Pigs*. Or at least they think they do. But I'll let you in on a little secret. Nobody knows the real story, because nobody has ever heard MY side of the story." In 1993, when NBC News was caught faking footage of a collision of a GM car, the public saw compelling evidence of the way in which news and information can be distorted and constructed to represent a slanted point of view. Children's picture books that play with this theme can be useful tools to develop critical viewing and thinking skills as children experiment with familiar tales told through new perspectives. Examining several versions of the same story can also help children see the way different authors and artists interpret and represent the same story. This concept can be easily applied to the way different newspapers and networks cover the same story.

Suddenly, in classrooms and libraries across the country, children want to rethink and retell traditional tales through the eyes of other characters. What happens if *Jack and the Bean Tree* (Haley 1986) is told through the eyes of the giant Ephidophilus or his wife, Matilda? What are the educational implications of asking children to conceptualize alternative points of view? The child's imagination is liberated to play with the plot, to examine motivation, and to explore closure beyond the traditional "and they all lived happily ever after" ending. Set free to construct their own texts, children begin to explore and experience stories through their own imaginations and their own eyes.

New ways of seeing can also be promoted through thematic approaches using a variety of picture books. *Knots on a Counting Rope* (Martin, Archambault, and Rand 1987), for example, presents the character of a blind boy who recognizes that there are many different ways of seeing. Another useful book to explore the concept of critical viewing skills is David Wisniewski's *Elfwyn's Saga* (1990). Ostensibly an old Norwegian tale, the story actually has contemporary relevance. The cold crystal at which the villagers stare endlessly, until they lose contact with their own culture and community, might well be regarded as a metaphor for television. Like the *Knots* Native American tale, this story also features a blind child who is sighted in other ways.

Of course, those who create for children have always tapped into this inner vision. Shirley Hughes said, "I think the best pictures any child sees are in his or her own head. The power of inner visualization is one of the most amazing attributes" (1991, 17). The concept that children negotiate and construct their own meaning is also evident to Caldecott medal recipient David Wiesner. In his acceptance speech for *Tuesday* (Wiesner 1991), he said, "[A]s the author of a wordless picture book, I don't have to concern myself about whether the reader's interpretation of each and every detail is the same as mine. My own view has no more, and no less validity than [that] of any viewer" (1992, 421).

David Macaulay has also provided an outstanding opportunity to link the picture book to critical viewing and thinking skills, inviting his young readers to construct their own meaning from his work. In his Caldecott medal winner, *Black and White* (Macaulay 1990), the title page confronts the reader with a boxed warning label: "This book appears to contain a number of stories that do not necessarily occur at the same time. Then again, it may contain only one story. In any event, careful inspection of both words and pictures is recommended."

Inviting readers to enter a book on their own terms is, of course, not a new trend in children's literature. *The Green Man* (Haley 1979) opened by proclaiming: "The story you are about to read may have happened just this way—or perhaps it came about in a different manner in some other place entirely." The readers are clearly invited to make of the story what they will. The invitation is made all the more intriguing by the fact that the images deliberately contradict the text in some places, forcing the child to recognize and reconcile levels of meaning in the story. *A Story, A Story* (Haley 1970) drew upon Ashanti oral tradition and opened with a further invitation to the reader or listener to explore the tale on his or her own terms: "We do not really mean, we do not really mean that what we are about to say is true. A story, a story, let it come, let it go."

While the author's words can invite readers to explore the story, the artist's pictures, even when visually engaging, can actually engender fear and anxiety in the viewer. This "great intimidation," wrote *Wilson Library Bulletin*, "lies in that nebulous area called ART. Most of us, or all of us, are at least a little confused as to what art is and what it should really be doing for books" (Lorraine 1977a, 145). "I don't know much about art, but I know what I like," the saying goes, and so it is with many of those working with children's books. Many teachers and librarians have had little or no training in art, and thus are confronted with the problem of not knowing how to use the pictures in picture books. Being able to work successfully with these images involves what Steig has called "problems of affective content, aesthetic value, meaning . . . and the status of this work as a children's book" (1985, 139). Illustrators themselves have articulated the need for broader education. Robert McCloskey said, "[P]eople must be trained to look and see; I find a great lack of real perception" (Heins 1988, 192). In his Caldecott medal acceptance speech, David Macaulay said that reading a drawing means that "we must pay equal attention to both what is said and what is left unspoken." Macaulay also articulated the need for visual literacy. "Lack of curiosity is the first step toward visual illiteracy . . . [I]t threatens to turn us into isolated, insensitive, incapable and ultimately helpless victims of a world of increasing complexity and decreasing humanity" (1991, 419–23).

Just where does one turn for help in understanding these concepts? Cover notes may provide some clue as to what techniques were used in developing the illustrations, but space constraints usually limit such notes to one or two lines, which are of little help to teachers and librarians. In *Aïda* (Price, Dillon, and Dillon 1990), for example, we are told that the illustrations were done with acrylics on acetate and marbleized paper. Most teachers and librarians would have difficulty in processing this information so that it meaningfully contributes to an understanding or appreciation of the book.

Reviews are generally regarded as a useful source of information about picture books. Although reviews can be a good source, too often they seem intent on telling the reader what the reviewer knows, with little or no consideration of the child for whom the book was intended. A *School Library Journal* review for *Puss in Boots* (Kirstein and Vaes 1992) is a clear example of this. Though the review began by indicating that the book was for grades 1 through 4, the remainder of the review discussed, in great detail, various art styles, techniques, and subtle nuances, with references to the baroque, the rococo, El Greco, Watteau, and Velázquez (among others)—none of which would be understood, recognized, or appreciated by children in grades 1 to 4. Even a cursory inspection of reviews suggests that they can actually compound the problem of comprehension by providing strikingly disparate and irreconcilable views of a given book. Hence we find *Publishers Weekly*, *Horn Book,* and *Kirkus Reviews* lauding both the text and illustrations in *Mountain Jack Tales* (Haley 1992a) whereas *School Library Journal* found fault. Whereas some reviewers described "a lucid and vibrant voice," saying, "Haley's use of metaphor, hyperbole and dialect captures the playful spirit of mountain lore" (*Publishers Weekly* 1992, 86), another reviewer found the voice "matter-of-fact" and said the dialect "seems artificial" (*School Library Journal* 1992, 96). Unable to agree on the language of the text, the reviewers seemed similarly divided when it came to discussing the art for the book. *School Library Journal*'s reviewer said, "[E]ach story is illustrated with one or two bland, black and white wood engravings that seem too stilted for what should be lively tales" (1992, 96). This opinion was in stark contrast to other reviews, which described the illustrations as "full of energy, comedy and magical creatures," noting that "the emotive, elaborate wood engravings . . . enrich this buoyant anthology" (*Publishers Weekly* 1992, 86).

Reviewers are, of course, free to differ on their responses to books. When those responses are so contradictory, however, the validity of the reviews must seriously be called into question. For teachers and librarians, reliance on any single review to understand a book is dangerous. One suitable strategy might be to use contradictory reviews of the same book to help children develop their own evaluative criteria.

Confronted by the contradictions of the review process, some educators might seek shelter and sanctuary in the world of the award winners, dealing only with those titles that have been proclaimed "good." Such a strategy also quickly unravels in the light of the reviews. Maurice Sendak's *Outside Over There* (1981), for example, garnered a Caldecott honor, but was described by one critic as "drearily nostalgic and sentimental" (Steig 1985, 139). Another called it "a paranoid vision" and "a shallow, icy surrogate for a literature which will benefit humanity" (Hankla 1982, 347). Nor did the Caldecott medal for *A Story, A Story* (Haley 1970) save it from one critic who assailed it as "facile stylization without meaning or force" (Bader 1975, 281). In a particularly outspoken interview that raised concerns about the objectivity of the review process, Newbery winner Cynthia Rylant complained about "the incestuous literary community in New York" and said, "I truly believe that a lot of people get the *New York Times* cover review because they were good friends with somebody and they were at the right cocktail party" (Antonucci 1993, 26). A recent chair of the Newbery Committee described the choice as a consensus reflecting "the wisdom and biases of 15 people from various regions of the country" (Naylor 1991, v).

# Ignorance of Imagery

Although reviews may differ in their responses to any given book, one thread of remarkable consistency and continuity running throughout the review research is the predisposition to ignore or downplay the role of the visuals in picture books. In an important article published in *The New Advocate*, one author explored research related to the treatment of illustrations both in reviews and in children's literature textbooks. The review research indicated that "most of the reviewing journals focused more on texts than pictures." In the case of the textbooks, the author concluded, "while they do describe pictures, they give little explicit direction about classroom activities to help children learn to read pictures. Thus, most classroom teachers, whose own visual education is spotty at best, simply don't know what to DO with the visual half of a picture book" (Stewig 1992, 11).

The lack of attention given to the illustrations in picture books is by no means new, nor are concerns about it. Blair Lent complained many years ago that "too often the art in picture books is considered to be a mere decoration for the text" (Lent 1977, 161). At the same time, Kenneth Marantz observed that "picture books are reviewed as if they were pieces of literature" (Marantz 1977, 149). Both authors drew attention to the fact that picture books were reviewed and cataloged according to literary criteria such as age level, complexity of syntax, and vocabulary. The fact that these criteria are not appropriate for how children read and process pictures has never deterred either reviewers or catalogers.

One of the most important studies examining how reviews respond to illustrations was published in *The Journal of Youth Services in Libraries* in 1989. Included in the study were *Horn Book, Booklist, School Library Journal,* and *Wilson Library Bulletin*. The authors analyzed the reviews in terms of information related to the style of the art, the relationship between image and text, and elements such as color, composition, line, detail, and medium. With the exception of *Wilson Library Bulletin*, all reviews devoted less than 25 percent of the total space to discussing the artwork. The authors "found little evidence that reviewers are knowledgeable about many aspects of art employed in illustrations of picture books for children" (Busbin and Steinfirst 1989, 265).

Such problems might make readers more cautious in reliance on reviews. A more constructive approach, however, is to recognize that the limitations of reviews are the logical and inevitable outgrowth of how and where reviewers are educated. Although the review format, with its time and space constraints, obviously compounds the problem, the real issue goes back to the scant attention given to visual teaching strategies and visual processing skills in the preparation of teachers, librarians, and media specialists. Any significant attempt at understanding the paucity of attention given to the picture book as a serious teaching tool must look holistically at the limited role traditionally accorded to visuals in the training of educators.

Central to this problem is the hemispheric bias that pervades our education system, despite the increasingly visual and right-brained direction of our communication modes. Some two decades have now elapsed since John Debes, the acknowledged founder of the visual literacy movement, made this clear. In a paper presented to the National Council of Teachers of English, Debes said, "American educators have been concentrating on the left hemisphere of the brain in which the verbal skills, including reading and writing, develop, ignoring the right hemisphere of the brain in which visual sequencing, visual literacy and visual patterning develop" (1974). In 1981, Roger Sperry won the Nobel Prize for his work related to brain functions. The implications of this work for how we teach and how students learn are potentially enormous. As of the moment, however, they have still failed to radically change teacher preparation or classroom practice. The result, as has increasingly been noted, is a widening gap between the world our students live in and the world we try to make them learn in. The failure to address the right-hemisphere, high-technology electronic environment in which they live separates school from society (Considine and Haley 1992) and creates competing curricula (Postman 1985).

The body of research related to visual literacy and its potential contribution to the teaching/learning process is extensive (McKim 1972; Pressley 1976; Dwyer, Szabo, and DeMelo 1981; Wilson 1986). The research also makes it quite clear that, when properly used and understood, the integration of imagery into instruction can result in an increase in student comprehension and recall. That such strategies and skills can be nurtured in the classroom is well established. "Any basic visual process can be developed into a visual skill through practice, and any visual skill can be developed into a useful learning strategy through training" (Winn 1982, 17). Despite this significant body of research documenting a relationship between imagery and learning, little of the information filters through to the classroom. Noting that "imagery exists as a powerful influence on composing and comprehending," Sinatra (1986, 49) documented the low impact of these potentially significant findings. Concepts associated with visual literacy, he says, "weren't covered in college coursework" (p. 48). Nor is the research related to visual literacy readily accessible in the data banks educators traditionally use. One search of ERIC, for example, located 7,511 studies related to reading research, 1,916 related to writing research, and only 6 addressing visual literacy research. For visualization to assume a greater role in the teaching/learning process, the research related to it must become more visible and, by that process, more useful.

But access to information is not the only problem associated with visualization in education. One of the major obstacles to integrating imagery into instruction is the degree of hostility, both latent and manifest, that confronts any attempt to redefine *literacy*. In part, this springs from our cultural assumptions that "seeing is believing," "the camera never lies," and "what you see is what you get." Dondis notes the paradox at the heart of the problem: "How can you study what you already know? The answer to this question lies in a definition of visual literacy as more than just seeing, more than just making visual messages. Visual literacy implies understanding, the means for seeing and sharing meaning with some level of predictable universality" (1973, 182).

Those who seek a greater role for visuals in education must assume the responsibility for more clearly articulating the relationship between learning from words and learning from pictures. Clearly, both words and images are associated with human communication. In reality, however, the child begins to process visually well before the language of words is understood. "Seeing comes before words. . . . [T]he child looks and recognizes before it can speak" (Berger 1972, 7). Recognizing an object or word, however, is not the same as understanding or comprehending the reality to which the word relates. So it is with the image. In a high-tech world of computer simulations and virtual reality, we must move beyond the notion that seeing is believing and provide our students with the skills to read pictures as well as words.

Support for this concept is now gaining strength within the world of children's literature. In a 1993 cover story called "Reading the Image," *School Library Journal* noted that visual images saturate the world of young people and are often "a major part of the tools they use to reflect upon their world." Tellingly, the journal noted that "the skills and abilities needed to decode and interpret visual images are probably as demanding as those required for reading print" (Vandergrift and Hannigan 1993, 20). *Horn Book* also acknowledged the electronic environment in which our children live. "Children are being raised today amid visual media and are bombarded from television and other visual media and are consequently much more sophisticated" (Evans 1992, 763). Though there is little doubt that our children are increasingly surrounded by visual messages, we must guard against confusing *access* to, with *understanding* of, these visual messages. John Naisbitt argued that "we are drowning in information and starved for knowledge" (1982). Psychologist David Elkind says the media promote "pseudosophistication"; he argues that "children today know much more than they understand" (1981, 77). Adults also have difficulty processing all the information they now have access to. In *Democracy Without Citizens,* Entman argues that "despite any improvement in access to news, Americans do not know more about politics now than they did twenty years ago" (1989, 4). Those who wish to promote media literacy must be careful to link the concept to the iconic information forms of our culture and to make it clear that, as these forms proliferate, we must provide our children with the skills to process these messages.

In an age of iconic information, children need to be taught to read visual messages and to communicate through the pictorial formats that increasingly surround them. (Calvin and Hobbes. Copyright © 1992 by Bill Watterson. Reprinted with permission of Universal Press Syndicate.)

Some progress has begun to occur in this movement. Ernest Boyer, president of the Carnegie Foundation for the Advancement of Teaching, said, "It is no longer enough to simply read and write. Students must also become literate in the understanding of visual messages as well" (1988, xxiv). Writing in *Educational Leadership,* Elliot Eisner said, "[W]e think about literacy in the tightest, most constipated terms" (1991, 15), and he called for a broader definition of literacy based upon the communication forms of the culture. Hence, as long as print was the central information form in society, the ability to read and write print constituted an appropriate definition of literacy. The advent of computers, telecommunications, and distance learning, and the ubiquitous presence of television at all levels of our society, now necessitate a broader definition of literacy that encompasses these aspects of the communication culture.

Although this may seem both obvious and logical, some remain intent on clinging to an outmoded and increasingly irrelevant definition of literacy. The "Back to Basics" cry of the early 1980s was one simple example of this. Other signs are all around, most notably manifested in anti-media rhetoric. Symptomatically, media are persistently perceived and positioned as the enemy in the struggle for literacy. Perhaps nowhere was this better exemplified than in an article in *Educational Leadership* entitled "Reversing the Literacy Decline by Controlling the Electronic Demons" (Shenkman 1985, 26). The anti-media stance has also gained significant publicity from several successful books (Bloom 1987; Hirsch 1988).

Unfortunately, such attitudes have also penetrated the work of highly respected academics. In *Illiterate America* (Kozol 1985), for example, the author defines *literacy* as the ability to decipher words and decode their connotations. The definition seems far removed from the reason words need to be read: Words must be read because they contain ideas. The concept of finding, storing, or producing ideas in nonprint form seems to be ignored or irrelevant. The hostile attitude toward nonprint forms is evident in Kozol's chapter called "Technological Obsession." The author sees print as a panacea for the excesses of the mass media. Literacy, he suggests, can in part "counteract the visual and aural violence of the mass media," providing "calm aesthetic satisfactions that transcend the hedonistic thrill of instantaneous and often mesmerizing exaltations" (p. 177). Rather than helping students to recognize the effect mass media have on their lives, and teaching them to read media content and form, the author turns

## 8 Information and Imagery: Expanding the Use of the Picture Book

his back on what he clearly regards as the unworthy products of a pop culture. Kozol argues that "scholars in colleges of liberal arts ought to take an active role in helping to reverse the technological momentum that has overtaken literacy work" (p. 174). Kozol sounds a call to arms against the onslaught of the media menace: "We would do best to hold to an archaic faith in the persistent value of the written word. Books will endure. Literacy will continue to depend upon the power to decipher words and decode their connotations" (p. 161–62).

Such language continues to promote conflict rather than cooperation between the worlds of print and picture, between the traditional and emerging communication forms of our society. The result is increasingly evident in the "tension between the print-oriented curriculum of the school and the electronically oriented curriculum of the learner" (Chiarelott 1984, 19). Until this antagonism is addressed, our students will continue to suffer in an education system based more on the past than the present. In such a system, too much emphasis has been placed on *what* teachers cover. The time has come to recognize that *how* teachers cover the material has a major effect on what students derive from it. In both the presentation and the processing of information, visuals can make a major contribution. Although computers, video, and other image-based technologies are an obvious part of this arsenal, so too is the children's picture book.

The artificial barrier between children's literature and popular culture may at last be breaking down. In a recent publication, Nodelman articulated the relationship between these areas. "TV," he said, "equips children with a repertoire of basic story patterns" (1992, 49). According to Nodelman, film, television, toys, and video games "have a powerful influence on children's expectations and attitudes—not only about literature, but about life in general." Rather than lamenting this, the author argues that we now need to consider the "implications of the context that popular culture creates for children's understanding and enjoyment of literature" (p. 43).

## Beyond "Kiddy Lit"

The opportunity to use picture books to develop critical viewing and thinking skills has been greatly enhanced in recent years by the development of audiovisual materials providing behind-the-scenes views of the production process. One of the best sources for such materials is the highly acclaimed Weston Woods Studio in Connecticut. In addition, an increasing number of books are being specifically designed to facilitate the visual recognition and discrimination skills of young readers. At the most basic level, this includes the well-known *Where's Waldo?* (Handford 1987). A more sophisticated and challenging example can be found in *Errata* (Alles 1992). The book—subtitled "What's Wrong with This Picture?"—features 12 scenes from history, each containing 10 visual errors. Although some of the mistakes are instantly identifiable, such as the presence of the television at the Norman Christmas feast, others require a much greater understanding and awareness of both history and cultures.

The mere presence of these materials, however, is not sufficient. The greatest barrier to visual literacy and media literacy has less to do with the materials available than it does with the mindset, perceptions, and preconceptions we have about those materials. Before changing the way picture books are used in education, we must first change the way we as adults think about children's books and children's literature in general.

In 1982, the President of the Children's Literature Association, speaking at the University of Florida, echoed the view of *Horn Book* that there remains "persistent condescension" toward children's books and their writers (Lukens 1982, 20–21). A decade later, in an article called "The Trashing of Children's Literature," Francelia Butler lamented "the time honored practice by mainly male faculty of treating children's literature as a second rank course," concluding that "hundreds of bright teachers of children's literature live lives of quiet desperation in unsympathetic departments" (1992, 61). This second-class status was also documented by Peter Hunt, who said that the children's literature course in academia tends to have "a somewhat tenuous existence on the periphery of university departments" (1984, 192). Nor are the artists and authors themselves immune to the denigration of their field. Although handsome advances, substantial royalties, and a marginal degree of fame may go with the job, most of those involved in the creative side of children's books are well aware that few people understand the amount of work involved in creating for children, and many do not regard it as work at all. Speaking at a children's literature conference in Australia, Shirley Hughes commented on the suspicion with which outsiders view those in children's literature. "Anyone who works in a child-centered idiom tends to be slightly suspect as far as the general public is concerned. There is some embarrassment and social unease in case we should all be discovered skipping about in short white socks and pinafores, trying to re-enter the world of childhood" (Hughes 1991, 17).

For children's literature to assume a larger role in learning, its advocates must begin to articulate its contribution to these areas, as well as its relationship to art, social studies, and history.

Of these areas, the line of least resistance seems to be in the realm of art education. Exploration of the technique and medium used in a picture book's art, as well as elements such as design and composition, falls well within the aesthetic goals of art education. Through such study, students become more aware of the production process and more fully appreciate the relationship between form and content. This process adds "pleasure to the text, the pleasure of understanding at a higher level" (Greenaway 1991, 3).

Recognizing how a painting or series of paintings are executed, however, is merely scratching the surface of children's literature. The question of both content and effect must also be addressed. Those who work with children's books must also recognize the messages contained in these texts and the impact these views and value systems have—individually or cumulatively—on young readers. Traditional fairy tales, for example, are much more than just good entertainment. The mythic and archetypal elements of the stories represent historical and psychological continuity that can actually help children deal with the world around them. In *The Uses of Enchantment*, Bettelheim said, "[T]he fairy tale enlightens him about himself and fosters his personality development. It offers meaning on so many different levels, and enriches the child's experience in so many ways" (1977, 12). This theme was taken up again recently by a Jungian analyst in *Women Who Run with the Wolves* (Estes 1992). "Stories," said the author, "are embedded with instruction which guide us about the complexities of life. . . . Stories are medicine. They have such power, they do not require that we do, be, act, anything—we need only listen. The remedies for repair or reclamation of any lost psychic drive are contained in stories" (p. 15–16).

Beyond the world of fairy tales and analysts, there exist an increasing number of children's book titles that teachers and librarians would recognize as contemporary lessons in life. Such fare might well be termed *social-realism*. A child might be helped to deal with the death of a pet in *The Tenth Good Thing About Barney* (Viorst and Blegvad 1975); with ecological issues in *Noah's Ark* (Haley 1971); and *The Great Kapok Tree* (Cherry 1990); or with divorce *My Mother's House, My Father's House* (Christiansen 1992). Of all these books with contemporary themes, clearly the most controversial are those intended to help children understand gay lifestyles and in particular, gay parents, such as *Heather Has Two Mommies* (Newman and Souza 1989); *Daddy's Roommate* (Willhoite 1991). Yet so-called message books are merely the tip of the iceberg when it comes to understanding children's books as agents of socialization.

Beneath the seemingly innocent exterior of traditional children's literature, a powerful ideology is at work, molding the minds and attitudes of young readers. Although most classroom teachers and librarians seldom think of children's books in such terms, the failure to recognize the presence and power of these forces must be seen as the logical outcome of the rather shallow way in which they are introduced to children's books. Once one steps beyond the superficial confines of most children's literature textbooks, the social, psychological, and political aspects of the stories are not difficult to document. Writing in *Children's Literature in Education,* Sutherland described "the hidden persuaders" and "political ideologies" present in children's literature (1985, 143). Exploring the classic tales of Perrault and the Brothers Grimm, Tatar documented the socializing role played by traditional fairy tales. "Children's literature," she wrote, "has always been more intent on producing docile minds than playful bodies. From its inception it has openly endorsed a productive discipline that condemns idleness and disobedience along with other forms of social resistance" (Tatar 1992, cover notes).

Given the apolitical nature of American education, it is quite likely that the political and ideological aspects of children's books will be met with denial and rejection by many who work in the field. Such denial, however understandable, is in and of itself political. The issues of class, gender, and race implicit in multicultural education cannot be swept under the rug, nor adequately responded to by simply selecting more titles about particular groups in our society. Children have to be helped to understand that "all knowledge is socially constructed . . . all knowing is political" (Edelsky, Altwerger, and Flores 1991, 67). The knowledge contained in children's books represents a slice of life—it is part of the picture, but not the whole picture. Nevertheless, those stories and the images that accompany them are capable of profoundly shaping young lives. The Council on Interracial Books for Children has been very clear about the social consequences and outcomes of children's literature:

> [I]n any given society, children's books generally reflect the needs of those who dominate society. A major need is to maintain and fortify the structure of relations between dominator and dominated. . . . Children's books play an active part in maintaining that structure by molding future adults who will accept it (1976, 1).

Children's literature and the images in picture books are but one factor in the complex lexicon of life, but they may constitute a contributing and causal factor in the lives our children come to lead. Relinquishing our tendency to view these books as single, independent entities permits us to see them as the products of an industry, driven like all industries by the profit motive. What stories are told, who tells them, whose eyes they are seen through, and what stories are not told: These issues are central to any understanding of how information is produced in our society. Even though some teachers may be uncomfortable in addressing what seem like political issues, they must realize that "not making connections is as political as making connections" (Edelsky, Altwerger, and Flores 1991, 67). Nor does such an approach have to dwell on differences or division. In fact, the growth of multicultural titles for children makes it increasingly possible for teachers to stress continuity and similarity in cultures. In this way, African Ananse in *A Story, A Story* (Haley 1970) can be connected to Appalachian Jack in *Jack and the Bean Tree; Jack and the Fire Dragon* (Haley 1988) through the theme of the hero quest or journey, well documented in *The Hero with a Thousand Faces* (Campbell 1975). (See transparency master.) Today's children of all colors and cultures can begin to recognize the universality and the continuity of themes evident in the stories of so many lands. They may follow Jack underground, to the home of the fire dragon, and recognize that Alice, too, made such a journey to Wonderland. They may climb the beanstalk with Jack, or the spiderweb with Ananse, and recognize the presence of this sky journey in *Arrow to the Sun* (McDermott 1974), *The Wizard of Oz* (1939), and *Star Wars* (1977). Merely recognizing the similarity of stories is not enough, however. Critical viewing skills and critical thinking skills require more than understanding what the stories are about. They require some understanding of where those stories came from, the relationship between form and content, and the potential effect of those stories on the intended audience. Such an approach locates the study of children's literature within the mainstream of the media literacy movement, where it can be examined like any other product created in the communication conglomerates of corporate America. Such an approach requires that we step beyond the pages and pictures of the bound work, beyond the imagination of the child exploring the story, beyond even the creative process as the author and illustrator labor over the work. A thorough understanding of children's books requires an awareness of their dual nature as both an art form and an industry. Only then can we truly comprehend that there is, in fact, much more to it than meets the eye.

Beyond "Kiddy Lit" 11

# APPALACHIAN JACK

## SIMILARITIES

## DIFFERENCES

## AFRICAN ANANSE

Use this transparency master to have children brainstorm similarities and differences in these African and Appalachian sky journeys. (From *Jack and the Bean Tree*, retold and illustrated by Gail E. Haley, and *A Story, A Story* written and illustrated by Gail E. Haley.)

## Stories That Tell; Stories That Sell

The dual natures of the children's book as both a commercial and an artistic creation, though not necessarily incompatible or in conflict with each other, are nonetheless different enough that anyone seeking to really understand children's literature must recognize both its economic and educational imperatives. Nor can the issue of literacy and children be divorced from the broader issue of literacy in adult society.

Teachers, parents, and librarians struggling to interest children in reading must do so in a culture that, on the surface at least, does not value reading. In 1991, 60 percent of U.S. households failed to purchase a single book, prompting an editorial in *The Nation* to proclaim that "publishing needs all the help it can get" (1991, 1). "Think about it," wrote *USA Today*, "6 out of 10 households didn't buy a work of serious fiction or non-fiction, much less a mystery, a romance novel, a diet guide or a kid's book" (Donahue 1992, D1). One could, of course, argue that these figures do not reflect the true picture—that Americans are actually reading what they borrow from libraries—but, taken with the decline in newspaper readership and the growth of specialty magazines narrowly targeted to particular audiences, there seems ample reason to believe that Americans are reading less and that what they do read lacks substance.

In the midst of these depressing figures, the children's book industry has experienced a boom. In fact, sales of children's books represent the fastest growing segment of the industry, with 1991 sales topping one billion dollars for the first time, more than doubling the sales figures in 1985. But quantity is not the same as quality. The top three paperbacks for children in 1990, for example, were *Teenage Mutant Ninja Turtles*, *Teenage Mutant Ninja Turtles: The Final Lesson*, and *Teenage Mutant Ninja Turtles: The Final Battle* (Sussman 1991, 65–66). The fact that children are reading, even if we disapprove of their choice of reading material, should not be overlooked. Nor can educators ignore the growing relationship between mass media such as motion pictures and spinoff merchandising targeted and marketed to the young consumer. Though many parents and educators no doubt lament this trend and question the quality of the resultant publications, they should also recognize once and for all the fallacy of the old argument that television and other mass media prevent students from reading. In reality, film, television, and rock music are quite capable of motivating children and adolescents to read. The problem, of course, goes back to the quality of what they read. The issue of content, as media literacy suggests, cannot be separated from the question of ownership. The industrial and commercial nature of the publishing industry, including its links to huge communication conglomerates, means that what is published is frequently related to toys, movies, records, posters, and a vast array of other merchandise. In this sense, the independence and sanctity of children's literature has now been consumed by larger economic interests.

This represents a radical departure from the past, and is characterized by the emergence of the electronic storyteller. The oral tradition and even print have given way to this technological tide. For George Gerbner, Dean Emeritus at the Annenberg School of Communication, the implications are enormous:

> For the first time in human history most children are born into homes where most of the stories do not come from their parents, schools, churches, communities...but from a handful of conglomerates who have something to sell. These changes have profound consequences. They have altered the ways we grow up, learn and live (1991).

Gerbner's comments force us to investigate children's literature beyond a simple discussion of what children read, challenging us to consider also where the stories come from.

Other concerns must also be addressed. The issue of *what* children read should not be isolated from the issue of *who* buys the books or even *where* they buy them. The who and the where questions of children's book sales remove educators from the confines of the classroom and curriculum and force us to address the commercial nature of the picture book. In the process, it potentially liberates us by empowering us as consumers. The consumer advocacy movement recognizes the role of the consumer/customer in shaping the products that are available and the way they are marketed and packaged. Educators are not the main consumers of children's books from retail stores. According to 1992 statistics, mothers purchase 41 percent of the books, teachers 16 percent, children 11 percent, and grandparents 10 percent (*USA Today* 1992, D1). With parents and grandparents accounting for more than 50 percent of retail sales, any attempt to improve how much children read and what they read should seek the support of these family members. Like most consumers, particularly those who are not buying for themselves, the adult purchasers of children's books will buy only what is available. They will also buy from a location that is both familiar and accessible, which, in the United States, more often than not, means a mall. Malls have traditionally not been the home of specialty bookstores for children. The book chains that dominate the nation's malls usually have small children's sections with a limited number of titles. This tradition is now giving way, but the changes, though promising, are driven by economic factors, not questions of artistic, literary, or educational merit. The bottom line, as in all industry, remains the buck! As *Publishers Weekly* put it, "[W]ith the growing retailization of children's books ... publishers need newer and bigger markets" (Rosen 1992, 29). The result is the trend on the part of major book chains to open specialty stores for children's books in major shopping malls. Waldenbooks set up Basset Book shops. Barnes and Noble joined the trend, and B. Dalton set up a series of stores called P. B. Pages that actually look like an open book. Another recent development has been the merger between Western Publishing and Toys–R–Us, a strategy designed to put children's books in toys stores where the children are. This may suit consumer convenience—reports have suggested a preponderance of Golden Books on the shelves—which raises serious questions about the quality of the literature available to children in these megastores.

This marketing strategy has both positive and negative implications. On the positive side, more titles aimed at children will become available in outlets where children and their families traditionally shop. On the negative side, this competition might be damaging to quality, independent children's bookstores such as Pooh Corner in Madison, Wisconsin, and The Red Balloon in St. Paul, Minnesota. By 1993, the boom in children's books was already leveling off and *Publishers Weekly* reported that the independent stores were hurting. "Many of the existing children's bookstores are feeling the pinch of the recession and the increased competition from superstores, warehouses, clubs and discount stores. Booksellers are complaining about overpublishing and they're running out of room on their shelves" (Roback 1993, 31). The mass marketing of children's books beyond the school and library market may also result in a conservative, no-risk publishing policy, restricting innovation and diversity in what is published. It may also lead to the increased use of slick marketing and sales techniques, aimed more at catching the eye and wallet of the adult consumer than engaging the heart and mind of the child reader. Ethel Heins, a respected voice in the field of children's literature, said, for example, that "in many contemporary picture books, color and brilliance and sophistication and ornamentation are taking the place of inner substance" (1988, 189).

Such trends are already evident in the publication of picture books by individuals from outside the field of children's literature. The high name recognition of individuals such as Carly Simon or Whoopi Goldberg gives them entree into the children's book field where their names alone guarantee sales. Another likely result of targeting children's books to adult buyers is the continued publication of numerous versions of classic tales such as *Puss in Boots* and *Beauty and the Beast*. Because such titles are instantly familiar to adults, and possibly rekindle memories from their own childhoods, publishers are likely to continue retellings of these time-tested favorites. Recently, there has also been a tendency on the part of publishers to select what would normally be considered adult fare and transform it into picture books.

## 14 Information and Imagery: Expanding the Use of the Picture Book

Two examples are *South Pacific* (Michener and Hague 1992 ) and *Aïda* (Price, Dillon, and Dillon 1990).

There has, of course, always been debate about what really constitutes a children's book, including discussion of what is or is not appropriate for children. One can, for example, find the journals of the field discussing the work of Roald Dahl, acknowledging that "it's about children and it's for children—but is it appropriate?" (Culley 1991, 59). Maurice Sendak, whose children's books have irked some adults, complained about "those who feel that the book has to conform to some set of ritual ideas about childhood.... [U]nless this conforming takes place, they are ill at ease" (Lorraine 1977b, 156). There is little doubt that children and adults respond to stories in different ways. The notion is perfectly consistent with a key tenet of media literacy: Audiences negotiate meaning. In the case of the fantasy genre, Susan Cooper made an interesting observation about the difference between children and adults. "The child knows that the fantasy is true," she has said, "but the adult tends to be handicapped by the fact that it isn't real" (1988, 6). Research also suggests that what an adult thinks is a good children's book is not a very reliable indicator of how children will respond. In a study that examined the relationship between "The Adult as Critic and Child as Reader," researchers reported a negative correlation between books praised by critics and those most frequently borrowed from libraries by children (Nilsen et al. 1980).

Creating children's books for adult eyes is not a new development. A decade ago, in an article entitled "Children's Literature Without Children," Kimmel wrote, "What we are witnessing is the emergence of children's books for adults... exotically illustrated, high-priced picture books that appear to be far too unusual or sophisticated to attract many children" (1982, 41). Earlier, *School Library Journal* complained about "sly sophistication" in publishing, which "ignores a child's experience and is little more than a slightly veiled attempt to lure adult buyers of children's books" (Lewis 1976, 82). *Wilson Library Bulletin* also seized on the trend, describing illustrators whose time "is spent polishing their technique rather than exploring ways of communicating ideas which is, after all, the heart and soul of the picture book" (Lorraine 1977a, 145). One does not have to look very far to find examples of picture books for children in which the pictures seem to be for adults. Technically skillfull and visually stunning books like *The Boy Who Held Back the Sea* (Locker 1987) pay tribute to Vermeer and the Dutch masters. Although books like this often win critical acclaim from adults, and may introduce children to fine art, there is often a coldness in the art that does not communicate with many children. Of all the major journals to highlight this problem, none was perhaps more prestigious nor more controversial than *Horn Book*. In a 1986 editorial called "Could Randolph Caldecott Win the Caldecott Medal?" the distinguished publication lamented the trend toward what it called "high art, high gloss decoration and emotionless embellishment" (1986, 85).

Those who work with children and children's books need to be aware of this development. Careful attention must be given to the overall value of the book for the child reader. Often that means trying to see the book through the eyes of the child. It also means being alert as consumers. In advertising there is a saying, "unseen is unsold." Like it or not, children's literature is advertised and marketed like any other product. To catch the eye of the adult buyer, the book jacket must be splashy. Teachers and librarians would do well to remember that you can't judge a book by its cover. Nor can a book be judged by gimmicks and tricks posing as technological advances. Such sales devices provoked one newspaper to observe that "a book that doesn't move, squeak, bang or pop up is in falling demand" (Walden 1992, 18).

For the moment, however, literature-based learning and multicultural education seem to be fueling a steady supply of quality literature for children. Those who welcome this trend should also be aware that publishers have simply responded to the marketplace and to economic demands. Although this gives teachers and librarians a great deal of power, that power may be eroded as the commercialization of children's literature continues. In the recent past, there has still been room for small, quiet books for children. Jane Yolen's *Owl Moon* (Yolen and Schoenherr 1987) surprisingly managed to win a Caldecott, but the author knew what she was contending with and thought she would be lucky to sell out the first printing.

"Splashy books get the attention. Conventional wisdom is what makes publishing run most of the time" (Yolen 1989, 200). It is now time for the question of what makes publishing run to receive serious consideration in courses for teachers and librarians. Only by understanding the conditions and the context in which these products are created can the traditional custodians of children's literature begin to exert an active influence on a market that may soon succumb to the lure of quantity over quality. With the publishing industry now so firmly a part of great business conglomerates, those who wish to fully understand children's literature cannot separate the look of the book from the targeted market, the telling of the tale from its selling.

# References

Alles, Hemesh (1992). *Errata: What's Wrong with This Picture?* New York: Green Tiger Press.

Antonucci, Ron (1993). Rylant on Writing. *School Library Journal*, May: 26–30.

Bader, Barbara (1975). Picture Books, Art and Illustration. In *Newbery and Caldecott Medal Books, 1966–1975*. Boston: Horn Book.

Berger, John (1972). *Ways of Seeing*. Middlesex, England: Penguin.

Bettelheim, Bruno (1977). *The Uses of Enchantment: The Meaning and Importance of Fairy Tales*. New York: Vintage.

Bloom, Allan (1987). *The Closing of the American Mind*. New York: Simon & Schuster.

Boyer, Ernest (1988). Preface. In *Television and America's Children: A Crisis of Neglect*, edited by Edward Palmer. New York: Oxford University Press.

Busbin, O. Mell, and Susan Steinfirst (1989). Critics of Artwork in Children's Picture Books: A Content Analysis. *Journal of Youth Services in Libraries* 2 (3): 257–65.

Butler, Francelia (1992). The Trashing of Children's Literature. *Ms. Magazine,* September/October: 61.

Campbell, Joseph (1975). *The Hero with a Thousand Faces*. London: Abacus.

Cherry, Lynne (1990). *The Great Kapok Tree: A Tale of the Amazon Rain Forest*. San Diego, CA: Harcourt Brace Jovanovich.

Chiarelott, Leigh (1984). Cognition and the Media-ted Curriculum: Effects of Growing Up in an Electronic Environment. *Educational Technology* 24 (5): 19–22.

Christiansen, C. B. (1992). *My Mother's House, My Father's House*. New York: Atheneum.

Considine, David M., and Gail E. Haley (1992). *Visual Messages: Integrating Imagery into Instruction*. Englewood, CO: Teacher Ideas Press.

Cooper, Susan (1988). Preserving the Light. *Magpies,* no. 2: 5–9.

Council on Interracial Books for Children (1976). *Human and Anti-Human Values in Children's Books*. New York.

Culley, Jonathan (1991). It's About Children and It's for Children, But Is It Appropriate? *Children's Literature in Education* 22 (1): 59–73.

Debes, John (1974). Paper presented at the annual convention of the Teachers of English, New Orleans, LA, January 29.

Donahue, Deidre (1992). Books Pushed to the Back of the Shelf. *USA Today*, June 24, D1.

Dondis, Donis (1973). *A Primer of Visual Literacy*. Cambridge: MIT Press.

Dwyer, Frank, M. Szabo, and H. DeMelo (1981). Visual Testing: Visual Literacy's Second Dimension. *Journal of Visual Verbal Languaging* 1 (1): 37–47.

Edelsky, Carole, Bess Altwerger, and Barbara Flores (1991). *Whole Language: What's the Difference?* Portsmouth, NH: Heinemann.

Eisner, Elliot (1991). What Really Counts in Schools? *Educational Leadership* 48 (5): 10–11, 14–17.

Elkind, David (1981). *The Hurried Child: Growing Up Too Fast, Too Soon*. Reading, MA: Addison-Wesley.

Entman, Robert (1989). *Democracy Without Citizens: Media and the Decay of American Politics*. New York: Oxford University Press.

Estes, Clarissa Pinkola (1992). *Women Who Run with the Wolves: Myths and Stories of the Wild Woman Archetype*. New York: Ballantine.

Evans, Dilys (1992). An Extraordinary Vision: Picture Books of the 90s. *Horn Book*, November/December: 759–63.

Gerbner, George (1991). Draft correspondence.

Greenaway, Peter (1991). *Teaching the Visual Media*. Milton, Queensland, Australia: Jacaranda Press.

Haley, Gail E. (1970). *A Story, A Story*. New York: Atheneum.

———. (1971). *Noah's Ark*. New York: Atheneum.

———. (1979). *The Green Man*. New York: Scribners.

———. (1986). *Jack and the Bean Tree*. New York: Crown.

———. (1988). *Jack and the Fire Dragon*. New York: Crown.

———. (1992a). *Mountain Jack Tales*. New York: Dutton.

———. (1992b). Puppetry as Illustration, Part 1. *The Puppetry Journal* 43 (3): 11–14.

Handford, Martin (1987). *Where's Waldo?* Boston: Little, Brown.

Hankla, Susan (1982). Letter. *Horn Book,* June: 347.

Heins, Ethel (1988). From Mallards to Maine: A Conversation with Robert McCloskey. *Journal of Youth Services in Libraries* 1 (2): 187–93.

Hirsch, E. D. (1988). *Cultural Literacy: What Every American Needs to Know.* New York: Vintage.

*Horn Book* (1986). Could Randolph Caldecott Win the Caldecott Medal? August: 85.

Hughes, Shirley (1991). "Word and Image." In *On Writing for Children: Nine Papers from the Annual Lecture Series in Children's Literature* 17–19. Brisbane, Australia: Queensland University of Technology.

Hunt, Peter (1984). Narrative Theory and Children's Literature. *Journal of the Children's Literature Association Quarterly* 9 (4): 191–94.

Kimmel, Eric (1982). Children's Literature Without Children. *Children's Literature in Education* 13 (1): 38–44.

Kirstein, Lincoln, and Alan Vaes (1992). Review of *Puss in Boots. School Library Journal,* April: 108.

Kozol, Jonathan (1985). *Illiterate America.* Garden City, NY: Anchor Press.

Lent, Blair (1977). There's More to the Picture Than Meets the Eye. *Wilson Library Bulletin* 52 (2): 161–64.

Lewis, Marjorie (1976). Back to Basics: Reevaluating Picture Books. *School Library Journal* 22 (7): 82–83.

Locker, Thomas (1987). *The Boy Who Held Back the Sea.* New York: Dial.

Lorraine, Walter (1977a). The Art of the Picture Book. *Wilson Library Bulletin* 52 (2): 145–47.

——— (1977b). Interview with Maurice Sendak. *Wilson Library Bulletin* 52 (2): 152–58.

Lukens, Rebecca (1982). The President's Message. *Proceedings of the Ninth Annual Conference of the Children's Literature Association,* University of Florida, Gainesville, FL, March 26.

Macaulay, David (1990). *Black and White.* Boston, MA: Houghton Mifflin.

——— (1991). Caldecott Medal Acceptance Speech. *Horn Book,* July-August: 419–23.

Marantz, Kenneth (1977). The Picture Book as Art Object: A Call for Balanced Reviewing. *Wilson Library Bulletin* 55 (1): 148–51.

Martin, Jr., Bill, John Archambault, and Ted Rand (1987). *Knots on a Counting Rope.* New York: Henry Holt.

McDermott, Gerald (1974). *Arrow to the Sun.* New York: Viking.

McKim, Robert H. (1972). *Experiences in Visual Thinking.* Monterey, CA: Brooks Cole.

Michener, James, and Michael Hague (1992). *South Pacific*. San Diego, CA: Harcourt Brace Jovanovich.

Mikolaycak, Charles (1986). The Artist at Work: The Challenge of the Picture Book. *Horn Book,* March/April: 167–73.

Naisbitt, John (1982). *Megatrends*. New York: Warner Books.

*The Nation* (1992). Public Publishing. February 3: 1.

Naylor, Alice (1991). Eight Dilemmas of the Newbery Committee. *Perspectives* 7 (3): v–viii.

Newman, Leslea, and Diana Souza (1989). *Heather Has Two Mommies*. North Hampton, MA: In Other Words.

Nilsen, Aileen Pace, et al. (1980). The Adult as Critic Versus the Child as Reader. *Language Arts* 57 (5): 530–39.

Nodelman, Perry (1992). *The Pleasures of Children's Literature*. New York: Longman.

Postman, Neil (1985). *Amusing Ourselves to Death*. New York: Viking.

Pressley, G. M. (1976). Mental Imagery Helps Eight-Year-Olds Remember What They Read. *Journal of Educational Psychology* 68 (3): 355–59.

Price, Leontyne, Leo Dillon, and Diane Dillon (1990). *Aïda*. San Diego, CA: Harcourt Brace Jovanovich.

*Publishers Weekly* (1992). Review of *Mountain Jack Tales*. November 9: 86.

Robak, Diane (1993). Bookstores Applying the Brakes. *Publishers Weekly,* January 11: 31.

Rosen, Judith (1992). Children's Books in the Chains. *Publishers Weekly,* October 12: 26–29.

*School Library Journal* (1992). Review of *Mountain Jack Tales*. December: 96.

Scieszka, Jon, and Lane Smith (1989). *The True Story of the Three Little Pigs*. New York: Viking.

Sendak, Maurice (1981). *Outside Over There*. New York: Harper & Row.

Shannon, George (1989). *Arnold Lobel*. Boston,: Twayne.

Shenkman, Harriet (1985). Reversing the Literacy Decline by Controlling the Electronic Demons. *Educational Leadership* 42 (5): 26–30.

Sinatra, Richard (1986). *Visual Literacy: Connections to Thinking, Reading, and Writing*. Springfield, IL: Charles C. Thomas.

Steig, Michael (1985). Reading *Outside Over There*. In *Children's Literature*. Vol. 13. New Haven, CT: Yale University Press.

Stewig, John Warren (1992). Reading Pictures, Reading Texts: Some Similarities. *The New Advocate* 55 (1): 11–22.

Sussman, Vic (1991). Best Books for Kids. *U.S. News and World Report*, December 23: 65–66.

Sutherland, Robert (1985). Hidden Persuaders: Political Ideologies in Literature for Children. *Children's Literature in Education* 16 (3): 143–57.

Tatar, Maria (1992). *Off with Their Heads: Fairy Tales and the Culture of Childhood.* Princeton, NJ: Princeton University Press.

*USA Today* (1992). Who Buys the Most Children's Books? April 9, D1.

Vandergrift, Kay, and Jane Anne Hannigan (1993). Reading the Image. *School Library Journal,* January: 20–25.

Viorst, Judith, and Brik Blegvad (1975). *The Tenth Good Thing About Barney.* New York: Macmillan.

Walden, P. (1992). Show Me a Closed Library and I'll Show You a Closed Mind. *Daily Telegraph,* February 27, 18.

Wessell, Frances (1992). Catholic Connections to Media Literacy: Who Tells the Stories? Newsletter, *Center for Media and Values.*

Wiesner, David (1991). *Tuesday.* New York: Clarion.

——— (1992). Caldecott Medal Acceptance Speech. *Horn Book,* July-August: 417–22.

Willhoite, Michael (1991). *Daddy's Roommate.* Boston: Alyson Wonderland.

Wilson, Trudy (1986). Visual Literacy: Survey of Experimental Research, 1981–1985. *Visual Literacy Newsletter* 15 (1): 1–7.

Winn, William (1982). Visualization in Learning and Instruction: A Cognitive Approach. *Educational Communication and Technology Journal* 30 (Spring): 3–25.

Wisniewski, David (1990). *Elfwyn's Saga.* New York: Lothrop, Lee & Shepard.

Wolcott, John (1992). Land of Hype and Glory: Spin Doctors on Parade. *U.S. News and World Report,* February 10: 6.

Wood, Don (1986). The Artist at Work: Where Ideas Come From. *Horn Book,* September-October: 556–65.

Yolen, Jane (1989). On Silent Wings: The Marketing of *Owl Moon. The New Advocate* 2 (4): 199–211.

Yolen, Jane, and John Schoenherr (1987). *Owl Moon.* New York: Philomel.

## Other Reading

Bang, Molly (1991). *Picture This: Perception and Composition*. Boston: Little, Brown.

Baum, Susan (1985). How to Use Picture Books to Challenge the Gifted. *Early Years K8*, April: 48–49.

Benedict, Susan, and Lenore Carlisle (1992). *Beyond Words: Picture Books for Older Readers and Writers*. Portsmouth, NH: Heinemann.

Bogen, J. (1975). Some Educational Aspects of Hemispheric Specialization. *UCLA Educator*, Spring: 24–32.

Debes, John (1978). Cultural Symbolism, Visual Literacy and Intellectual Equality. *Educational Media International*, no. 22: 27–31.

Kensinger, Faye (1987). *Children of the Series and How They Grew*. Bowling Green, OH: Bowling Green State University Popular Press.

Kunen, Seth, D. Green, and D. Waterman (1979). Human Memory and Learning: Spread of Encoding Effects Within the Nonverbal Visual Domain. *Journal of Experimental Psychology*, Spring: 574–84.

Probst, Robert (1984). Visual Literacy. In *Adolescent Literature: Responses and Analysis*. Columbus, OH: Charles Merril.

Richey, Virginia, and Katharyn Puckett (1992). *Wordless and Almost Wordless Picture Books: A Guide*. Englewood, CO: Libraries Unlimited.

Stewig, John Warren (1980). What Do Reviews Really Review? *Top of the News* 37 (1): 83–84.

Williams, Clarence (1978). The Concept and Purpose of Visual Literacy. *Educational Media International*, no. 3: 26–29.

Chapter 2

# *Pictures and Pedagogy*

There are many ways to see.
—*Knots on a Counting Rope,*
    Martin, Archamault, and Rand, (1987)

## Imagery and Instruction

As the last decade of the twentieth century began, the iconic information revolution continued to sweep the western world, transforming the way we produce, store, access, and process information. Despite the high-visibility of these image-based technologies including distance-learning, interactive video, and multi-media, our classrooms and curricula have been slow in responding to these technologies as delivery systems for the traditional curriculum and as content and competencies, constituting a completely new curriculum. Recognizing the problem, former Secretary of Education, Terrel Bell said "[C]hildren today live in a world of visual images and modern technology. . . [A] technological revolution is transforming and restructuring all aspects of society-except its schools. Schools cannot continue to stagnate in this nineteenth century mode" (1992, 10). Agreeing with Bell, the Director of the Institute for the Transfer of Technology to Education reported that "chalkboard lectures and textbooks continue to dominate instruction" (Mecklenburger 1990, 106).

For teachers and students to make full use of the visual materials continuing to flood the educational marketplace, visual learning must be given greater prominence and respect in teacher preparation. Some 75 years have passed since the first course in visual instruction offered for credit was presented at the University of Minnesota in 1918. Just five years later, in a major report that remains relevant today, researchers said, "The movement for visual education will progress in direct ratio to the number of teachers who are trained in the technique of visual instruction. . . . [T]eachers must be given an opportunity to learn the advantages and disadvantages of visual instruction through formal and informal instruction" (McClusky 1923, 193).

Despite the seemingly obvious nature of these conclusions, there is widespread evidence to suggest that although schools continue to acquire visual media and image-based technologies, teachers are seldom fully trained in how to maximize these materials in the teaching/learning process. This was among several conclusions reached by the 1988 OTA Report, *Power On!: New Tools for Teaching and Learning* (U.S. Congress, Office of Technology Assessment 1988). It has often been argued that teacher use of these materials would increase with greater access, but the issue must now be addressed in terms of qualitative use of media and technology. Research also indicates that even when materials are available, teachers still tend not to use them (Proctor 1983; Smith and Ingersoll 1984; Seidman 1986). Significantly, there is also a body of research indicating that teacher use of media tends to be attitudinal

## 22  Pictures and Pedagogy

(Bellamy et al. 1978; Seidman 1986). Which is to say, how teachers feel about media and technology often influences their willingness to use them.

The attitudinal research emphasizes ways of motivating teachers to use media, technology, and visual teaching strategies. For teachers to integrate such techniques and materials into their methodology, they must first value the contribution these materials can make to them as professionals. Again, the history of instructional technology tells us that the present has failed to learn from the past. A 1923 study of teacher preparation noted that "much training in-service has been concerned with the technique of handling visual equipment rather than the technique of instruction" (Saettler 1968, 132). Today, whether in the area of computers, educational media, or audiovisual instruction, it is quite common to find the nation's student teachers being trained how to operate hardware, with very little understanding of how to evaluate software, design and produce their own products, or link materials and strategies to learner characteristics, media attributes, and educational objectives. The demands of such courses often seem so unrewarding to these young teachers that, even after this training, they fail to use the materials they have been prepared for (Carter and Schmidt 1985). It is hardly surprising that research shows teachers to be suspicious not only of media, but also of the media specialist (Willis 1981). Such a climate is not an accident; it is the creation of teacher training still rooted in the past and the primacy of print.

Our universities and teacher training colleges tend to perpetuate outdated methods of instruction in outmoded courses even while school reform and restructuring propels public schools toward outcome-based education. Waggoner (1984) saw the lecture tradition in institutes of higher learning as a major barrier to innovation. Hand-in-hand with the dominance of the lecture tradition is the prevalence of print and a testing/teaching system predisposed almost entirely to reading and writing. As a result, when colleges of higher education should be preparing tomorrow's teachers for instructional innovation, too often they actually lag behind, lacking the expertise to model changes and new techniques. "The average university in this country, in terms of its use of information technology in teaching, is substantially behind the typically elementary and secondary school" (Staman 1990). Although this may represent something of an overstatement, there is too much research, conducted over too long a time period, to discount or discredit the piecemeal, fragmented response to media and technology in teacher training. As the 1980s came to an end, *Educational Technology* said: "[V]ery few universities currently prepare teachers to use instructional technologies by modeling the use of technology in classes taught in the university. . . . [F]or most faculty in teacher education, technology is a bother, a mystery, a blur, a largely incomprehensible phenomenon" (Gooler 1989, 20).

Before public school teachers can make better use of new technologies and methods, those who are responsible for training them must undergo their own major reeducation. Faculty development was a central recommendation of the OTA report. Those who take on the responsibility for this task would do well to consult the literature of management as well as that of technology. Teachers have traditionally resisted technology because of the way it has been presented to them. Faculty will also resist any attempt to change what or how they teach until the issue of motivation is addressed. The Concerns Based Adoption Model (Hall and Wallace 1973; Naidu 1988) offers an important opportunity to plan in-service and preservice training programs that address the nature and needs of the client. This technique matches innovation with the day-to-day concerns and career stage of the individuals who must implement the changes. Ideally, such an approach would look holistically at education to make sure that administrators in higher education, as well as those in the public schools, were exposed to courses and training programs that enabled them to value the role of media and technology in teaching. If teachers are to change the way they teach, they must do so in an organizational culture and climate where the leadership is predisposed to the role these new materials and methods can play in education (Merck and Fleit 1988; Pritchard and Busby 1991). The starting point for such a change is to assemble the body of research that has accumulated in the area of visual learning. The next stage is to disseminate it.

# Visual Literacy

Sless and others have argued that "the current imbalances in the curriculum are due to educational policies and philosophies that came about historically . . . in terms of the kinds of skills that were thought necessary for the education of factory workers and administrators in the nineteenth century" (Sless 1984, 226). Today, faced with fierce global economic competition, the United States needs an education system that creates individuals with fundamentally different skills and abilities. In 1991, the Secretary of Labor received a copy of the report from the Secretary's Commission on Achieving Necessary Skills. Addressing the skills that workers in the twenty-first century would need, the document pinpointed the ability to evaluate, process, and use information in all its forms and the ability to understand and use technology. The increasingly iconic nature of information and information technologies requires workers with more than the technical ability to operate a piece of equipment. Increasingly, those who work with these information systems will need the vision competencies associated with visual literacy. The workplace is already responding to this realization. The Federal Office Systems Exposition in Washington, D.C., for example, recently added a new visual applications training track. Discussing the need for such skills, *Training and Development* wrote that, "well trained for it or not, many office workers already work with desktop publishing that involves image-manipulation" (Kirrane 1992, 58).

With an anticipated decline in the cost of such technologies, it is expected that pictorial information systems will proliferate, with enormous significance for society and all our assumptions about literacy. The ability to read print from the page, for example, is not the same as the ability to read projected print (Stevenson 1984). The ability to write for the printed page does not automatically transfer to information displayed on a screen. Design elements, based on an understanding of human perception and media characteristics, become a vital contributor to the success of any such communication. "With the display screen, such traditional print media concerns as use of illustration and color take on a new navigational significance. Illustration becomes a way of breaking the monotony of the text; color becomes a key to use and retrieval" (Bradford 1984, 14). Our understanding of the processes of both reading and writing must change in response to our new information systems. Our schools must now recognize that "the potential for 'visual culture' to displace 'print culture' is an idea with implications as profound as the shift from oral culture to print culture" (Kirrane 1992, 58). Just as schools in the nineteenth century evolved to meet the needs of the industrial age, today's schools must now change in response to the social and economic realities of the information age. Central to that shift is a recognition of the role pictures play in shaping our beliefs and attitudes, whether those images are illustrations in children's books or the increasingly sophisticated images of television, computer graphics, video games, or educational software.

Comprehending today's world requires an understanding of visual information. Imagery is a central element of human communication. Some 65 percent of information imparted between people is nonverbal in nature (Kundu 1986). Research recognizes the "relative universality of visual literacy" through all countries and cultures, suggesting that "it appears that it is normally distributed and that all of us possess this talent to some degree" (Dwyer 1978, 58). At an early age, children begin naturally to process their visual environment. They are, in fact, "capable of reading pictures long before they are capable of reading words" (Pettersson 1984, 2). But, although they can see visuals, their pictorial proficiency is rudimentary and must be nurtured. Research has indicated, for example, that children arrive at school "lacking pictorial concept mastery" (Snyder 1984).

Some may see such skills as peripheral to the role of schools. In reality, though, these vision competencies are central to traditional schooling. Properly understood and cultivated, they support reading, writing, and thinking skills. For children between the ages of four and eight, images facilitate formation of concepts about themselves and their world (Bruner 1960).

## 24 Pictures and Pedagogy

From their earliest encounter with reading, visual discrimination skills are central to children's ability to recognize letters and words (Whisler 1984). Perception problems, such as those associated with distinguishing between the letters *b* and *d* or *p* and *b*, are also directly related to their success with reading. Whereas most educators clearly recognize that how the child sees will affect how the child reads, other relationships between visualization and learning are often less understood. In a fascinating chapter called "Draw Me a Word, Write Me a Picture," Newkirk shows the print bias in education and the language links between pictures and prose. "School culture," he says, "is wordcentered; while we might admire the drawings of young children, we're not terribly concerned when the interest in drawing gives way to an interest in print" (1989, 36). In reality, as many authors know, visualization can actually facilitate written expression (Graves and Hansen 1983; Dyson 1986). In her visits to classrooms and libraries throughout the country, author-illustrator Gail Haley often employs such strategies to promote the flow of language. Guided imagery activities may be used to help children project themselves into a story, where their imaginations allow them hear, see, smell, and touch the developing ideas. The fragments of stories that begin to emerge from the imaginings of these students may be transferred as words to pages, or they may become drawings on paper. In stimulating the creative process, Haley employs many strategies to unlock the stories she believes each child has inside. One visual technique that she has used for many years involves the use of paper figures and shadow puppets employed with an overhead projector. Children who have difficulty verbalizing a story, or committing print to paper, often experience a form of language liberation through playing with the shadows cast by the puppets. These pictures serve as a catalyst for children's creativity and are quite consistent with learning-styles research related to visual and tactual kinesthetic learners.

Haley's methods are rooted in her own experience of learning, but the idea of using visuals to promote writing skills is well documented in academia. In *Visual Literacy: Connections to Thinking, Reading and Writing*, Sinatra argues that "the teaching of separate disciplines, reading, writing and the arts, prevents children from letting different forms of expression emerge from and into one another. In other words, the creation of a toy or puppet or painting can be the impetus for an oral or written composition" (1986, 32). Using illustrations from popular magazines, slides, photographs, and other visual materials, Sinatra has demonstrated the role pictures can play in developing composition. These materials are particularly useful with students classified as language deficient, who have difficulty imagining what to write about. Students whose language skills are influenced by visual/spatial input also benefit from the use of imagery in instruction, because it facilitates their right-hemisphered learning style (Sinatra 1983).

Although pictures can stimulate students to write, pictures and symbols, in and of themselves, actually constitute their own form of writing. Teachers who have worked with rebus writing will be familiar with how successful this approach can be. Rebus activities can also be integrated into several areas of the curriculum (for instance, they could be used in the study of Egyptian hieroglyphics or Native American picture writing). Because visual literacy includes the ability to both comprehend (read) and create (write) visuals, teachers using rebus methods should have students make their own visual stories as well as read those created by the teacher or other students. These encoding (writing) and decoding (interpreting) functions address the two key components of visual literacy.

Similar techniques have proven to be successful with editorial cartoons, which can be used very creatively in social studies classes. Work with these cartoons provides another link between the visual language of the picture book and the iconic modes of communication in film, television, advertising, and computer graphics. Students can examine these cartoons in terms of their graphic design and artistic technique. They can explore the relationship between image and text. Their thinking skills can be developed by applying semantic mapping strategies from reading education to help them "compare, contrast, classify and identify patterns and relationships" (Steinbrink and Bliss 1988, 218). The analysis of political and editorial cartoons has been shown to be especially useful in "helping young learners to recognize bias, satire and exaggeration" (Steinbrink and Bliss 1988, 217). Thus, working with cartoons develops information skills that can be transferred to the analysis of visual media, including broadcast news and advertising. Like rebus writing, the use of editorial cartoons should not be restricted to the interpretation of existing materials, but should also include the opportunity for students to make their own cartoons based on the issues or individuals they are studying.

Educators who are interested in promoting the concept of visual literacy need to be aware of these and other ways in which vision competencies can promote and support traditional literacy skills, as well as critical thinking skills. Too often in the past, media literacy and visual literacy have been relegated, like the study of art, to a matter of appreciation and aesthetics lurking on the periphery of the curriculum. Such competencies have been tolerated (at best) but never given the central role they now demand based on the realities of how western society communicates. Visual literacy is about much more than the appreciation of pictures. It "includes the ability to understand and use images, including the ability to think, learn and express oneself in terms of visuals" (Braden and Hortin 1982, 41). As the critical thinking skills movement gathers momentum in American education, another opportunity exists for visual literacy proponents to articulate their case. The ability to think critically cannot and should not be restricted to the contemplation of the classics, as some educational elitists would have it. Critical thinking must be related to the information forms of our culture and society. If that society now communicates through mass media and iconic modes, our schools must begin to teach students to think *about* those visual messages. In addition, emphasis must be placed on the concept of thinking *with* and *through* visual modes. Robert McKim, with his *Experiences in Visual Thinking* (1972), was an early advocate of the role of visualization in thinking. Since that time, research with concepts such as mental rehearsal continues to demonstrate a relationship between seeing and thinking. Writing in the *Newsletter of the International Visual Literacy Association*, John Hortin articulated this relationship, saying, "[V]isual thinking is the ability to create visuals in our own minds to help us solve problems, interpret the past, relive moments, process external visual stimuli and create our own meaning" (1984, 3).

The children's picture book and visual literacy research offer a compelling opportunity for teachers and librarians to dramatically redefine literacy and improve the thinking skills of their students. Such a development represents much more than another fad or passing phase. It is firmly rooted in the industrialtechnological development of the nation and in a solid body of research related to the role pictures play in human perception.

## Learning from Visuals: What the Research Shows

The adage "A picture is worth a thousand words" seems well supported by a body of research that indicates, among other things, that pictures can improve comprehension (Levin and Lesgold 1978) and facilitate both short-term and long-term recall (Haring and Fry 1979). A number of studies conducted with K–6 students support the contention that, when properly used, visuals can make a major contribution to learning. "Both males and females benefit from pictures. So do children at all ages between 6 and 12. Picture facilitation has been obtained in both rural and urban communities and with children drawn from both middle-class white populations and lower-class black populations" (Levin and Lesgold 1978, 238).

For those who believe that these techniques require the use of expensive and sophisticated computer graphics and other materials, the research offers food for thought—and cause for celebration. In fact, visual literacy research proves that schools do not require expensive technology to improve learning. Line drawings, cartoons, flashcards, and picture books can all improve recall and comprehension of verbal and print material, when properly used. Studies indicate that proper use includes employing "story-relevant" (Levin et al. 1979) visuals to support learning. Such visuals anchor the concepts in the child's mind and promote cueing and retrieval operations. In addition to visual materials used by the teacher, research also indicates that "internal representations" and "visual imagery have been found to facilitate children's recall of story information" (Levin et al. 1979, 89). In other words, when children imagine a visual related to the concept they are learning, that internal picture or mental image helps them understand and remember the idea. Inspecting illustrations and then describing them in a visual/verbal interface has also been shown to "significantly increase the amount of constructive visual thinking in which both children and adults engage" (Kunen and Duncan 1983, 372).

The illustrated children's book offers a perfect opportunity for teachers to engage students in activities like this. Addressing the illustrations as both information and decoration, students can analyze the pictures in terms of both form and content, exploring the relationship between what is shown and how it is shown. At a more advanced level, students can go beyond an internal reading of the frame to an external evaluation of how the representation relates to the real world. In the case of multicultural education, this process is of great importance, raising questions of visual validity and artistic authenticity (see chapter 8).

Throughout the 1980s, research continued to support the role of visual teaching strategies. One study concluded that "illustrations can and do often increase children's learning of meaningful verbal materials" (Pressley et al. 1982, 151). Two years later, *Instructional Innovator* wrote: "Pictures are a very versatile instructional tool. Pictures, for example, are better remembered than words. They can make complex and abstract ideas more meaningful and concrete. They can affect emotions and attitudes, and students find them interesting" (Brody 1984, 21). Several schools throughout the country served as useful demonstrations of the role visual literacy could play in the curriculum. Work in Milford, Ohio; Roanoke, Virginia; and Lafayette, Indiana, among other sites, resulted in the following conclusions: 1) identifiable visual skills that can be taught do exist; 2) schools should be teaching these skills; 3) teachers can be taught these techniques; and 4) school systems have the financial resources necessary to implement such training (Burbank and Pett 1983).

Training teachers to effectively use visual instruction techniques is a necessary prerequisite for students to benefit from visuals in instruction. The acquisition and purchase of visual materials without accompanying teacher training will undermine the potential benefits of such materials. As part of a teaching strategy, visuals cannot simply be injected into lesson plans. They must be selected and applied based on the characteristics of the learners and the instructional objectives. "A picture will improve instruction only if the desired learning outcome is appropriate for the picture's capabilities, and if the picture serves the necessary instructional functions" (Brody 1984, 21).

Although sections of our society still seem inclined to accept the propositions that "seeing is believing," or "what you see is what you get," in fact there is more to it than meets the eye. There is a vast difference between looking and actually seeing—a difference that might best be described in terms of critical viewing skills, which is the analytical or "reading" component of both media literacy and visual literacy. Simply showing children pictures does not mean that they will learn from them. "It has been observed that learners frequently overlook details in complex illustrations *unless they are prompted to pay attention*" (Beck 1984, 207). The process of prompting becomes one of the most important strategies teachers can engage in. Through verbal and written directions, teachers can encourage students to look more carefully at illustrations. Simple statements such as "pay attention to," "look carefully at," or "what do you see?" raise the expectations of young learners and focus their attention more fully. Research has clearly demonstrated that the attitudes and assumptions learners have about the instructional task and medium will influence the level of learning they derive from the materials. Working with sixth-graders' preconceptions about print and television, Salomon and Leigh concluded that "the amount of mental effort they invest in utilizing or processing what they see and hear" (1984, 119) is related to their expectations of the media. Students tend to think of television as "easy," so they invest little mental energy when viewing. This process is called *cognitive economy* or *shallow processing*. This is one reason why instructional television and new projects like *Channel One* have had less impact than might be expected. Too much emphasis has been placed on *what* programs children watch, while too little attention has been directed to *how* they watch (Considine and Haley 1992). When teachers function as instructional intermediaries between the students and what they are looking at, educational outcomes are profoundly altered. In the case of television, researchers have concluded, "changing the effects of television depends on interventions with viewers" (Huston et al. 1992, 6).

For Salomon and Leigh, the concept of AIME (Amount of Invested Mental Energy) is the basis of this intervention. If children are to more fully benefit from the use of visual media in the classroom, teachers must change the expectations children have about those media. If children see the illustrations in picture books as decorations, they are less likely to devote time to thinking about their form and content. If, in contrast, the teacher suggests that the pictures contain information that is not in the text, the children have reason to process the pictures on a higher level. If the teacher asks the students to think about what technique the artist used, or why a vertical or horizontal format was chosen, once again children are provided with reasons to reconceptualize the form and content of the picture book.

In *The Interaction of Media, Cognition and Learning* (1979), Salomon provided further opportunity for teachers and media specialists to dramatically increase the instructional strategies available to them when working with picture books. Arguing that media "affects the mastery of mental skills through the symbolic modes they employ" (p. xx), Salomon demonstrated that if the content remained the same, but the media format changed, there would be a change in learner outcome. Applied to the children's book, this concept has far-reaching implications. Audiovisual versions of these stories, whether on video, filmstrip, or cassette, offer teachers an opportunity to explore the same story in different ways, to affect different learner skills. A single filmstrip, for example, can be presented without the visual to foster critical listening skills. Children can be asked to visualize and illustrate characters and events from the story. This independent use of imagination cannot take place after they have seen the illustrations in the book, video, or filmstrip version of the story.

By selecting and varying the approach to any given story, teachers can target specific competencies to be developed. Research with Gail Haley's *A Story, A Story* (1970) clearly demonstrated how different outcomes could be generated by different approaches. The African folktale was presented to one group in picture-book form, which was read to them, while the other group watched a television version of the story. Significant differences were revealed as to what each group derived from the experience of the story. When asked to retell the story in their own words, the children who saw the television version "include[d] more character actions, more active verbs in their accounts.... [C]hildren's memory for story events improved from seeing the characters in action" (Brown 1986b, 38). By contrast, the children who heard the story "retained more of the author's vocabulary in their retellings; for example, they more often repeated phrases such as 'by his foot' and referred to characters by their formal names, Ananse and Osebo" (p. 38). The television viewers tended to mention these characters more generally, as "the man" or "the leopard." What the children derived from the story was clearly affected by the form, or what Salomon refers to as the media attributes or symbol systems. With less picture information to draw upon, "the book audience seemed more attentive to the sound of the language" (p. 38). When vocabulary was new or unfamiliar, as in the case of words like *calabash*, the television version provided vocabulary enhancement information.

Brown's research with *A Story, A Story* and other books is reported in detail, with illustrations, in *Taking Advantage of Media* (1986a). Among other findings, the research suggests:

- Preschool children can recall the order or narrative sequence of a story better when it is conveyed visually rather than orally

- Moving pictures can reinforce verbal messages

- Still pictures can facilitate prose learning.

For these outcomes to actually occur, more emphasis has to be placed on how children are introduced to these materials. With video, filmstrip, and audio versions of so many children's books now available, it is important that educators understand that each format represents a different learning experience for the child, even though the story remains the same. The benefits to be derived from these materials can be achieved only when the process, not just the program, is stressed.

## How Children See Pictures: Preferences and Processes

Knowing that pictures facilitate learning, and that teacher intervention can nurture the process of learning from visuals, is only part of the concept. As reading teachers need to understand children's developmental levels and their vocabulary acquisition skills, those who work with visuals must also understand the ways in which children recognize and read visual stimuli. As Higgins said, "[T]he empirical study of inference drawing based on pictures is becoming increasingly relevant to the educational enterprise" (1978, 217). One of the potential pitfalls of working with pictures is the assumption that everyone sees a picture in the same way. Too often, too much reliance is placed on the content of the picture rather than the process by which the child encounters, explores, and experiences the picture. The reality of the picture as object does not necessarily conform to how that reality is perceived by the child. "We sometimes overlook the fact that different learners may use pictures in different ways. We also overlook the fact that different learners experience different levels of success in gaining information from pictures in various instructional tasks" (Hurt 1989, 24).

Studies that address the way children respond to pictures have often focused on their preferences. Typically, these studies either looked at children's response to picture content, or considered their response to picture form, such as color and artistic style. One study worked with fourth-, fifth-, and sixth-graders, measuring their picture preferences in children's books. Notably, the study indicated that the students did not select Caldecott award books as their first choice. Drawing on a broad body of research, Myatt and Carter (1979) concluded that:

- Children prefer color to black-and-white

- The majority of children prefer photographs

- Children tend to prefer realism in form and color

- Younger students prefer simple illustrations to complex ones

- No significant difference exists in regard to preference for artistic style, nor gender or race variables.

Teachers and librarians might begin to evaluate this data by observing how children respond to various picture books. If children are not inclined to like black-and-white illustrations, what accounts for the success, for example, of Chris Van Allsburg? *Jumanji* (1981), *The Garden of Abdul Gasazi* (1979), and *The Widow's Broom* (1992) are all black-and-white and have all been very successful. Does the story carry the pictures? Do the children like these particular black-and-white drawings? Do they prefer Van Allsburg's books *The Polar Express* (1985) or *The Wretched Stone* (1991), which feature colored illustrations? Does the fantasy genre in which Van Allsburg works lend itself to black-and-white art more than other genres? How, for example, do children respond to the black-and-white art in John Steptoe's award-winning *The Story of Jumping Mouse* (1972)?

In light of the expressed preference for realism, teachers might also want to monitor the way children respond to abstraction in picture books. Prevailing assumptions about this suggest that "abstract art is contentless; and that abstraction is inappropriate for young children" (Dressel 1985, 103). *The Stonecutter* (McDermott 1975), *The Golem* (Brodsky-McDermott 1976), and *The Mouse Couple* (Malotki and Lacapa 1988) are several books that offer an opportunity to explore young readers' responses to abstract art. If these books are not isolated as literature, and if art activities are integrated into their study, children may be provided with new means for expressing themselves. In *The Arts, Human Development and Education* (1976), Elliot Eisner says that the emphasis upon representational art often frustrates children. If children are given the opportunity to express themselves in nonrepresentational forms, this might actually encourage them to be more sensitive to form, shape, and style. Educators should also recognize the implicit culture bias in Western representational art. Exposing children to abstract art should be a supportive strategy facilitating their introduction to the stories, myths, and folktales of other cultures and countries. It may well be that by relying too much upon "that which has been traditionally accepted, i.e., representational art and literature, we are encouraging lower levels of thinking. . . . [I]t may well be that in exposing children to the abstract . . . one can encourage extension to higher levels of thinking" (Dressel 1985, 110–11).

The issue of children's picture preference is particularly important when using pictures to gain and maintain the attention of students. These motivational factors must be taken into account when selecting appropriate visuals. The way in which the visuals are actually used, however, requires some understanding not just of what children like, but of how they actually see, read, and think about visuals. Clearly, children do not all see the same way even when they all look at the same picture. Their age and corresponding developmental level are important variables in this process. Research with third-grade students, for example, suggested that they see only partial elements of pictures in their textbooks. They tended to look at pieces of the picture and to see items in isolation rather than as part of a whole (Miller 1983). Although older students are more responsive in the way they process pictures, they are still "likely to remain descriptive and haphazardly selective when reporting information derived spontaneously from pictures" (Higgins 1978, 215–16). Salomon's concept of Amount of Invested Mental Energy supports the belief that the way children process pictures can be altered through teacher intervention. Pettersson links the information retrieved from a picture to the utility or need for information. "When we first look at an image, we see only that which is necessary to perceive and identify objects and events in a reasonable and meaningful manner" (1988, 53). Pettersson distinguished between high and low cognitive processing of pictures. On the low level, "recognition and meaning of the image content is formed very quickly." In the higher cognitive process, "information is processed again, maybe several times, detail by detail. The process demands attention and is sequential . . . [as] various hypotheses about the image content are weighed and tested" (p. 53).

If we can change the way children think about illustrations, it seems highly likely that we will change their ability to retrieve and process information from pictures. For the most part, children look at pictures within the narrow framework represented by the question, "What is happening in this picture?" Most of their energy addresses the way the picture conveys the narrative chain of events. The picture is therefore examined in terms of what is happening, who it is happening to, and where it is taking place. In short, the visuals are used to support the literary elements of plot, characters, and setting. The means by which this information is carried and conveyed, for the most part, continues to be obscured by the educational process. How the picture achieves meaning, the technique the artist has used, the design and composition of the page, and the relationship of all these elements to the content

## 30 Pictures and Pedagogy

are for the most part ignored. A 1993 children's literature textbook, though making some headway, continued this process. In *The Essentials of Children's Literature* (Lynch-Brown and Tomlinson 1993), the authors outline the form and style of picture books. They name five broad categories of artistic style and discuss concepts such as framing, type, and the size and shape of pictures. Typically, these areas are dealt with in a cursory way, with few, if any, examples and no supporting illustrations. Equally disturbing is the failure to relate the book's style and form to its content. Asking whether the pages are square or rectangular, for example, is rather meaningless unless that decision is seen as a question of composition and design related to content and theme. The artistic decisions made about the look of a book should not continue to be isolated from the study of the story. Higher order thinking skills can be promoted if children are encouraged to see a relationship between form and content by exploring the decisions the illustrator has made.

Considerations of design and composition must, of course, take into account the content of the illustration. In quality picture books, the illustrations do more than support the text; they extend it by including information not available in words. Stewig's extensive analysis of *Jack and the Bean Tree* (Haley 1986) indicates just how much information the pictures contain that is not also carried in the text. When young Jack first meets the giant's wife, Matilda, the text simply says, "There stood the biggest, strangest woman Jack had ever seen." As Stewig points out, "artist Haley tells us much more in pictures. . . . This is an exotic looking woman of leisure, wearing a dress with elaborate shirred and piped sleeves. . . . Matilda is proud of her body, an inference supported by noticing her elaborate coiffure" (Stewig 1992, 17–18). Continuing to process information contained in the illustrations but not the text, Stewig draws on the pictures to further understand the lifestyle of Matilda and her husband. "Long fingernails and the rather impractical slippers she wears suggest that Matilda is not overburdened by household tasks, an inference supported by the magnificence of her house. The giant and his wife obviously live in comfort, even elegance" (p. 18).

"There stood the biggest, strangest woman Jack had ever seen." This minimalist text and rich illustration provide a wealth of detail to be processed from the picture says John Warren Stewig. (From *Jack and the Bean Tree*, retold and illustrated by Gail E. Haley.)

Stewig's sophisticated analysis shows the role visuals can play in helping young readers make inferences and construct meaning from the images encountered in picture books. This approach has been well documented by Meringoff (1980). The Harvard researcher worked with six- to ten-year-olds and *A Story, A Story* (Haley 1970). Through a series of tasks, including sequential picture ordering and inference drawing beyond story content, the study was able to document the role visuals played in helping children understand the stories, including concepts such as the time and space in which the tale took place. For classroom teachers and librarians, this approach can be duplicated by asking students several simple questions. When Ananse binds the leopard Osebo and hangs him in the tree, students can be asked: "Was it difficult to put Osebo in the tree?" In answering this question, students will have to rely on their exposure to the words and pictures in the book. If they see the video version of this action, they have numerous visual cues to call upon rather than the one picture that depicts this incident in the book.

In asking questions of students, it is always important that the key question be followed by asking, "How do you know that?" This second question reveals how students make inferences from stories, including their predisposition to process words or pictures. The implications of this process are extremely important in a visual culture, and they have applications to media literacy and critical viewing skills, particularly in terms of television viewing. The research related to television viewing can quite clearly be related to how children process picture books. "Most of the time, children construct meaning for television content without even thinking about it. They attend to stimuli and extract meaning. How well television content is understood varies according to similarities between viewers and content, viewers' needs and interests, and the age of the viewer" (Adams and Hamm 1989, 8). "The ability to process pictures, whether illustrations in a book or the video imagery of television, is a developmental outcome that proceeds from stage to stage with an accumulation of viewing experience. . . . [I]mprovement in comprehension occurs with maturity but substantial understanding of the medium requires training" (Adams and Hamm 1989, 8). By observing how children respond to images in picture books and by structuring activities that expand their understanding of the form and content of these illustrations, educators can prepare the groundwork for the wider area of media literacy.

Obviously, younger children encounter both television and picture books with "limited operational facility" (Higgins 1978, 217), which restricts how well they make inferences based on pictures. This is, of course, totally consistent with the work of Piaget and substantiated by research arguing that "the pre-operational child can forge only a partial and necessarily centered view of any situation" (Higgins 1980, 100). Research with four- to seven-year-olds looked at the ability to process information from partial pictures. When children were shown illustrations with part of a dog out of the frame, they concluded that the dog could not run—that it was incomplete—even when words and text told them otherwise. "A substantial proportion of the children responded as if an element out of sight in a picture either did not exist or was incomplete . . . as if out of sight in a picture signified that the element concerned was also out of existence" (Higgins 1980, 100, 119). At this stage of their development, students described by the researcher as "the picture book population" (p. 116) tend to base their interpretation of pictures on literal, not inferred, properties.

This research offers teachers working with picture books and young children an opportunity to further explore how children read pictures. *Sea Tale* (Haley 1990) contains one picture that can be used this way. In the illustration, we see the mermaid Falilah combing her hair as she sits in the small dinghy. In the front left-hand side of the frame, we see extended hands playing a concertina. The hands belong to the hero, Tom. The text indicates that "Falilah sat opposite Tom, combing her hair. . . . Tom sang songs to her that told her of his feelings." Because Tom is disembodied, extrapolation from research indicates that very small children would consider him out of sight and mind. Older children would, of course, be able to bring closure to this frame. The concertina is not mentioned in the text, so teachers might also monitor at what age level students begin to process its presence in this picture.

## 32 Pictures and Pedagogy

A significant issue of closure and visual maturity. At what age can the child complete the picture, by assigning wholeness to the partial person? (From *Sea Tale*, witten and illustrated by Gail E. Haley.)

Another interesting example of the out-of-sight/out-of-mind response of small children can be found in *Puss in Boots* (Marcellino 1990). Early in the story, Puss convinces the Marquis of Carabas to go swimming. In the illustration of the event, Puss stands on a tree limb and calls out to the Marquis. In the foreground of the picture, the artist presents the disembodied Marquis, showing only the tips of his toes protruding above the waterline. Can young children close this picture by recognizing the out-of-frame body?

Visual sophistication can also be tracked with Haley's version of *Puss in Boots* (1991). In the scene where Michael buys the cat fine new boots, the exchange of money is obscured behind the cat's back. The money passing hands between the master and the cobbler is shown, but it appears as a reflection in a mirror. The use of reflection is combined with the out-of-frame figure in *Jack and the Bean Tree* (Haley 1986). Late in the story, Jack creeps into the sleeping giant's bedroom. In the foreground of the frame we see the young hero lacing together the giant's shoes. This action is described in the text. But we do not see all of Ephidophilus—the giant's feet extend into the frame from the foreground. In the rear of the frame, behind Jack's head, the giant and his wife appear as reflections in a mirror. Interpreting the complexity of this illustration requires a visual sophistication not present in very small children.

As children mature, however, both through their own natural development and through the educational experiences provided for them, they become capable of more sophisticated visual analysis. Rather than drawing all understanding from the internal content of the frame, these students can now contribute meaning based upon their own inferences and knowledge base. "Concepts and principles are retrieved from memory and selected as being compatible with the information given in the picture, thereby enabling the individual to categorize the depicted event and actors in it and to forge reasoned links between the scene that is presented, and possible antecedent, concomitant, and subsequent events" (Higgins 1978, 217). At this stage, these students can interpret images, in both static and dynamic visual formats, by drawing upon their awareness of visual codes, conventions, and cues of the culture. In doing so, they combine the actual content of the image with the form and style of the picture. "A Guide for Using Visuals in Teaching Culturally Diverse Children" offers some interesting observations in this respect. Describing elements such as shadow, depth, texture, distance, and horizon, Hurt argues that a child "experienced with visuals and interpretation might recognize that a shaded area indicates a shadow" (Hurt 1989, 25). Teachers wishing to test this competency can select images in picture books that include shadows. In the Weston Woods filmstrip, *Creating Jack and the Bean Tree: Tradition and Technique* (Haley and Considine 1987), the artist describes the use of shadow, depth, posture, and perspective to convey the size of the giant bean tree. Because the book was horizontal in format, the size of the tree was limited, so Haley relied heavily upon shadow to convey the sense of size. The roof of the house is covered with the shadow of the stretching tree. In the distance across the valley and up the hill, the shadow of the tree spreads out. By structuring appropriate questions, teachers can begin to see whether students consider shadow, posture, proportion, and other techniques as they process the picture. Students in the pre-operational mode are, of course, much more likely to rely only on the parts of the tree that they can actually see to ascertain its size.

Hurt also addresses what he calls "cues that refer to motion" (1989, 25). Citing techniques such as wake lines, vibration marks, and blurred images, he notes that such conventions must be learned. "Correct interpretation of these cues necessitates having had prior experience with them in pictures" (p. 25). Anyone who is familiar with the work of Van Gogh knows how movement and energy are represented through line and the dynamic application of paint to canvas. The copyright/dedication page of *Jack and the Fire Dragon* (Haley 1988) unmistakably evokes this technique. In a different way, Duchamp's *Nude Descending a Staircase* also uses line to convey the sense of movement. Sometimes a particular artistic technique or medium lends itself very well to creating movement. Gail Haley used linoleum cut in *Sea Tale* (1990) because the movement of sea, sky, and wind can be clearly expressed through the swirling lines of linoleum cut. This is evident on the title page of the book. The wind blows across the frame from right to left, moving the clouds, buffeting the small boat, blowing the hair and clothes of the characters, sweeping through the trees and grass on the shore, tossing the waves and the great distant clipper ship on the horizon. If we ask children to examine this image and to describe the climate or weather, we can help them to derive information from the content and style of the picture. At the same time we have the opportunity to observe their ability to interpret this information. If the students tell us that the day is windy, we can follow up, for example, by asking which way the wind is blowing and how they know it is windy.

Helping children explore the images they encounter in picture books is neither busy work nor an activity to be isolated in art classes. Properly presented, this procedure develops their thinking and viewing skills and lays a solid groundwork for visual literacy and media literacy. Although the picture book can be a bridge to the electronic media that surrounds today's children, it also has its own unique characteristics and properties. As Shirley Hughes said, in an age when the reactions of even young children are "hotted up to a lightning speed by television and where fantasies are often pre-packaged by huge publicity juggernauts, picture books may be the only non-photographic imagery they may be exposed to in a relaxed and intimate way, without a built-in hard-sell" (1991, 18). With this in mind, it is now time to turn our attention to the techniques used in creating picture books, and the strategies and activities that can be used to facilitate children's understanding and enjoyment of this unique medium.

Visual clues, or what Hurt refers to as "motion cues," evident here in the windblown clouds, hair, and clothing, offer teachers an opportunity to focus children's attention on such detail to promote visual acuity. (From *Sea Tale*, written and illustrated by Gail E. Haley.)

# References

Adams, Dennis, and Mary Hamm (1989). *Media and Literacy: Learning in an Electronic Age*. Springfield, IL: Charles C. Thomas.

Beck, Charles (1984). Visual Cueing Strategies: Pictorial, Textual and Combinational Effects. *Educational Communication and Technology Journal* 32 (4): 207–16.

Bellamy, R., et al. (1978). *Teacher Attitudes Toward Non-Print Media*. Frankfort, KY: State Department of Education. ERIC Document No. 174, 197.

Braden, Roberts, and John Hortin (1982). Identifying the Theoretical Frameworks of Visual Literacy. *Journal of Visual Verbal Languaging* 2 (2): 37–42.

Bradford, Annette (1984). Conceptual Differences Between the Display Screen and the Printed Page. *Technical Communication*, 3rd quarter: 14–16.

Brodsky-McDermott, Beverly (1976). *The Golem*. Philadelphia: Lippincott.

Brody, Philip (1984). A Research-Based Guide to Using Pictures Effectively. *Instructional Innovator* 29 (22): 21–22.

Brown, Laurene Krasny (1986a). *Taking Advantage of Media*. Boston: Routledge Kegan Paul.

——— (1986b). What Books Can Do That TV Can't and Vice Versa. *School Library Journal*, April: 38–39.

Bruner, J. (1960). *The Process of Education*. New York: Random House.

Carter, Alex, and Kenneth Schmidt (1985). An Assessment of the Production and Utilization of Instructional Media by Student Teachers. *Educational Technology*, November: 30–32.

Considine, David M., and Gail E. Haley (1992). *Visual Messages: Integrating Imagery into Instruction*. Englewood, CO: Teacher Ideas Press.

Dressel, Janice Hartwick (1985). Abstraction in Illustration: Is It Appropriate for Children? *Children's Literature in Education* 15 (2): 103–12.

Dwyer, Francis (1978). Is Visual Literacy Teachable? *Audiovisual Instruction,* February: 58.

Dyson, Ann (1986). Transitions and Tensions: Interrelationships Between the Drawing, Talking and Dictating of Young Children. *Research in the Teaching of Writing* 20: 279–409.

Eisner, Elliot (1976). *The Arts, Human Development and Education*. Berkeley, CA: McCutchan.

Gooler, Dennis (1989). Preparing Teachers to Use Technologies: Can Universities Meet the Challenge? *Educational Technology,* March: 18–21.

Graves, Donald, and Jane Hansen (1983). The Author's Chair. In *Composing and Comprehending,* edited by Julie Jensen. Urbana, IL: National Council for Research in English.

Haley, Gail E. (1970). *A Story, A Story*. New York: Atheneum

—— (1986). *Jack and the Bean Tree*. New York: Crown.

—— (1988). *Jack and the Fire Dragon*. New York: Crown.

—— (1990). *Sea Tale*. New York: Dutton.

—— (1991). *Puss in Boots*. New York: Dutton.

Haley, Gail E., and David Considine (1987). *Creating Jack and the Bean Tree: Tradition and Technique*. Weston, CT: Weston Woods Studios. Audiocassette and filmstrip.

Haring, Marilyn, and Maurine Fry (1979). Effects of Pictures on Children's Comprehension of Written Text. *Educational Communication and Technology Journal* 27 (3): 185–90.

Higgins, Leslie (1978). A Factor Analytic Study of Children's Picture Interpretation Behavior. *Educational Communication and Technology Journal* 26 (3): 215–32.

—— (1980). Literalism in Young Children's Interpretation of Pictures. *Educational Communication and Technology Journal* 28 (2): 99–119.

Hortin, John (1984). Important Aspects of Visual Literacy, Visual Thinking and Visual Rehearsal. *International Visual Literacy Association Newsletter* 13 (2): 11–15.

Hughes, Shirley (1991). Word and Image. In *On Writing for Children: Nine Papers from the Annual Lecture Series in Children's Literature*. Brisbane, Australia: Queensland University of Technology.

Hurt, Jeffry (1989). A Guide for Using Visuals in Teaching Culturally Diverse Children. *Tech Trends* 34 (1): 24–26.

Huston, Aletha, et al. (1992). *Big World, Small Screen: The Role of Television in American Society*. Lincoln: University of Nebraska Press.

Kirrane, Diana (1992). Visual Learning. *Training and Development* 46 (9): 58–64.

Kundu, Mahima Ranjan (1986). Visual Literacy Training: Teaching Non-Verbal Communication Through Television. *Educational Technology,* August: 31–33.

Kunen, Seth, and Edward Duncan (1983). Do Verbal Descriptions Facilitate Visual Inferences? *Journal of Educational Research* 76 (6): 370–73

Levin, Joel, et al. (1979). Pictures, Imagery and Children's Recall of Central Versus Peripheral Sentence Information. *Educational Communication and Technology Journal* 27 (2): 89–95.

Levin, J. R., and A. M. Lesgold (1978). On Pictures in Prose. *Educational Communication and Technology Journal* 26: 233–43.

Lynch-Brown, Carol, and Carl Tomlinson (1993). *Essentials of Children's Literature*. Boston: Allyn and Bacon.

Malotki, Ekkehart, and Michael Lacapa (1988). *The Mouse Couple*. Flagstaff, AZ: Northland Press.

Marcellino, Fred (1990). *Puss in Boots*. New York: Farrar, Straus & Giroux.

McClusky, F. Dean (1923). *The Administration of Visual Education: A National Survey,* Report to N.E.A. (unpublished).

McDermott, Gerald (1975). *The Stonecutter*. New York: Viking.

McKim, Robert H. (1972). *Experiences in Visual Thinking*. Monterey, CA: Brooks Cole.

Merck, Edwin, and Linda Fleit (1988). Is Higher Education Too Old for Technology? *Educational Technology International,* no. 12: 3-7.

Meringoff, Laurene (1980). Influence of the Medium of Children's Story Apprehension. *Journal of Educational Psychology* 72 (2): 240–49.

Miller, W. A. (1983). What Do Children See in Pictures? *Elementary School Journal* 39: 280–88.

Myatt, Barbara, and Juliet Mason Carter (1979). Picture Preferences of Children and Young Adults. *Educational Communication and Technology Journal* 27 (1): 45–53.

Naidu, Sam (1988). Developing Instructional Materials for Distance Education: A Concerns Based Approach. *Canadian Journal of Educational Communication,* Fall: 167–79.

Newkirk, Thomas (1989). *More Than Stories: The Range of Children's Writing*. Portsmouth, NH: Heinemann.

Pettersson, Rune (1984). Factors in Visual Language: Emotional Content, Part 2. *International Visual Literacy Association Newsletter* 13 (4): 1–4.

——— (1988). Interpretation of Image Content. *Educational Communication and Technology Journal* 36 (1): 45–55.

Pressley, Michael, et al. (1982). Picture Content and Pre-schoolers' Learning from Sentences. *Educational Communication and Technology Journal* 30 (3): 151–61.

Pritchard, William, and John Busby (1991). A Blueprint for Successfully Integrating Technology into Your Institution. *T.H.E. Journal,* Special Issue: 48–54.

Proctor, L. F. (1983). Student Teacher Utilization of Educational Media. Ph.D. diss., University of Indiana. ERIC Document No. ED 244 620.

Saettler, Paul (1968). *A History of Instructional Technology.* New York: McGraw-Hill.

Salomon, Gavriel (1979). *Interaction of Media, Cognition and Learning.* San Francisco: Jossey-Bass.

Salomon, Gavriel, and Tamar Leigh (1984). Predispositions About Learning From Print and Television. *Journal of Communication* 34 (2): 119–35.

Seidman, Steven (1986). A Survey of School Teachers' Utilization of Media. *Educational Technology,* October: 19–23.

Sinatra, Richard (1983). How Visual Compositions Aid Visual and Verbal Literacies. In *Readings from the 14th Annual Conference of the International Visual Literacy Association*, edited by Roberts Braden and Alice Walker. Blacksburg, VA: Virginia Polytech Institute and State University.

——— (1986). *Visual Literacy: Connections to Thinking, Reading and Writing.* Springfield, IL: Charles C. Thomas.

Sless, David (1984). Visual Literacy: A Failed Opportunity. *Educational Communication and Technology Journal* 32 (4): 224–28.

Smith, C. B., and G. M. Ingersoll (1984). Audiovisual Materials in U.S. Schools: A National Survey on Availability and Use. *Educational Technology* 24 (9): 36–38.

Snyder, D. C. (1984). A Study of Visual Literacy Skills of Kindergarten Children on the Title One Schools of the Allentown School District. Ph.D. diss. Abstract in *Dissertation Abstracts International* 45:1926a. University Microfilm No. DA 8418400.

Staman, E. Michael (1990). An Action Plan for Infusing Technology in the Teaching/Learning Process. *Cause/Effect* 13 (2): 34–40.

Steinbrink, John E., and Donna Bliss (1988). Using Political Cartoons to Teach Thinking Skills. *The Social Studies,* September/October: 217–20.

Steptoe, John (1984). *The Story of Jumping Mouse.* New York: Mulberry.

Stevenson, Dwight (1984). The Effect of CRT Display on Reading Speed and Comprehension of Readers of Technical Documents. Presentation to IBM Interchange Group, January, Boca Raton, FL.

Stewig, John Warren (1992). Reading Pictures, Reading Texts: Some Similarities. *The New Advocate* 55 (1): 11–22.

United States Congress, Office of Technology Assessment (1988). *Power On!: New Tools for Teaching and Learning*. Washington, DC.

Van Allsburg, Chris (1979). *The Garden of Abdul Gasazi*. Boston: Houghton Mifflin.

——— (1981). *Jumanji*. Boston: Houghton Mifflin.

——— (1985). *The Polar Express*. Boston: Houghton Mifflin.

——— (1991). *The Wretched Stone*. Boston: Houghton Mifflin.

——— (1992). *The Widow's Broom*. Boston: Houghton Mifflin.

Waggoner, Michael (1984). The New Technologies Versus the Lecture Tradition in Higher Education: Is Change Possible? *Educational Technology* 24 (3): 7–12.

Whisler, Nancy (1984). Visual Memory Training in First Grade: Effects on Visual Discrimination and Reading Ability. *Elementary School Journal*, October: 50–54.

Willis, K. F. (1981). Educational Technology Research: Teacher and Library Media Specialist Knowledge of Instructional Design and Media Selection and Utilization. *Educational Technology*, April: 47–51.

## Other Reading

Bailey, Gerald, and John Hortin (1983). Mental Rehearsal: A Method to Improve Classroom Instruction. *Educational Technology*, August: 31–34.

Bernard, Robert, et al. (1981). Can Images Provide Contextual Support for Prose? *Educational Communication and Technology Journal* 29 (2): 101–8.

Cennamo, Katherine, et al. (1991). Mental Effort and VideoBased Learning: The Relationship of Preconceptions and the Effects of Interactive Covert Practice. *Educational Technology Research and Development* 39 (1): 5–16.

Fleming, Malcolm (1977). The Picture in Your Mind. *Audiovisual Communication Review* 25 (1): 43–62.

Fredericks, Anthony (1986). Mental Imagery Activities to Improve Comprehension. *The Reading Teacher*, October: 778–81.

Hittleman, Daniel (1985). A Picture Is Worth a Thousand Words . . . If You Know the Words. *Childhood Education*, September/October: 32–36.

Holub, Brenda, and Clifford T. Bennett (1988). Using Political Cartoons to Teach Junior/Middle School, U.S. History. *The Social Studies,* September/October: 214–16.

Maher, John, and Howard Sullivan (1982). Effects of Mental Imagery and Oral and Print Stimuli on Prose Learning of Intermediate Grade Children. *Educational Communication and Technology Journal* 30 (3): 175–83.

Smith, D. Larry, and Nancy Smith (1985). The Visual Medium: A Curriculum Model for Learning, Growth and Perception Art. *International Journal of Instructional Media* 12 (4): 331–40.

Chapter 3

# The Look of a Book

A book doesn't really exist until it is read, looked at
and thought about. My picture books need the reader
to fill in the blank spaces between one page and the next.
How each reader makes a book come to life is unique.

—Gail Haley, *Wood and Linoleum
Illustration* (filmstrip, 1978)

## Toward Critical Thinking Skills

"Simply being surrounded by visuals," John Stewig noted, "doesn't mean that we have automatically become more sophisticated in interpreting them and reacting to them" (1989, 70). For that to occur, we need to develop new ways of looking at both the picture book as product, and teaching as process. The critical thinking skills movement has begun to focus attention on the assumptions, values, and practices that have traditionally pervaded education. In the introduction to *The Critical Thinking Handbook K-3rd Grades,* the authors argue that the traditional approach to teaching has unwittingly "taken the motivation to think away from students" (Paul, Binker, and Weil 1990, 3). In this teachercentered classroom, students tend to be passive listeners, not actively engaged in the learning process. "Most teachers' utterances are statements, not questions. When teachers ask questions, they typically wait only a couple of seconds before they answer their own questions. Knowledge is taken to be equivalent to recall" (p. 3). Because the picture book is both a visual and a hands-on format, it is ideally positioned to be used for individual, independent, discovery-learning and for groupinvestigation techniques associated with cooperative learning. As such, it can shatter the paradigm of the teacher-centered classroom, transforming students from passive listeners into active explorers and learners.

For the librarian, the media center offers "a natural setting to employ critical thinking skills with students" in a subject that "lends itself to both a content and a process approach" (Craver 1989, 16). This content and process format, as we have argued, can be used to help students examine not only the content of the story or the illustrations, but also their structure and style. The process of deconstructing and demystifying the form and content of the picture book facilitates critical thinking skills and can be transferred to the information skills necessary to analyze and evaluate any print and pictorial communications in society.

The old concept of the teacher showing children pictures in a book as the story is read to them can now give way to individual or group exploration of a single story, a group of stories, an author, an illustrator, or the visual design, artistic technique, or recurring motifs used in picture books. Although group work must obviously guard against the "free rider effect" (Slavin 1990, 16), in which one or two persons do all the work, the properly monitored and managed picture book experience can provide almost limitless resources for both critical thinking and cooperative learning. Even when students work on the same title, conceptual frameworks make it possible for them to explore completely different elements of the book, including artistic technique, social construction, genre, composition, and the relationship between image and text. Reworking the picture book means rethinking the picture book in terms of several major questions. These include defining what constitutes a picture book, as well as understanding the relationship between what a book says and how it says it. The effect of the book must also be taken into account, linking an internal reading of the theme and message to the nature of the child reader, as well as to the origin of the story and the social and cultural context in which it operates.

There is no doubt that multicultural education, the whole language movement, and literature-based learning, among other developments, have encouraged a more serious response to children's literature. The shared inquiry method promoted by Junior Great Books, for example, seeks to "develop readers who think for themselves and have the persistence of mind to reach for meaning" (Plecha 1992, 104). Through discussion, analysis, and interpretation, this method develops students who are "able to relate what happens in a story to their subjective experience in a heartfelt and intelligent way and so learn to incorporate what they have read into their understanding of life" (Plecha 1992, 105). By developing questions with several plausible answers, teachers lead shared inquiry discussions that help students explore their own understanding of stories. Working with *Jack and the Bean Tree* (Haley 1986) as a model of this technique, James Plecha developed the following structure:

- Why does Jack go up the tree for a third time?

- Why does he risk his life by stealing the harp?

- Why does he take the harp against its will?

There are no right or wrong answers to these questions. By asking them, teachers help children think about the motivations of the characters and understand what makes them tick. The technique helps children get inside the heads of the characters, to see things through their eyes, and often to extend the tale beyond the closure of the text. Gail Haley has often encountered children who want to know, for example, why the Sky God wanted the leopard, the hornet, and the fairy (*A Story, A Story* 1970); and what happened to the giant's wife, Matilda, after his death, in her version of *Jack and the Bean Tree* (1986). This natural curiosity and questioning that children bring to stories can be tapped to help them explore the stories from different perspectives. The "What If You Did That" approach, for example, is one way of helping children relate behavior in a story to their own conduct and actions. The actions of the children in *Hansel and Gretel* and Jack's behavior in "Jack and the Bean Stalk" would, in our time, result in an appearance in juvenile court. Why, then, do we share such morally ambiguous tales with our children? How do children respond to these moral and ethical questions?

Another technique to develop critical thinking skills involves asking children to find relationships between stories that, on the surface, seem quite different. One interesting example is to compare and contrast the African tale in *A Story, A Story* (Haley 1970) to the Appalachian story in *Jack and the Bean Tree* (Haley 1986). Though the tales come from completely different countries and cultures, and though there are clear differences between them, there is also a remarkable degree of consistency and continuity, which can be used to help children realize what they have in common with other people. At the opening of *A Story, A Story*, the author explains that it is a spider story, because it tells how a small, defenseless individual outwits someone who seems much more powerful. Given Jack's encounter with the giant, and his reliance on his brain rather than his brawn, one could make the case that *Jack and the Bean Tree* is also a spider story. There are many other similarities between the two tales:

- Both Jack and Ananse journey to the sky—one climbs a web and the other a tree

- Both encounter a powerful, larger-than-life male figure in the sky

- Both engage in three tasks or quests.

It is also important to stress the differences between the stories. Whereas Ananse performs three tasks at the request of Nyame, the Sky God, delivering three things to him, Jack steals three things from the giant, Ephidophilus. Ananse works by himself, but Jack is helped by Matilda, the giant's wife. Jack is a youth, whereas Ananse is an old man. Finally, Jack and his mother keep all that he steals from the giant, whereas Ananse shares his reward with his village and the world.

Comparing and contrasting the two stories provides a perfect venue for helping children recognize universal themes and archetypes. The giant in conflict with the common man is a universal theme. Bettelheim says that "it is common to all cultures in some form, since children everywhere fear and chafe under the power adults hold over them" (1977, 28). In developing *Jack and the Bean Tree*, Gail Haley was well aware of the universal and archetypal elements of the story. Writing in *Children's Literature Association Quarterly*, she compared the bean stalk to Yggdrasil, "the ancient Norse tree of life" (1986, 119). Jack was described as Everyman Jack (the Norse Everyman) and Ephidophilus the giant was seen as All Father. The young male's sky journey in search of the Great Father cuts across time and cultures. It is clearly present in the Pueblo story *Arrow to the Sun* (McDermott 1974), and is profoundly present in Luke Skywalker's search for his dead father in *Star Wars* (1977).

The three tasks found in both the African and the Appalachian story also reflect the universality of the triad, which can be located, for example, in stories like *The Fool of the World and the Flying Ship* (Ransome and Shulevitz 1968). Children are quite capable of making a list of all the stories they know in which *three* appears, as three brothers, three tasks, three journeys, and so on. Obvious examples include *Goldilocks and the Three Bears*, *The Three Little Pigs*, and *The Three Feathers*. In part, the presence of three family members, as in *Jack and the Fire Dragon* (Haley 1988), enables the story to explore different aspects of the human character, in the same way that three tasks provide time to examine the progress of the hero or heroine when confronted with adversity. Referring to the recurring presence of the number three in so many stories, Bettelheim says that "three in fairy tales often seems to refer to what in psychoanalysis is viewed as the three aspects of the mind; id, ego and superego" (1975, 102). Beyond the psychological significance of the stories, students can develop their analytical skills by exploring the broader themes that link stories together.

Of these themes, perhaps the most significant element is the journey motif, or what Campbell calls the hero-quest (1975). The universality of this motif can be brought home to children by reference to popular culture, particularly to film and television. One way of doing this is simply to ask children what Luke Skywalker has in common with Ananse or Jack. Another way is to have students list all the stories they know in which the hero or heroine makes a journey or quest in the sky. Students must distinguish between a character who simply travels and one who has to perform various tasks or missions as part of the journey. Dorothy's adventures in Oz might also qualify as a good example of the journey or quest motif. Building on this theme, students could then explore travel or quests that go beneath the ground. *Jack and the Fire Dragon* (Haley 1988) is a good example of this, especially if it is related to the popular film *Legend* (1985), in which Tom Cruise played Jack in the Green. Other underground journeys to be explored might include *Alice in Wonderland* and *Journey to the Center of the Earth*. The theme can be further expanded to include journeys beneath the sea. Represented graphically, the concept of the hero quest could be mapped out in terms of vertical and horizontal journeys, with examples of sky, sea, subterranean, and earth journeys.

Activities such as these clearly contribute to the development of critical thinking skills. They shift students from the lower-order thinking skills, usually categorized as memory and translation, moving them into areas such as interpretation, application, analysis, synthesis,

## 44 The Look of a Book

and evaluation (Bloom 1956; Sanders 1966; Soar et al. 1969). Although this is a valuable process, well worth cultivating in children, it is also currently limited almost exclusively to exploring the literary elements of books in terms of "what happens in a story" (Plecha 1992, 105). What is needed in addition is a conceptual framework for applying critical thinking skills to *how* the story happens, with particular emphasis on how pictures carry and convey the story.

## Format and Features of Picture Books: A Framework for Analysis: Activities and Strategies

The physical structure, organization, layout, design, and look of the picture book contribute to its overall feel and effect. Too often, however, as John Stewig said, the books are simply considered "as containers for stories, rather than visual artifacts to be examined" (1989, 71). In many cases, as we have noted, reviews are written with scant attention to such elements as cover design, type, endpapers, even artistic medium or technique. Nevertheless, each of these elements is usually carefully selected to blend with or complement the theme, mood, setting, and period of the story. In a thoughtful review of *The Stinky Cheeseman* (Scieska and Smith 1992), *School Library Journal* acknowledged this role: "The broad satire extends even to book design and a skewed table of contents. . . . [T]he type face, text size and placement var[y] to become a vital part of the illustration of some tales" (1992, 210).

The complexity of the design of *Mountain Jack Tales* (Haley 1992) did not go unnoticed in the review process where the look of the book was connected to audience appeal. "The black and white wood engravings," said *The Bulletin*, "have a skillfully textured, artistically homespun strength to match, and the book design is handsome enough to attract young readers as well as adult storytellers" (1993, 7).

By exposing students to an examination of the book as a physical object, as well as for the story it contains, teachers and librarians can foster understanding of the creative process involved in making a picture book. Accepting the Caldecott medal in 1958, Robert McCloskey articulated his own interest as an illustrator in having readers who were more visually literate. "I think it is important," he said, "for everyone really to see and evaluate pictures and really to see and evaluate his surroundings . . . to develop a visual sense . . . to 'read' pictures . . . to know when someone is fooling us with pictures" (McCloskey 1965, 188–93). This examination process also fosters children's ability to analyze and evaluate materials and to recognize the relationship between form and content. By focusing attention on the look and design of the book, teachers can also help students recognize that even though a book usually carries the name of one author and/or illustrator, many other people are involved in the production process. The collaborative nature of the picture book was clearly acknowledged by Peter Spier in his acceptance speech for the Caldecott medal. Noting that a successful book is the result of teamwork, Spier said, it has "to run a long and risky gauntlet before it finally staggers into your libraries" (Spier 1986, 191–200). During this production process, an editor—"with the best of intentions—might make changes which could ruin the book." The company making the color separations "could demolish the artwork." The printer, said Spier, "could ruin the sheets in countless different ways and the bookbinder could do the same." Even when the book has finally made its way through the production stage, it must then pass muster at the marketing stage and, here too, "publicity and advertising . . . can be done the right way or the wrong way." A behind-the-scenes look at the production process often helps children recognize the research, time, and effort that goes into the creation of a picture book. Weston Woods Studios in Connecticut has several outstanding programs that demonstrate this process to children, including Steven Kellogg's *How a Picture Book Is Made* (1981). This program introduces students to various stages of the production process and the various individuals who work on the book, including the editor, designer, color separator, and printer.

The following framework can be used to help children think about the design decisions that have contributed to the creation of a book, as well as to the story contained in its pages. Utilization of the framework can motivate the child to "look more carefully, notice new relationships and to consider more thoroughly, reactions to what is seen" (Stewig 1989, 71).

## *The Cover*

The dust jacket or cover of a picture book serves many functions. It can provide a preview and insight into the characters, plot, events, mood, or period of the story. Because of the need to sell and promote the book, especially in a visual culture, it must also serve as a marketing mechanism, reaching out to attract the attention of the browser in a bookstore. Although the artist and author are involved in designing the cover, it is also highly likely that the salespeople in the publishing house will have their own ideas about what the cover should look like. These ideas may not match, and the final product is often the result of compromise between these interests.

Traditionally, covers also tell us the title of the book and the names of the author and illustrator. In recent times, however, there has been much more variety in the design of book covers. *Puss in Boots* (Marcellino 1990) represented a radical departure from tradition, featuring a close-up of the cat's face with no book title and no author's name. *The Widow's Broom* (Van Allsburg 1992), like *Jumanji* (Van Allsburg 1981), gave the book title but not the name of the author or illustrator. In a very lavish cover design, *Pish, Posh, Said Hieronymous Bosch* (Willard, Dillon, and Dillon 1991) used expensive paper stock and a raised or embossed image. The front and back covers both feature different illustrations, as distinct from the wraparound cover art used for books such as *The Polar Express* (Van Allsburg 1985), *Noah's Ark* (Spier 1977), *Puss in Boots* (Haley 1991), *Knots on a Counting Rope* (Martin, Archambault, and Rand 1987), and *Love Flute* (Goble 1992).

Divide the class into groups, or have students work individually, to examine cover designs and how they relate to the form and content of the book. Students can work with a single category of covers, or they may compare and contrast different styles.

1. *Wraparound covers* are often found in books with horizontal formats. The wraparound usually enables a scene or location to be established. Simply looking at the cover of one of these books usually provides information about where the story is set and something about some of the characters. The village of Ananse is represented in detail on the cover of *A Story, A Story* (Haley 1970). Ananse is seen climbing down the web ladder, with the box of stories in his hand. (This is actually a reverse image of the same scene in the book.) The costume, landscape, activities depicted, and vegetation all create a strong sense of the location and origin of this story.

Other good examples of wraparound covers include *Lon Po Po* (Young 1989), *Elfwyn's Saga* (Wisniewski 1990), *Noah's Ark* (Spier 1977), *Ten Little Rabbits* (Grossman and Long 1991), *Shadow* (Brown 1982), *Sukey and the Mermaid* (San Souci and Pinkney 1992), *Thirteen Moons on Turtle's Back* (Bruchac, London, and Locker 1992), and *Hey, Al* (Yorinks and Egielski 1986). Ask students to examine this artwork in terms of what aspects of the story it represents, why it was selected for the cover, and whether these covers are new art or repeat an illustration used in the book. Students may also look for books where the image continues across the spine of the book, such as *Jack and the Fire Dragon* (Haley 1988), and books where the spine breaks the wraparound illustration, such as *The Polar Express* (Van Allsburg 1985) and *Puss in Boots* (Haley 1991). The spine of the book is often used to break a wraparound illustration so the title and author's name will be clearly seen.

2. *Single-image covers* feature one strong picture on the front of the book, often with a smaller design on the back. The back cover may also be blank; this space is often used to print reviews in the paperback version. Covers that use this format appear on *Mirette on the High Wire* (McCully 1992), *Encounter* (Yolen and Shannon 1992), *Dream Peddler* (Haley 1993), *Rumpelstiltskin* (Zelinsky 1986), *Tuesday* (Wiesner 1991), and *Hurricane* (Wiesner 1990). Again, students can be asked to examine these covers in terms of the role they play and the way they create a sense of place, character, time, or circumstance. The covers for *Tuesday* and *Hurricane* offer an interesting contrast.

3. *Separate-scene covers* or jackets contain two illustrations, usually the same size, representing different elements of the story. *Little Red Riding Hood* (Hyman 1983) uses the front cover to show the young girl entering the woods; the back cover shows her leaving, repeating the final image from the book. In *Saint George and the Dragon* (Hodges and Hyman 1984), different images also appear on the front and back covers. The back cover, however, is of particular interest, as it does not repeat a picture from inside the book and does not seem related to events and characters from the story. The illustration actually depicts the working artist, while the author, Margaret Hodges, and her husband are seen delivering the manuscript of the book to the artist. Other examples of this type of cover design include *The Sleeping Bread* (Czernecki and Rhodes 1992) and *Aïda* (Price, Dillon, and Dillon 1990).

4. As a final activity for students, have them look at the cover of each book listed above and ask them if they can do it better. Ask if they think the cover detracts from or does not significantly further the effect of the book. Ask for their ideas and suggestions to make the cover different or perhaps more powerful.

## *Endpapers*

Like cover design, the selection and variety of endpapers can easily be grouped into several types, which makes it easy to assign individual students, or groups of students, to separate investigative and analytic tasks.

Immediately inside the cover of the opened book are the endpapers. In quality pictures books, these papers are selected and designed to support and enhance the mood, period, or location of the story. Sometimes these endpapers simply use a color that dominates the book. In *Sea Tale* (Haley 1990), the sky and ocean motifs are continued in the endpapers. Similarly, *Puss in Boots* (Haley 1991) repeats the coloring of the feline's fine cloak and the grandeur of the king's court. In *Amazing Grace* (Hoffman and Binch 1981), the bright yellow endpapers connect to the exuberance of the central character.

Sometimes endpapers feature designs and motifs that run throughout the story. Good examples of this can be found in *Anancy and Mr. Dry-Bone* (French 1991), *Ten Little Rabbits* (Grossman and Long 1991), *Aïda* (Price, Dillon, and Dillon 1990), and *Borreguita and the Coyote* (Aardema and Mathers 1991). In addition to using colors, motifs, and graphic design, endpapers can also feature central locations or elements of a story. *Rumpelstiltskin* (Zelinsky 1986) features a panorama of the landscape of the story. *The Great Kapok Tree* (Cherry 1990) endpapers feature a world map, indicating tropical rain forests and the native flora and fauna. In *Dream Peddler* (Haley 1993), the endpapers were creatively used to represent the world and wares of the eighteenth-century chapman. Based on authentic cries of the period and derived from her own collection of chapbooks, Haley designed the endpapers so readers could photocopy them, fold them, and make their own chapbooks.

**Format and Features of Picture Books: A Framework for Analysis 47**

The color or design of endpapers often reinforces the mood or period of the book. In this case, the endpapers are designed for duplication that will enable young readers to make their own eighteenth-century chapbooks, like those sold by the hero of the story. (From *Dream Peddler*, written and illustrated by Gail E. Haley.)

Other books with useful examples of endpapers to discuss with students include *The Napping House* (Wood and Wood 1984), *Lon Po Po* (Young 1989), *Brother Eagle, Sister Moon* (Jeffers and Seattle 1991), *The Golden Deer* (Hodges and San Souci 1992), *The Lost Lake* (Say 1989), *Pish, Posh, Said Hieronymous Bosch* (Willard, Dillon, and Dillon 1991), *Fox's Dream* (Tejima 1985), and *Strega Nona* (dePaola 1975). Discuss the use of color, motif, design, and scene with students, using several different examples, until they are comfortable with the concept of endpapers and the relationship between form and content. Then have them select one example, or a number of different examples, explaining how the endpapers are related to the mood, period, location, or characters of the story.

## *Front Matter*

After the endpapers but before the first line of the story begins, a picture book usually contains a half-title page, a title page, and copyright and dedication information. These are generally referred to as the *front matter*. Librarians developing children's reference skills can help children explore these pages to find out the name of the author, illustrator, and publisher; the date of publication; and the city of publication. The same section of the book can be used when children are learning to work with the card catalog, or a computerized catalog. In recent times, publishers have also begun to include some information about the artwork and type in this section of the book. Examples of this can be found in *Encounter* (Yolen and Shannon 1992), *Heckedy Peg* (Wood and Wood 1987), *Sukey and the Mermaid* (San Souci and Pinkney 1992), and numerous others. But the front matter may also be used to start the story, serving as an *establishing shot* or *opening sequence*, to borrow some cinematic terms. Failure to process the characters, events, and locations represented in this front matter, before the text actually begins, has been compared to arriving for a movie 10 minutes late (Haley 1992b). The role of front matter in advancing and introducing the story is examined in some detail in chapter 4, which explores the relationship between picture and print.

Introduce students to the concept of front matter and the various bits of information contained in this part of a picture book. Have them locate examples of each of these elements in a book of their own choice. Note that some books now include this matter at the back of the book, as in *Lon Po Po* (Young 1989), *The Stinky Cheese Man* (Scieska and Smith 1992), and *Knots on a Counting Rope* (Martin, Archambault, and Rand 1987).

## *Author/Artist Notes*

A growing number of picture books now contain sections, usually at the back of the book, in which the author or artist or both indicate something of the process involved in writing and illustrating the story. Examples of this can be found in *Tar Beach* (Ringgold 1991), *Dream Peddler* (Haley 1993), *Elfwyn's Saga* (Wisniewski 1990), *Rumpelstiltskin* (Zelinsky 1986), *Sukey and the Mermaid* (San Souci and Pinkney 1992), *Encounter* (Yolen and Shannon 1992), and *Orpheus* (Mikolaycak 1992).

Assign students the task of reading these author notes, once they are familiar with a story, to see what problems or perceptions sharpen the writer's words and the artist's images. What do the student's learn about the creative process that they did not previously know?

## Type

The term *type,* or *typeface,* refers to more than the words that appear on a page to tell the story. The selection of the typestyle or lettering is part of the overall design of the book. The decision may be based on word density, length of line, and legibility, or it may relate to the time, era, or period in which the story is set. Technical information related to the typeface and paper stock is now often contained in the front matter.

Sometimes a unique typestyle is used to create a special feeling for a book. For *Pish, Posh, Said Hieronymous Bosch*, Leo Dillon and Diane Dillon designed their own hand-lettering. Careful examination of the words reveals the use of both uppercase and lowercase letters. Medieval manuscripts are often famous for their use of illuminated letters. When working on *Mountain Jack Tales* (1992), Gail Haley drew upon this technique, designing a special capital letter to begin each story. The hand engravings depict characters, events, and motifs from the tales and contribute to the overall appeal of the book.

In addition to selecting a specific typeface, design decisions also have to be made about the organization and layout of the type. This format is either *ragged-edge* or *justified* type. For justified type, the sentence lines are even, or balanced, giving a formal appearance. Examples of this technique can be seen in *The Green Man* (Haley 1979), *Little Red Riding Hood* (Hyman 1983) and very formal books like *The Boy Who Held Back the Sea* (Locker 1987), and *Puss in Boots* (Marcellino 1990).

Sometimes a book contains both elements. In *Birdsong* (Haley 1984), the text appears in justified type but the poems are ragged-edge. The ragged-edge, or uneven format, is quite common and often enables text to be blended around an illustration or design. This format can be seen in *Hey, Al* (Yorinks and Egielski 1986), *Sea Tale* (Haley 1990), and *Heckedy Peg* (Wood and Wood 1987).

In addition to the typeface, the overall position and placement of the type must also be considered. The narrow vertical column of type in *Owl Moon* (Yolen and Schoenherr 1987) echoes the giant trees that dominate the landscape of the pages and contrasts very well with the horizontal lines of the snowy fields. Two other Caldecott medal winners provide good examples of type design. A careful examination of *Where the Wild Things Are* (Sendak 1963) shows the diversity and variety of text in relation to picture. White space is used liberally, often with only two or three words on a page. For emphasis, capital letters are employed. A single sentence may spread across a double page, be confined to one line on one page, or be broken into several short, sharp lines. At the height of the adventure, the words vanish completely as three double-page illustrations take over the role of telling the story. *A Story, A Story* (Haley 1970) also reveals some interesting design decisions. The introduction of the book is a white page completely filled with text. When the page is turned, Ananse the storyteller looks out at the reader, while the storyteller's greeting is confined to the upper left of the double-page spread. Throughout the book, the text moves from the left to the right of the frame according to the function of the visual. Sometimes the text is integrated into the color and design of the page and picture; on other occasions it is separated into a white space apart from the illustration. When Ananse meets the leopard, and later in the Gum Baby sequence, the text is divided to create balance on the left and right of the frame. This organization of the text and type not only creates visual variety, but also enables the story to progress and flow as the pages are turned and the text weaves in and out like the jungle and web of the story.

- Introduce students to the concept of justified type and ragged-edge type. Have them find examples of each format in books of their own choosing.

- Using *Where the Wild Things Are* and *A Story, A Story*, show students how the position, size, and organization of type can contribute to the variety and effect of a book. Have them select a book and describe the way in which the typeface, style, size, and position of the type relate to the story and contribute to its impact.

## Shape

Two of the most obvious, but most ignored, aspects of the picture book are its size and shape. The shape of the book obviously contains and controls the space in which the artist-illustrator functions. A story requiring vistas and landscapes may be more suited to a horizontal than a vertical format. In *Owl Moon* (Yolen and Schoenherr 1987), for example, the woodland setting and subject matter (a bird) meant that a tall, vertical format would almost certainly be more appropriate than a square or horizontal book. The shape of the book may also reflect marketing decisions related to positioning and display in stores or housing on a library shelf. Between 1973's *Jack Jouett's Ride*, and 1991's *Puss in Boots*, all of Gail Haley's picture books were oblong, shaped with an emphasis on horizontal design. Haley's decision to work exclusively in this format is particularly interesting because *A Story, A Story* (1970) using a square format, won the Caldecott medal. New to the book industry, Haley researched successful books including Marcia Brown's *Once a Mouse* (1961) and settled on the square format. For her next book, *Noah's Ark* (1971), the illustrator continued to work with this shape. It would be the last time.

The reason for the shift in direction was partly commercial and partly artistic. Association with Weston Woods Studios on the production of the film version of *A Story, A Story* had shown Haley how the screen dimensions gave her greater scope in which to work. She also recognized the financial opportunities available to her in designing books that Weston Woods could more easily transfer to film or filmstrip. Beyond the commercial incentives, however, the real decisions about design centered around what had to be shown and said. For her next project, *Jack Jouett's Ride* (1973), the horizontal format of the double-page spread would allow her to convey the terrain and landscape through which Jouett would ride. Exteriors account for 13 of the 16 double-page spreads in the book. The shape of the book also related to Jouett's horse, as it galloped forth, spread out across the pages.

The decision about the shape of the book is often integral to the story. In *The Post Office Cat* (Haley 1976) the next-to-last page of the book gives a clue to the design decision. In this image, Clarence the cat stretches out across two-thirds of the double-page spread. The shape of the cat was a significant factor in determining the look of the book. Haley's reliance on the horizontal in *Go Away, Stay Away* (1977), *Birdsong* (1984), *Sea Tale* (1990), and others usually resulted in landscapes and interiors crowded with creatures and characters. She wanted to create books that children could rest their elbows on and mentally step into. In cinematic terms, this enabled her to use a series of long or establishing shots to introduce key locations and characters. These long shots are very evident in the front matter of *The Green Man* (1979), *Sea Tale* (1990), and *Puss in Boots* (1991).

By contrast, books designed around a vertical format or composition use considerably fewer long shots. Typically, such books feature medium or close-up images of characters and interiors, with few landscapes or double-page spreads. *Rumpelstiltskin* (Zelinsky 1986) establishes the location in the endpapers and then quickly moves indoors, opening and closing with a medium close-up of a key character. With two exceptions, *Encounter* (Yolen and Shannon 1992) also restricts its illustrations to single-page, vertical art. The claustrophobic frame and the relatively tight compositions tend to trap the viewer like the Taino culture that Columbus encountered. From the front cover to the final page, Marcellino's *Puss in Boots* (1991) also features more interiors and close-ups of characters than environments and landscapes. Arnold Lobel's *Fables* (1980) contains only vertical, single-page illustrations. *Ashanti to Zulu* (Musgrove, Dillon, and Dillon 1976) also shows the strengths and limitations of the vertical format. Beautifully designed, each picture manages to convey, in a relatively small space, something of the unique characteristics, culture, costumes, and artifacts of each tribe. Only on the title page is the vertical format replaced with a double-page spread of the African landscape. With twenty-six letters and tribes to deal with in this alphabet book, the content of the 32-page picture book made it highly unlikely that a horizontal format using a double-page spread could be effectively integrated into the design of the book. Contrasting this book to *Mufaro's*

*Beautiful Daughters: An African Tale* (Steptoe 1987), which uses several horizontal spreads, shows how format both contains and restrains the art.

Although there are, of course, traditions, there are few hard-and-fast rules governing the size of a picture book or how the illustrator conceptualizes the layout of the art. The vertical format of *Heckedy Peg* (1987) certainly did not confine Don Wood. The layout and composition of the book bring a surprise with each new page. Students will appreciate books more if they understand the design decisions involved in creating them. Though they will enjoy discovering examples of traditionally designed books, they will also enjoy finding books that break the rules. *The Widow's Broom* (Van Allsburg 1992) is one popular book that fails to conform to the traditional shape. Introduce students to the book and ask them to think about why the artist chose this shape.

Divide the class into groups, each group working with books of a different shape. What do the books have in common? Why do the students think the artists selected this shape? How is the content of the book related to the form or look of the book?

Here are some useful examples of the basic book shapes:

*Square*: These books are not all exactly square, but the overall look suggests a square format. Does the illustrator use a square format for the art or vary its composition? Look at *A Story, A Story* (Haley 1970), *The Inch Boy* (Morimoto 1986), *The Golden Deer* (Hodges and San Souci 1992), *Treasure* (Shulevitz 1979), *Why the Sun and the Moon Live in the Sky* (Daynell and Lent 1968), *Why Mosquitoes Buzz in People's Ears* (Aardema, Dillon, and Dillon 1975), and *The Talking Eggs* (San Souci and Pinkney 1989).

*Vertical*: There is no shortage of books with a vertical format. Some good examples are *Shadow* (Brown 1982,) *Fox's Dream* (Tejima 1985), *King Bidgood's in the Bathtub* (Wood and Wood 1985), *Black and White* (Macaulay 1990), *The Weaving of a Dream* (Heyer 1986), *Dream Peddler* (Haley 1993), and *Song and Dance Man* (Ackerman and Gammell 1988).

*Horizontal*: Look at *The Lost Lake* (Say 1989), *Hurricane* (Wiesner 1990), *The Polar Express* (Van Allsburg 1985), *Everyone Knows What a Dragon Looks Like* (Williams and Mayer 1976), *Sea Tale* (Haley 1990), *Noah's Ark* (Spier 1977), *The Glorious Flight* (Provensen and Provensen 1983), and *Tuesday* (Wiesner 1991).

Assign students the task of comparing and contrasting different versions of the same story that have been illustrated in differently shaped formats. How does each shape affect the content and impact of the illustrations? Interesting examples to work with are *Puss in Boots*, which has been published in both vertical (Marcellino 1990) and horizontal formats (Haley 1991); and *Noah's Ark*, which has appeared square (Haley 1971), horizontal (Spier 1977), and vertical (Ray 1990). Haley's vertical *Dream Peddler* (1993) can be compared to *Treasure* (Shulevitz 1978), which is a square version of the same story.

Gail Haley indicated that in preparing *A Story, A Story*, she selected a square format because successful books like *Once a Mouse* (Brown 1961) were square in shape. In studying Caldecott medal books, ask students to complete a table or chart indicating the shape of all the award-winning books in a given period. What trends, if any, emerge?

## *Gutter*

Irrespective of size or shape, all picture books have a *gutter* running through the middle of the book. Whether the gutter, or spine, simply divides the book into left and right sides or is actually used as part of the art is a technical design decision that often reflects the skill of the illustrator. In *Owl Moon* (Yolen and Schoenherr 1987), the dramatic appearance of the owl and the horizontal dimension of the outstretched wings dictated a double-page spread running across the gutter. The joint or seam of the page is integrated into the bird's left wing, in a clear, continuous line that does not disrupt or disfigure the art. Because she has spent two decades working with double-page spreads, Gail Haley's books usually feature interesting examples of an artist integrating the gutter into an illustration without disruption. *Birdsong* (Haley 1984) features 14 spreads that run across the gutter. In each case, the disruption is minimized by careful integration of the gutter into the design of the art. Landscape, Jorinella's cloak, a kitchen table, and an enormous net are all used to develop continuity of line, color, and object across the gutter. The careful composition and design of *Puss in Boots* (Haley 1991) and *Dream Peddler* (Haley 1993) clearly demonstrate the illustrator's technical skill in minimizing the potentially disruptive gutter; Haley positions her characters, objects, and scenery in such a way that the illustrations flow across the gutter.

Occasionally, examples of less successful spreads can also be found, even in quality picture books. John Steptoe's use of the gutter in the Native American tale *The Story of Jumping Mouse* (1984) and *Mufaro's Beautiful Daughters: An African Tale* (1987) provide examples of the gutter successfully employed but also disruptive. When landscapes and environments are used to cross over the gutter, the pictures seem to retain their unity. When key characters, or animals are placed in the center of the frame, the effect is less satisfying. In the African story, an exotic red bird is cut in half by the gutter, and the book has to be forced flat for the reader to see the whole image. In the Native American tale, large illustrations of a mouse, a buffalo, and an eagle spread across a gutter, with varying degrees of success. Outstanding use of the gutter can be found in *Free Fall* (Wiesner 1988), *Rumpelstiltskin* (Zelinsky 1986), *The Polar Express* (Van Allsburg 1985), *The Weaving of a Dream* (Heyer 1986), *Hurricane* (Wiesner 1990), and *Heckedy Peg* (Wood and Wood 1987).

Introduce children to the concept of the spine and gutter of a book. Show them examples of how the gutter can either disrupt an illustration or be disguised. Ask students to find their own examples of books where use of the gutter has been successful or unsuccessful. Have the students develop lists of subject matter that hurts or helps the artist use the gutter. When students do their own illustrations, assign the task of designing pictures that must disguise a gutter.

Once children have been introduced to these basic elements and features of a picture book, they become capable of examining the book as an artifact, rather than simply as a physical container to hold the story. This process prepares them for a greater understanding, awareness, and appreciation of the book, particularly the relationship between form and content. Such preparation establishes a foundation for a more sophisticated exploration of the visual components of picture books, including the design, composition, format, and artistic techniques.

The gutter, or spine, is always potentially disruptive to the illustration. Here, an excellent example shows the technical skill involved in integrating the gutter into the composition. (From *The Weaving of a Dream*, by Marilee Heyer. Illustration copyright © 1986 by Marilee Heyer. Reprinted with permission of Viking Penguin, a division of Penguin Books USA.)

# References

Aardema, Verna, Leo Dillon, and Diane Dillon (1975). *Why Mosquitoes Buzz in People's Ears*. New York: Dial.

Aardema, Verna, and Petra Mathers (1991). *Borreguita and the Coyote*. New York: Alfred A. Knopf.

Ackerman, Karen, and Stephen Gammell (1988). *Song and Dance Man*. New York: Alfred A Knopf.

Bettelheim, Bruno (1977). *The Uses of Enchantment: The Meaning and Importance of Fairy Tales*. New York: Vintage.

Bloom, B. S. (1956). *Taxonomy of Educational Objectives: Handbook 1, Cognitive Domain*. New York: David McKay.

Brown, Marcia (1961). *Once a Mouse*. New York: Charles Scribner's Sons.

——— (1982). *Shadow*. New York: Charles Scribner's Sons.

Bruchac, Joseph, Jonathan London, and Thomas Locker (1992). *Thirteen Moons on Turtle's Back*. New York: Philomel.

Bulletin for the Center for Children's Books (1993). Review of *Mountain Jack Tales*. January: 7.

Campbell, Joseph (1975). *The Hero with a Thousand Faces*. London: Abacus.

Cherry, Lynne (1990). *The Great Kapok Tree: A Tale of the Amazon Rain Forest*. San Diego, CA: Harcourt Brace Jovanovich.

Craver, Kathleen (1989). Critical Thinking: Implications for Research. *School Library Media Quarterly,* Fall: 13–18.

Czernecki, Stefan, and Timothy Rhodes (1992). *The Sleeping Bread*. New York: Hyperion Books.

Daynell, Elphinstone, and Blaire Lent (1968). *Why the Sun and the Moon Live in the Sky*. Boston: Houghton Mifflin.

dePaola, Tomie (1975). *Strega Nona*. Englewood Cliffs, NJ: Prentice-Hall.

French, Fiona (1991). *Anancy and Mr. Dry-Bone*. Boston: Little, Brown.

Goble, Paul (1992). *Love Flute*. New York: Bradbury.

Grossman, Virginia, and Sylvia Long (1991). *Ten Little Rabbits*. San Francisco: Chronicle Books.

Haley, Gail E. (1970). *A Story, A Story*. New York: Atheneum.

——— (1971). *Noah's Ark*. New York: Atheneum.

——— (1973). *Jack Jouett's Ride*. New York: Viking.

——— (1976). *The Post Office Cat*. New York: Scribners.

——— (1977). *Go Away, Stay Away*. New York: Scribners.

——— (1979). *The Green Man*. New York: Scribners.

——— (1984). *Birdsong*. New York: Crown.

——— (1986a). From the Ananse Stories to the Jack Tales: My Work with Folktales. *Children's Literature Association Quarterly* 11 (3): 118–21.

——— (1986b). *Jack and the Bean Tree*. New York: Crown.

——— (1988). *Jack and the Fire Dragon*. New York: Crown.

——— (1990). *Sea Tale*. New York: Dutton.

——— (1991). *Puss in Boots*. New York: Dutton.

——— (1992). *Mountain Jack Tales*. New York: Dutton.

——— (1993). *Dream Peddler*. New York: Dutton.

Heyer, Marilee (1986). *The Weaving of a Dream*. New York: Viking.

Hodges, Margaret, and Trina Schart Hyman (1984). *Saint George and the Dragon*. Boston: Little, Brown.

Hodges, Margaret, and Daniel San Souci (1992). *The Golden Deer*. New York: Charles Scribner's Sons.

Hoffman, Mary, and Carol Binch (1991). *Amazing Grace*. New York: Dial.

Hyman, Trina Schart (1983). *Little Red Riding Hood*. New York: Holiday House.

Jeffers, Susan, and Chief Seattle (1991). *Brother Eagle, Sister Moon*. New York: Dial.

Kellogg, Steven (1981). *How a Picture Book Is Made*. Weston, CT: Weston Woods Studios. (Audiocassette and filmstrip.)

Lobel, Arnold (1980). *Fables*. New York: Harper and Row.

Locker, Thomas (1987). *The Boy Who Held Back the Sea*. New York: Dial.

Macaulay, David (1990). *Black and White*. Boston: Houghton Mifflin.

Marcellino, Fred (1990). *Puss in Boots*. New York: Farrar, Straus & Giroux.

Martin, Jr., Bill, John Archambault, and Ted Rand (1987). *Knots on a Counting Rope*. New York: Henry Holt.

McCloskey, Robert (1965). Caldecott Medal Acceptance Speech. In *Newbery and Caldecott Medal Books, 1956–1965*, edited by Lee Kingman. Boston: Horn Book.

McCully, Emily Arnold (1992). *Mirette on the High Wire*. New York: Dutton.

McDermott, Gerald (1974). *Arrow to the Sun*. New York: Viking.

Mikolaycak, Charles (1992). *Orpheus*. San Diego, CA: Harcourt Brace Jovanovich.

Morimoto, Junko (1986). *The Inch Boy*. New York: Viking Kestrel.

Musgrove, Margaret, Leo Dillon, and Diane Dillon (1976). *Ashanti to Zulu: African Traditions*. New York: Dial.

Paul, Richard, A. J. Binker, and Daniel Weil (1990). *Critical Thinking Handbook, K-3rd Grades*. Rohnert Park, CA: Sonoma State University.

Plecha, James (1992). Shared Inquiry: The Great Books Method of Interpretive Reading and Discussion. In *Stories and Readers: New Perspectives on Literature in the Elementary Classroom*, edited by Charles Temple and Patrick Collins. Norwood, MA: Christopher Gordon.

Price, Leontyne, Leo Dillon and Diane Dillon (1990). *Aïda*. San Diego, CA: Harcourt Brace Jovanovich.

Provensen, Alice, and Martin Provensen (1983). *The Glorious Flight: Across the Channel with Louis Bleriot*. New York: Viking.

Ransome, Arthur, and Uri Shulevitz (1968). *The Fool of the World and the Flying Ship*. New York: Farrar, Straus & Giroux.

Ray, Jane (1990). *Noah's Ark*. New York: Dutton.

Ringgold, Faith (1991). *Tar Beach*. New York: Scholastic.

Sanders, N. M. (1966). *Classroom Questions—What Kinds?* New York: Harper & Row.

San Souci, Robert, and Brian Pinkney (1992). *Sukey and the Mermaid*. New York: Four Winds.

San Souci, Robert, and Jerry Pinkney (1989). *The Talking Eggs*. New York: Dial.

Say, Allen (1989). *The Lost Lake*. Boston: Houghton Mifflin.

*School Library Journal* (1992). Review of *The Stinky Cheese Man*. 38 (9): 210.

Scieska, Jon, and Lane Smith (1992). *The Stinky Cheese Man*. New York: Viking.

Sendak, Maurice (1963). *Where the Wild Things Are*. New York: Harper & Row.

Shulevitz, Uri (1979). *Treasure*. New York: Farrar, Straus & Giroux.

Slavin, Robert E. (1990). *Cooperative Learning: Theory, Research and Practice*. Englewood Cliffs, NJ: Prentice-Hall.

Soar, R., et al. (1969). *Florida Taxonomy of Cognitive Behavior K-1 Form*. Gainesville, FL: Institute for Development of Human Resources, College of Education, University of Florida.

Spier, Peter (1977). *Noah's Ark*. Garden City, NY: Doubleday.

——— (1986). Caldecott Medal Acceptance Speech. In *Newbery and Caldecott Medal Books, 1976-1985*, edited by Lee Kingman. Boston: Horn Book.

Steptoe, John (1984). *The Story of Jumping Mouse*. New York: Mulberry.

——— (1987). *Mufaro's Beautiful Daughters: An African Tale*. New York: Lothrop, Lee & Shepard.

Stewig, John Warren (1989). Reading Pictures. *Journal of Visual Literacy* 9 (1): 70–82.

Tejima (1985). *Fox's Dream*. New York: Philomel.

Van Allsburg, Chris (1981). *Jumanji*. Boston: Houghton Mifflin.

——— (1985). *The Polar Express*. Boston: Houghton Mifflin.

——— (1992). *The Widow's Broom*. Boston: Houghton Mifflin.

Wiesner, David (1988). *Free Fall*. New York: Clarion.

——— (1990). *Hurricane*. New York: Clarion.

——— (1991). *Tuesday*. New York: Clarion.

Willard, Nancy, Leo Dillon, and Diane Dillon (1991). *Pish, Posh, Said Hieronymous Bosch*. San Diego, CA: Harcourt Brace Jovanovich.

Williams, Jay, and Mercer Mayer (1976). *Everyone Knows What a Dragon Looks Like*. New York: Four Winds.

Wisniewski, David (1990). *Elfwyn's Saga*. New York: Lothrop, Lee & Shepard.

Wood, Don, and Audrey Wood (1984). *The Napping House*. San Diego, CA: Harcourt Brace Jovanovich.

——— (1985). *King Bidgood's in the Bathtub*. San Diego, CA: Harcourt Brace Jovanovich.

——— (1987). *Heckedy Peg*. San Diego, CA: Harcourt Brace Jovanovich.

Yolen, Jane, and John Schoenherr (1987). *Owl Moon*. New York: Philomel.

Yolen, Jane, and David Shannon (1992). *Encounter*. San Diego, CA: Harcourt Brace Jovanovich.

Yorinks, Arthur, and Richard Egielski (1986). *Hey, Al*. New York: Farrar, Straus & Giroux.

Young, Ed (1989). *Lon Po Po*. New York: Philomel.

Zelinsky, Paul (1986). *Rumpelstiltskin*. New York: Dutton.

# Chapter 4

# Design, Composition, and Visual Language

> A child can and must be trained in visual awareness
> if he is to become an aware adult.
> —Marcia Brown, *Lotus Seeds* (1986)

## Training the Eye to See

In her autobiography, Marcia Brown observes that "it is extremely difficult to be objective about a picture book because each of us brings something different to what he sees" (1986, 8). One's personality, character, and experiences do, of course, affect how one processes or negotiates picture books. Yet our appreciation, awareness, and understanding of the picture book can clearly grow and mature in the same way that our exposure to fine art, sculpture, and classical music deepens our understanding of these art forms. Though we will, of course, not all like the same art, or the same picture books, our understanding of them will grow as our eyes and minds become more discerning.

Training the eye to see, the development of critical viewing skills, the promotion of visual literacy; all these endeavors contribute to a culture that not only looks, but also sees. In the case of the picture book, consideration of the size, shape, and look of the book leads logically into analysis of the frame in which the artist constructs the visual component of the story. With new eyes, our children can now begin to see not simply what happens in the picture, but how the picture happens.

French film theory provides an interesting analytical tool or framework for conceptualizing the art of picture books. In *Understanding Movies* (1976, 48), Louis Giannetti says that mise-en-scène refers "to the arrangement of all the visual elements of a theatrical production within a given space—the stage." Applied to the picture book, the concept of mise-en-scène enables us to conceptualize the composition of the page or picture in terms of the way the cast, set, lighting, props, and other elements cumulatively contribute to the overall statement the illustrator is making. This theatrical and cinematic link is made very obvious by Lyn Lacy's discussion of *Where the Wild Things Are* (Sendak 1963). "Sendak as stage manager has regulated our responses to the various acts in his play by opening and closing the curtain of white space and by enlarging or telescoping the backdrops of ocean, forest and wild land" (Lacy 1986, 116). Describing Arnold Lobel's illustrations in *The Claypot Boy* (Jameson and Lobel 1973), George Shannon also saw cinematic techniques at work. "Images are frequently framed again within that frame, acting much like a zoom lens to intensify perspective and drama. . . . [A]fter beginning with a miniature wide shot of the couple . . . Lobel's camera moves closer, filling the doublespread screen with the couple to establish their roles in the story" (Shannon 1989, 32).

Teaching children to recognize and read these elements in picture books has implications well beyond that medium or the elementary school classroom. As a visual art form, the picture book inevitably draws upon the representational codes and conventions of Western culture. As such, the visual language of the picture book is related to other visual media, including advertising, motion pictures, and television. Children who become pictorially competent or visually proficient in their understanding of picture books are highly likely to be able to transfer these skills to their analysis of mass media messages, thereby fusing visual literacy with media literacy. This ability to analyze visual messages has been shown to succeed with both picture books (Considine 1986) and the electronic media (Considine and Haley 1992).

Anyone seeking to find a relationship between the language of film and the visual language of the picture book need only explore David Wiesner's *Tuesday* (1991). The half-title page (which actually contains no title) features three sequential vertical panels, representing a progression in time as the first frog begins to fly. The movement from the left to the right of the frame fulfills the same function as a camera panning across the scene. On the first full page of the book, where the text announces, "Tuesday evening around eight," the cinematic style is even stronger. This time the three panels are arranged horizontally, stretched out across the page like film frames for wide-screen projection. Adding further to the cinematic nature of the page is the way the illustrator has constructed the shots. The three panels constitute an establishing or opening shot, and their composition shows the camera progressively zooming in for a close-up. As a result, the turtle on the log, barely discernible in the upper panel, and just becoming visible in the intermediate shot, dominates the final frame. The expression on the turtle's face and its gaze upward herald the arrival of the floating frogs on the next double-page spread. The next page, which includes panels set against a double-page spread, can be equated to the cinematic concept of *montage*, which generally translates as the combination of several separate pictures. Wiesner's composition confronts us with various images of frogs, birds, and landscape, shown from different angles and strategically positioned at different distances in the background and foreground. Teachers wishing to relate the language of picture books to the language of film should be able to see the way the opening of *Tuesday* mirrors a classic use of establishing shots in *Psycho*, where Hitchcock's camera draws us slowly into the frame, progressing from a long shot of the city to one building and finally to one window.

Recognizing and reading visual compositions provides children with the skills to process pictorial information in all its forms. Although art appreciation has a role to play in this process, at a more basic level, this is an issue of language acquisition skills. By learning to read such elements of visual language as point of view, posture, props, position, and proportion, children become more adept at analyzing the form and content of picture books. Teachers can help children as they encounter these illustrations by carefully structuring strategies to promote information retrieval from the cues and clues contained in the visual language. Certainly this method can be applied as children read an entire book, but it is also quite possible to take individual pictures in isolation from the story and ask children to explain what they think is happening in the illustration. By doing this, the reliance on words can be relinquished and more emphasis can be placed on the narrative role of the visuals. Whether working with characters, location, or action, the same type of questioning can be employed to help children interpret the images:

LEAD QUESTION: Tell me about the people in this picture.

SECONDARY QUESTION: What do you see in the picture that makes you say that?

The secondary question is very important to the process, because it forces children to articulate the elements and aspects of the picture from which they unconsciously derive information. It will become very evident during this process that not all children come to the same conclusions and that not all of them assign processing priority to the same elements of the frame. While some may rely heavily on body language, posture, and gesture, others may work with clues contained in props, such as clothing or furniture; still others may respond to camera angle or point of view. It is quite informative to keep a record of what elements individual children seem most reliant on. With this knowledge, teachers can construct experiences that will facilitate the children's response to other elements of visual language.

# The "5P" Approach to Analyzing Pictures: Strategies and Activities

## *Element 1: Posture*

Of the five broad tools suitable for analyzing the meaning of images, the most obvious and natural deals with the role of body language in expressing human emotions. On a daily basis, children use facial expression, gesture, and posture to help them communicate with others. Because these skills are already part of their behavior, they represent a good starting point when children begin to process pictures. Although these exercises use picture books and are related to children's literature, they have social significance as well. Understanding and successfully using nonverbal communication skills can be an important attribute in many professions, including teaching, medicine, and law enforcement. Often doctors, teachers, and police officers must pay attention to how individuals act and appear, not just to what they say. The ability to read body language has also been applied to analyzing bias in broadcast news, where facial expressions may communicate the unspoken opinion of the anchor or reporter. In fact, the news is selected and presented as stories, told to us by a storyteller, so it seems logical that the teller's behavior could influence the way we respond to the story (Friedman et al. 1980; Moss 1986; Seidman 1984).

Before actually working with picture books, teachers can introduce students to the concept of body language through simple exercises. A line drawing of a face with smile can be accompanied by the question, "How does this person feel?" The secondary or follow-up question should, as always, ask students to explain why they arrived at the answers they gave. Mime can also be a useful ally in working with nonverbal communication skills. If a teacher has a box of index cards, each with the name of a different emotion written on it, students can be asked to select a card and communicate that emotion to the class without using words. This activity can be broken into two categories. On one occasion, students can employ only facial expression. On the other occasion, they may use posture and gesture as well as facial expression.

With this background, the picture book can now be analyzed in terms of the way the illustrator uses these elements to communicate. In many cases, this means dealing with the images in isolation from the story. If children are being asked to interpret the way a character feels, it is important that they focus attention on what the image tells them, not the words they read or that are read to them. In most cases, it is not necessary for children to use the text, because, consciously or otherwise, both the illustrator and the child audience draw on social codes and conventions relating to body language. Nodelman notes that picture books "depend to an astonishing extent on clichés of physical appearance" (1988, 112), particularly in regard to concepts such as good and evil. The good prince is traditionally tall, strong, and handsome, whereas the wicked witch or stepmother is often withered, misshapen, ugly, or deformed. These cultural assumptions and conventions contribute to the knowledge base we bring to body language and, as such, "they allow us to derive information from the gesture and posture of characters, both animals and human" (p. 117).

## 62  Design, Composition, and Visual Language

A simple example of this can be found in *The Garden of Abdul Gasazi* (Van Allsburg 1979). This is a thoroughly enjoyable story that children respond well to, but before they have even been exposed to the story, students can be asked to read the mood and feelings of the characters in the pictures. In the second-to-last image, a very sad Alan is comforted by Miss Hester as the faithful dog, Fritz, looks on. Alan has his hands in his pockets, his head is hung down, his expression is cheerless. Miss Hester, in a maternal gesture, pats him on the head and shoulder and bends over him. Without knowing anything about the characters or the plot, children will begin to read this picture. Simple teacher prompts, such as "What's happening in this picture?" and "How do these people feel?" should suffice. As always, the secondary question must always require students to explain why and how they arrived at their answers. For students who need more directed questioning to help them read this image, teachers can ask, "Are these people happy?" and "Do you think these people are angry?" Students may also play out the feelings of characters in the pictures by posing in the same way.

Almost any quality picture book contains numerous examples of body language that students can be helped to recognize and read. Children can work with an isolated image, or they may trace a character through a series of images. "Blue is happiness, Grandfather! I feel it in my heart," the young boy exclaims in *Knots on a Counting Rope* (Martin, Archambault, and Rand 1987). In the image that accompanies this text, the boy's face fills the frame. His eyes are wide, his mouth is open, smiling, and he gestures with his two hands. The artist provides the viewer with many cues about the character's mood. A more subtle example that relies almost entirely on facial expression can be found in *Tree of Cranes* by Allen Say (1991). "I don't want to go to bed," the sick boy protests to his mother, but go to bed he must. The boy's reaction is conveyed by his face and a slight stooping of the shoulders. The eyebrows, eyes, and down-turned mouth all suggest the child's unhappiness. *Song and Dance Man* (Ackerman and Gammell 1988) abounds with examples of posture providing insight into a character. The first image of Grandpa shows a passive, worn-out old man in an overstuffed chair. From the moment the children arrive at the door, Grandpa's facial expression and body language become energetic and animated.

Whereas sorrow and joy are rather easily communicated by expression and gesture, other human emotions are more difficult to convey. In *Encounter* (Yolen and Shannon 1992), the artist uses a close-up of a face staring at a gold coin. The text, told from the viewpoint of the child, says, "[I]t was the serpent's smile—no lips and all teeth." Even with the support of the text, it is likely that children will have some difficulty recognizing what the artist is trying to say about the character. Although they are likely to recognize an attraction to the golden coin, is this viewed as positive, or are concepts such as greed also read into the picture?

Another subtle attitude is present in Marcellino's representation of the ogre in *Puss in Boots* (1990). The text indicates that this is the richest ogre in the world and that he welcomed Puss "as affably as an Ogre can." As the cat enters the house, he sees the empty food trays coming from the ogre's dining room. A rack of ribs and something resembling a snake are all that is visible. When the ogre first appears, he is much less menacing than we may have anticipated. Without the benefit of beard, fangs, claws, tusks, or burning eyes, the bald-headed ogre is less than awe-inspiring. Breaking with visual conventions, Marcellino downplays the appearance of the ogre. The overall impact of the picture, fully supported by the point of view, suggests that the ogre is more imposing than menacing. There is perhaps even something a little humorous about his demeanor. Share this illustration with children without benefit of the text and see how they interpret the character.

Wordless or near-wordless picture books offer a good opportunity to explore body language. Without the support of text, these books must often use depictions of bodily expression and gesture to communicate. *The Bear and Fly* (Winter 1981) is a very good example. The filmstrip version, with its big images, offers teachers an opportunity to have the whole class respond to the expressions and gestures of the bear family. Stepping frame by frame through the story, children can detect the growing irritation of the father bear and the response of the rest of the family. As they become more involved in the story, they begin to anticipate what will happen in the next image.

### The "5P" Approach to Analyzing Pictures: Strategies and Activities 63

*Tuesday* (Wiesner 1991) employs facial expressions and gestures in both its human and animal characters to clearly convey how they feel as the flying-frog invasion takes place. Fish, birds, frogs, dogs, people, and pigs all emote clearly. On the page where the text reads "4:38 a.m.," a frog is seen in three horizontal panels, progressing from a state of contentment to fear and panic. In the middle frame, using broad body language, the frog pulls back on the lilypad—applying the brakes, as it were—to avoid the oncoming dog, which is barely visible to the right of the frame. In the final panel, wide-eyed, fearful, and hunkered down, the flying frog retreats with the dog in hot pursuit.

- In groups, or as individual assignments, give children a basic human emotion and ask them to find two or three examples from picture books that convey that feeling.

- Nodelman has suggested that physical appearance continues to support stereotypical notions. Ask children to describe the typical appearance of a hero, villain, prince, princess, or other broad archetype. Do they draw on physical appearance? What characteristics do they assign these characters?

- Have children conduct a simple content analysis of the physical appearance of heroes and villains in picture books. Develop a list of the attributes of all the good characters and all the villains. What roles do appearance, expression, and gesture play in these representations?

- Make a special study of the expression, posture, and body language of animal characters in picture books. As appropriate, introduce children to the concept of anthropomorphism. Study the changing body language of one character in one book, such as Clarence in *The Post Office Cat* (Haley 1976), Eddie the dog in *Hey, Al* (Yorinks and Egielski 1986), or Hannibal the cat in *Hurricane* (Wiesner 1990). Children could also work with a series of their favorite animal characters.

- Select a book with particularly strong use of body language and see how well students can interpret and act out the emotions of the key characters. An outstanding example is the many moods of Max manifested in *Where the Wild Things Are* (Sendak 1963). Other good examples include *Heckedy Peg* (Wood and Wood 1987) and *Rumpelstiltskin* (Zelinsky 1986).

- In the early part of *Mufaro's Beautiful Daughters: An African Tale* (Steptoe 1987), the differences between the two sisters are clearly reinforced by facial expression, body language, and posture. Working with stories from other countries and cultures, explore the universal nature of nonverbal communication. Are the gestures and mannerisms of the characters authentic, or have they been filtered through Western eyes for Western audiences? This approach to body language can be applied to the study of other cultures. Tourist information for Americans visiting Japan, Indonesia, Thailand, and other countries often makes reference to such things as eye contact, touching, and bowing. Open displays of affection, for example, which are quite common in the West, are not always acceptable in other cultures.

64 Design, Composition, and Visual Language

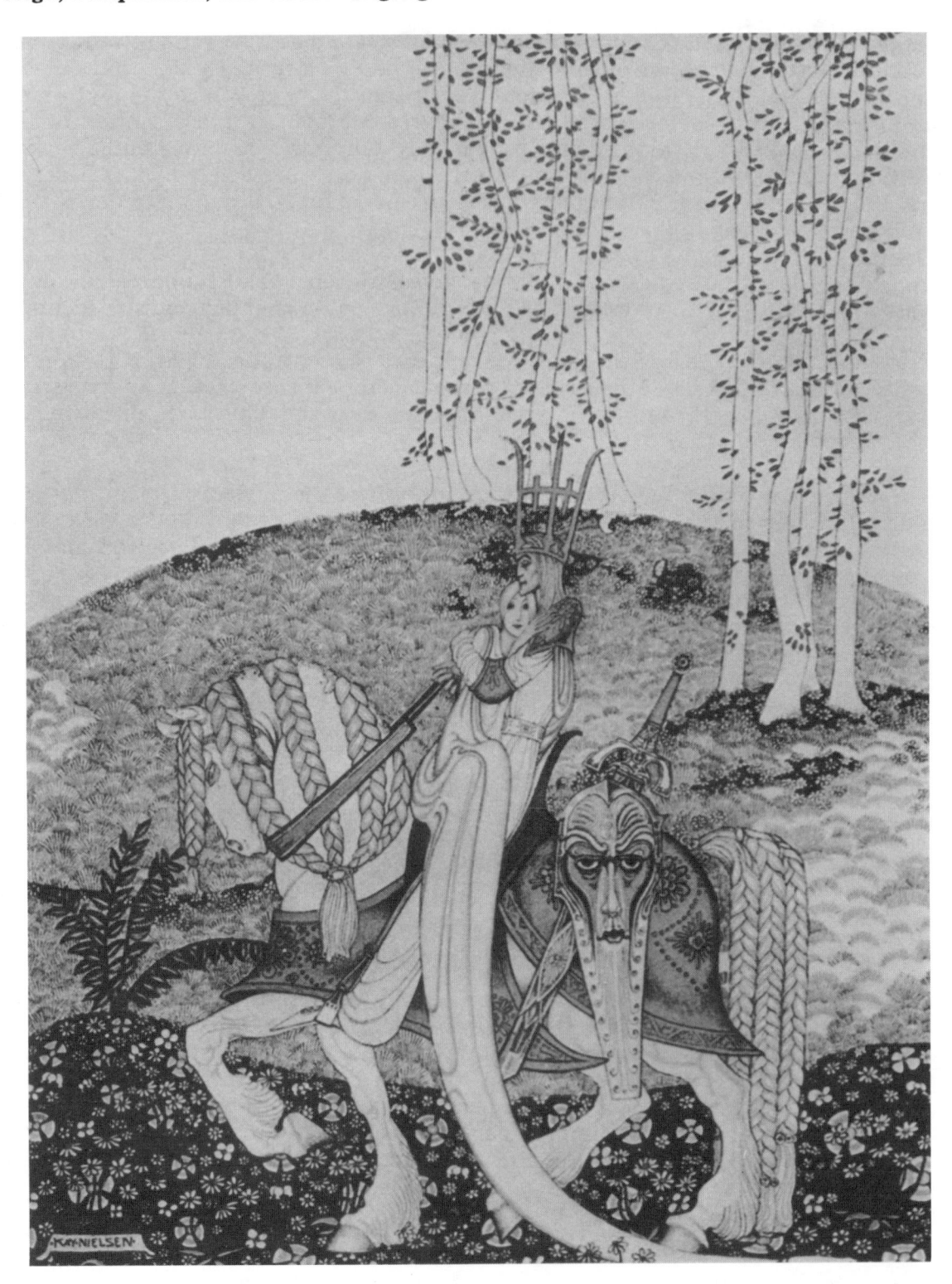

Pictorial processing. Ask children to tell you about the people in this picture. Typically, they will indicate that this is a prince or a king, tall, strong, wealthy, who has rescued the woman. The significant follow up question asks them to explain how they arrived at their conclusions. This process forces them to consciously acknowledge that they have read visual elements such as posture and props. The size of the sword and shield convey the warrior's strength. The crown signifies his royalty. The ornate trappings of the horse indicate wealth. The protective posture of the female suggests patriarchal control. (From *East of the Sun and West of the Moon*, by Kay Nielsen. Illustration copyright © 1914 by Kay Nielsen. Reprinted with permission of Brockhampton Press a division of Hodder & Stoughton Limited.)

## Element 2: *Point of View*

*Point of view* refers to the perspective or position from which the artist constructs the content of the frame. Two of the most used and most obvious techniques are what in film and television are called a *tilt up* and a *tilt down*. Traditionally, such techniques embody codes and conventions related to power and authority (Considine 1985). Placing the camera below the figure or object depicted usually conveys power. It may be physical power related to the strength and stature of the individual, or it may be emotional, sexual, or even spiritual power. This visual device has its origins deep in Western art. The structure and design of cathedrals, including elongated stained-glass windows, force our eyes upward to contemplate depictions of the Apostles, saints, and other figures. This concentration is documented in *A Concise History of Russian Art* (Rice 1963), which says: "[T]he tradition of depicting saints as taller than ordinary people is intended to underline the difference between the material and celestial world and size is often proportionate to ideological importance." Our language, with expressions such as "looking up to someone," also reflects the cultural context of this artistic device.

Point of view employing tilt up that confers power or authority on those seen this way. The concept is readily evident in television, motion pictures, and other visual media. (From *The Green Man*, written and illustrated by Gail E. Haley.)

The strength, authority, and power conveyed by the tilt up may be either benevolent or menacing. Villains as well as heroes are represented with this device. In the movie *Legend* (1985), excellent use is made of the tilt up in the underground scenes on the eve of the Devil's wedding. Consistently shot from below, the Satanic figure who has captured the unicorn looms across the screen as evil incarnate.

It should also be noted that the assignment of the tilt up has traditionally represented a gender bias. Given the patriarchal nature of the church and its role as patron of the arts during the Renaissance, it is hardly surprising that the foundations of Western art, later emulated by photography, film, and television, clearly assign power to males. In Western art and later in mass media, female figures are seldom represented through use of the tilt up. When they are, in classic films like *Mildred Pierce* (1945), *Johnny Guitar* (1954), and *Rebel Without a Cause* (1959), for example, they invariably disrupt the sexual balance and represent the dangers of matriarchy. When tilt ups are used to present females in other roles, whether in fine art or the mass media, they are traditionally positioned as madonnas or love-goddesses.

Whereas men are frequently represented through the power of the tilt up, women can only be assigned this device by relinquishing their femininity and taking on the role of spiritual or sexual divinity, or seductress and villain, in the tradition of the bloodsucking vamp. The way Western art has historically pictured and positioned women as the blessed Madonna or destructive Eve has been well documented (Brown 1975). Those concerned with women's issues, multicultural education, and social stereotypes must acknowledge this tradition and its presence in picture books and mass media.

The use of both tilt up and tilt down is clearly evident in the motion picture *Superman 2* (1980), in the sequence when Lois Lane discovers that Clark Kent is really Superman. The combination of point of view and posture throughout this sequence is used to choreograph the changing power perception of the two characters. Using brief clips from films like this, while studying these elements in picture books, can reinforce children's awareness of visual language in both electronic and non-electronic formats.

If the tilt up conventionally confers power on the figure or object depicted, the tilt down has the reverse effect, evident again in our day-to-day use of expressions such as "looking down on someone." The stature of an individual is diminished when the camera is placed above him or her. Such a device usually renders the figures weak, vulnerable, threatened, or inferior. A frequently used cinematic device, employing both the tilt up and tilt down, shows a staircase with a tilt up on the power figure at the head of the stairs and a tilt down on the weaker figure at the foot of the stairs.

It is not difficult to find examples of both the tilt up and the tilt down in picture books. *Saint George and the Dragon* (Hodges and Hyman 1984) uses both techniques. On the first page on which the dragon appears, it looms out of the landscape, dominating the frame and overflowing the formal borders. As viewers, we are clearly positioned below the dragon. As is usually the case when representing power in a threatening way, posture is also used to cumulatively convey the danger. The dragon's claws and expression, combined with the tilt up, create the overall impact of the image. Three illustrations later, in another battle sequence, we are again positioned below the beast. When the dragon is vanquished, in a cinematic technique, the "camera" pulls back and now tilts down on the defeated monster. In *Birdsong* (Haley 1984), the artist offers an early clue to the potential danger in Jorinella. When we first meet Jorinella, her body language and the point of view are neutral, though the text does tell us that she is greedy. On the next double-page spread, as the text tells us "something about the old woman frightened Birdsong," the artist employs a tilt up as Jorinella spreads out her cloak, dominating the frame. The potential danger is implicit in the angle and in the spiderweb design on her cloak. In *Sea Tale* (Haley 1990), the same artist used a similar technique to communicate the danger that faces Tom in Gertie's tattoo parlor. Here, using the tilt up, posture, and positioning, the illustrator creates an unmistakable message of menace. The young sea captain is positioned in the lower right of the frame, an area generally known as the *dead zone*, given Western art traditions that place the center of attention slightly left of center. But it is the tilt up on Gertie, and her exaggerated, outstretched hands and bony fingers, that pack the real power in the picture. Like Jorinella, Gertie's character is further established by props such as the octopus tentacles in the design of her dress.

An example of the cumulative use of major visual elements. The point of view, with its tilt up, empowers the evil Gertie. Her posture and body language menace the young hero, Tom. His position in the lower right of the frame banishes him to an area that, in most Western representations, signifies lack of authority. (From *Sea Tale*, written and illustrated by Gail E. Haley.)

*Tom Thumb* (Watson 1989), which received the Gold Kite Award, is perfectly suited to demonstrate both the tilt up and the tilt down. The interaction of the tiny boy and the giant permits the artist to play with point of view. The first image of the book is a tilt down on three cats, who watch while the tiny boy pours the milk. The image instantly establishes the dimensions of the story. Later, in a dramatic use of tilt up, we are placed in the position of the tiny boy as he gazes up at the giant Grumbong. *The Inch Boy* (Morimoto 1986), a Japanese version of *Tom Thumb,* is also rife with illustrations that demonstrate the role of point of view. The first illustration is an extreme tilt down on the old couple dwarfed by the giant Buddha. In a later illustration, the tilt up places us in the position of the boy as he stares up at the eight attendants who peer down at him. Later, when the boy encounters the Red Demon, the tilt up is used to stress the giant's size and power. Another book that demonstrates the role played by point of view is *The Rainbabies* (Melmed and La Marche 1992).

Although the techniques of tilt up and tilt down are often associated with size and physical power, they can also be used to suggest moral authority, weakness, or psychological vulnerability. *Jack and the Fire Dragon* (Haley 1988) contains one such example. After he has gone underground and killed the Fire Dragon, Jack is trapped by his brothers, who throw away his escape rope. After three days of searching for a way out, the despondent hero sits down and admits to himself, "Reckon I'm gonna starve and die down here." To convey Jack's vulnerability, the illustrator distances us from the hero by using a tilt down that dwarfs him in the subterranean tomb that threatens to become his grave. The picture of the funeral preparations for the miller in *Puss in Boots* (Haley 1991) also uses a tilt down, representing the loss and separation felt by the cat, who is shown with the miller on the half-title page immediately preceding the image of the casket. *Mirette on the High Wire* (McCully 1992) is another book in which the illustrator uses tilt down to convey loss and vulnerability. When the text tells us, "Mirette turned and ran to the kitchen as tears filled her eyes," the artist pulls back and tilts down on the child who, like Jack, sits forlornly on the floor.

**68  Design, Composition, and Visual Language**

Point of view employing tilt down that conveys a sense of weakness or vulnerability. Here Jack has been abandoned by his brothers in the underground home of the Fire Dragon and fears he will starve to death. Form and content therefore support each other. (From *Jack and the Fire Dragon*, written and illustrated by Gail E. Haley.)

Sometimes illustrators will employ point of view not to convey power, but because it enables them to play with space and perspective, or because the angle provides the only way of showing viewers what the artists want them to see. Marcellino's *Puss in Boots* (1990) provides numerous examples. The title page features a tilt down in the mill, which uses technical competency of the artist to re-create the mechanism of the mill and to show the threatened mice in the lower frame—who are, of course, examples of the visual victimization implicit in a tilt down. The next-to-last illustration in the book is an elaborate, double-page spread, without text, that establishes the opulence of the wedding and showcase the artist's skill in conveying depth and perspective. This use of point of view is significantly different from the more traditional application, evident in the same book in the depiction of the cat calling for help and in the first appearance of the ogre. In *Jumanji* (Van Allsburg 1981), the illustrator uses the tilt down because it is the only way he can visually tell us what he wants us to know. We know that the children, Peter and Judy, are bored. They find a board game and the artist uses words and pictures to make sure we believe this is just a game like any other. "It looked very much like the games they already had," the text says. To reinforce the message, Van Allsburg places our point of view above the children and the table so that we are looking directly down on the very ordinary board. When we turn the next page, Van Allsburg, who specializes in making the ordinary extraordinary, surprises us not just with the lion now lounging on the piano, but with the perspective that now places us in Judy's position. *Owl Moon* (Yolen and Schoenherr 1987), *Hurricane* (Wiesner 1990), *Free Fall* (Wiesner 1988), *The Weaving of a Dream* (Heyer 1986), and many other well-known picture books contain examples of point of view that can be shared with children.

## Element 3: Position

The position of characters or objects within a frame is often used to communicate their relationship to each other, as well as their relative weight or significance in the story or picture. The use of a close-up positions the characters forcefully on the page or screen, drawing attention to their physical appearance and emotions. The use of a long shot distances the individual from us, providing little evidence of how the character feels. The position of the character, either above or below another figure or object, also establishes a visual link with both point of view and posture, cumulatively creating the overall message of the illustration.

Books dealing with the journey motif are particularly illustrative of the way position can show movement, space, and a sense of progression, even within the confines of a static art form like the picture book. The pictures showing Max's journey to *Where the Wild Things Are* (Sendak 1963) effectively used position to advance the story.

*Saint George and the Dragon* (Hodges and Hyman 1984) also demonstrates this quite well. The title page is a double-page spread of a landscape. The image is an establishing shot that sets the scene. We are positioned in the place of spectators, witnessing the action that is about to begin. To the left of the spread, a fairy gestures right to the horizon, from whence our hero will come. At the bottom of the frame, three fairies stare out, directly engaging our eyes. This technique is consistently used throughout the book, creating a world in which we both see and seem to be seen. The copyright/dedication page repeats the landscape. This time, however, the Red Cross Knight and his party have just come into view at the point the fairy's gesture had directed us to. As the party enters the frame, the cinematic and theatrical device of characters entering and exiting is repeated as the fairies depart to the left of the frame. The progress of the party is now clearly established in a series of illustrations. Text occupies the right page. George and Princess Una appear on the left page, traveling from left to right across the frame. The dwarf, clearly the least significant member of the party, trails slightly behind in the distance, partially out of the formal frame. The next time we see the characters, they have been placed on the right page and they ride directly out of the frame toward us. The dwarf, who is now ahead of the knight, occupies the lower right of the frame. In Western art, center of attention usually is placed left of center, with the position here assigned to the dwarf carrying little in the way of significant information. Two pages later, when we again see the party's progress, they now have their backs to us. Una's pointing finger repeats the fairy's earlier gesture and directs our attention to the castle, which occupies approximately the same space in the frame that the party did when we first saw them. By repeatedly positioning her characters on different pages and from different perspectives, the artist creates continuity of movement, suitable to the journey motif.

The position of the characters within the frame also suggests their significance. In our first glimpse of the party, the characters are barely discernible. By the final image, George and Una loom large in the frame, filling it for the first time.

*Dream Peddler* (Haley 1993) also uses position to chronicle a journey. John Chapman's journey takes us from rural Swaffham to the hustle and bustle of London Bridge in the eighteenth century. The title page depicts the hero in the printing shop. He occupies the left of the frame, waiting for the printed sheets to come off the press. The copyright/dedication page moves him from left to right, from the print shop to the market square where he stitches the pages of the chapbooks that he will sell on his travels. The first full page of text shows the peddler, with his pack upon his back, as his travels begin. Throughout the book, the ebb-and-flow of the journey is clearly conveyed by how Chapman is positioned. His travels, the sequences in London, and even the dream sequences all depict a movement from the left to the right of the frame. The domestic scenes, showing the day-to-day needs of the family and household, all turn John away from the pull to the right. The ploughing sequence and the roof repair picture, for example, both show Chapman facing left. When the treasure is discovered, he again faces left, as if turning his back on the busy and congested world of the big city. He is repeatedly positioned, in the London sequence, as turning first one way and then another, resting only in the bookstore. The left and right movement throughout these images clearly

### 70 Design, Composition, and Visual Language

reflects his psychological state and his ambivalence about London. As he and his dog Caxton become lost in the throng, their position in the frame establishes their confusion. The final image in the book shows Chapman and Caxton, home again in Swaffham, in the cathedral he has built. Although he looks in the direction of London, he is positioned where he began, to the left of the frame. Caxton's gaze and the light streaming through the stained-glass windows hold him in place. The design of the page, with its emphasis on horizontal and vertical planes, repeats the earlier image from the bookstore and the passive posture evident in the family portrait. As the owner of the print shop, John no longer has to travel. His life can be spent in the quiet contemplation of his family, books, and God.

Share these examples with students and have them locate other books in which position is used to suggest a journey, a state of mind, or the significance of characters.

## *Element 4: Proportion*

Illustrators frequently employ proportion to convey meaning. This is one artistic device—one aspect of visual language—about which reviewers and academics do tend to comment. In *Lon Po Po* (Young 1989), we are told that "several illustrations show [how] the position and relative size of objects in a picture affect our interpretation of it" (Benedict and Carlisle 1992, 6). Describing a scene depicting three frightened girls and the shadow of the wolf, Carlisle and Benedict clearly address the function of both proportion and position. "The shadow's huge size in relation to the children and its position above them heightens the effect of the threat" (p. 6). Sometimes the design or proportion of the pages themselves contribute to the story. *Where the Wild Things Are* (Sendak 1963) begins with a small rectangular image in the middle of the page. The text, on the left, tells us, "That night Max wore his wolf suit and made mischief of one kind." When we turn the page, we see Max pursuing the family dog, and the frame has become larger. Turning the page again, we find the angry boy banished to his bedroom without supper, and the size of the image has increased again. Three illustrations later, as the bedroom is transformed into a jungle, the illustration fills the entire page. The changing proportion of the page is a clear reflection of the boy's liberation from both his bedroom and the confines of his imagination. For the next six illustrations, the world in which Max finds himself continues to expand.

*The Boy of the Three Year Nap* (Snyder and Say 1988) also gave reviewers the opportunity to discuss the relationship between proportion and posture. The *Horn Book* reviewer commented on the way the absence of visual details forces the reader to concentrate on the interplay between the two central characters. The calmness of the mother's expression and body language contrasts with the "range of emotions that play upon the boy's features.... When he first suspects his mother's disapproval, the child is drawn in smaller scale, apart from her and engulfed by a mildly threatening world. Later, secure in the certainty of his mother's love, he looms large on the page" (1991, 722).

Introduce students to the role of proportion in these and other picture books; then have them find their own examples. The object is not simply to have students spot this visual device. Students should also be able to explain how it relates to the mood, theme, plot, events, or characters in the book.

The "5P" Approach to Analyzing Pictures: Strategies and Activities  71

The vertical design and composition of this page enabled the illustrator to place emphasis on the planes and lines of the cathedral architecture with its vaulted ceiling. The height also permitted use of the stained-glass windows and the diagonal design of the intruding sunlight. (From *Dream Peddler*, written and illustrated by Gail E. Haley.)

The horizontal format running across a double-page spread with text in the upper left, enabled the artist to develop the congested crowd of eighteenth-century London, where the hero and his dog become lost and separated in the throng. (From *Dream Peddler*, written and illustrated by Gail E. Haley.)

## Element 5: Props

Children raised on film and television almost immediately appreciate the way props or artifacts can tell us something about a character's personality. Aided by elements like the zoom and close-up, both film and television frequently cue us to the importance of objects that would otherwise seem inconsequential. A close-up of a door knob announces an imminent arrival; in the same way, we expect a call when the telephone occupies the frame. A close-up of a pair of scissors heralds the demise of the killer in *Dial M for Murder* (1954). In *Ordinary People* (1980), director Robert Redford employed the symbolic language of props to convey Beth's character. The Academy Award-winning film features close-ups of napkin rings, cracked plates, and other objects that represent the fragmentation of the family and Beth's desperate need to hold herself together. Both films use props, but they employ them for different purposes. The scissors function on a manifest or obvious level. As they become central to the plot, we are made more aware of them. In *Ordinary People*, the props are given meaning beyond their objective existence. They are used to symbolically comment on a character in the way an artist may use color to convey a mood.

In children's picture books, there are numerous opportunities for children to learn from the clothes, tools, furnishings, and artifacts surrounding the characters, especially when this process is promoted by teachers and when it is also related to their mass media experiences. "Like practicing physiognomists, children plumb film and TV characters' appearance for demographic data.... [C]ostumes help viewers assign fictional characters to a time and place. ... Beards, breasts and other mile stones of maturity offer clues to a character's age" (Brown 1986, 70–71). Perry Nodelman observes that children "can learn to associate characters with their environments and to read the rooms and furnishings depicted in picture books for information about this owner's personalit[y]" (1988, 117).

In the crowded creations of Gail Haley, there is no shortage of visual evidence to piece together. Gertie's tattoo parlor in *Sea Tale* (1990) and Jorinella's cottage in *Birdsong* (1984) provide many insights into the interests and activities of both women. In illustrations exploding with detail, the artist depicts shrunken heads, cauldrons, candles, scales, chairs, chests, combs, curtains, nets, a menagerie of stuffed animals, and many of the kittens and cats that frequently peer out of the pages of her books. The austere world of Al and his dog Eddie in *Hey, Al* (Yorinks and Egielski 1986) is equally well conveyed by props. Our introduction to the book first presents us with a bucket, mop, and brush, the janitor's tools of the trade. Our first view of the apartment makes it clear that the two friends do not live the high life. The ceiling is cracked, the bed is broken, and the apartment is cramped. The final frame in *Free Fall* (Wiesner 1988) provides a wealth of objects for the discerning eye to recognize from the dream world that has preceded this illustration. The mirror and the comb depicted on the cover of *Mufaro's Beautiful Daughters: An African Tale* (Steptoe 1987) provide an instant insight into one character.

As we help children recognize the presence of props in pictures, and facilitate their ability to read these props, we must also be careful of the danger of reading too much into them. A review of *Sea Tale* (Haley 1990) attributed imagined meanings to simple objects, particularly a piece of jewelry that had no more or less significance the character's hat, coat, or shoes (Hodges 1990, F3). The necklace that consumed the reviewer's imagination was just a simple decoration, never referred to in the text.

Stories set in other periods and cultures provide an opportunity for teachers to help students identify objects and artifacts with which they are not familiar. In *The Green Man* (Haley 1979) and *Dream Peddler* (Haley 1993), the artist employs various trade signs to depict the different craftsmen in Claude's medieval village and in eighteenth-century London. Every page of *Ashanti to Zulu* (Musgrove, Dillon, and Dillon 1976) is crammed with African artifacts reflecting the lifestyle and customs of the various tribes. *The Legend of the Bluebonnet* (dePaola 1983), *The Girl Who Loved Wild Horses* (Goble 1978), and numerous other Native American stories offer other opportunities to explore the way props provide information about the various tribes depicted. The accuracy and authenticity of these artifacts can also be examined.

Although respected illustrators traditionally attempt to authentically capture the culture they are working with, at times social constraints and dramatic license impinge upon the historical accuracy of the art. David Shannon acknowledged this in the illustrator's notes for *Encounter* (Yolen and Shannon 1992). Trying to recreate the Taino culture was difficult, as "[m]ost of their artifacts were either melted down or burned." Shannon was aware that the "native people wore no clothing," but on that issue, historical accuracy had to give way. "I was faced with the problem of how to present them without offending those who object to nudity in a children's book." In his notes for *The Warrior and the Wise Man* (1989), David Wisniewski acknowledged the use of artistic license and dramatic and technical reasons for not always showing the truth. In one case, the artist omitted showing a weapon because "it would have been impossible to render in cut paper." In another case, he manipulated the presence of props because he wanted a character to be recognized immediately. "A warrior would probably not have brought his weapons into the Emperor's presence, but Tozaemon wears his sword here, so that his identity and character are immediately apparent to the reader." Both Shannon and Wisniewski endeavor to remain faithful to the spirit of the story and culture without slavishly replicating every aspect of it.

- Select illustrations from several books where the props provide clues and cues about the characters. Without introducing children to the story, ask them to describe the characters based on these props. Remember, props include clothing, artifacts, furnishings, and the environment.

- *The Green Man* and *Dream Peddler* (Haley 1993) both recreate graphics and trade signs from other centuries. Share these with students (e.g., The Mermaid and Bush pub referred to in both the text and images of *The Green Man*). Then have them design and create their own logos or emblems for contemporary occupations and professions. The Yellow Pages can be helpful in this process, and many banks have sheets of such designs for their business customers to use on their checkbooks.

- Tell students that they are working on a movie or television show about one of the following characters. Their job is to operate as wardrobe, property, and set designer/decorators. What materials would they select to enable audiences to visually recognize the characters?

Queen/Princess
King/Prince
Knight/Warrior
Wizard/Sorcerer/Witch
Mermaid/Sailor

The activity can be updated to contemporary times by having them make the same decisions for:

Attorney
Priest
Gangster
Detective
Doctor
Scientist
Homemaker

#### 74 Design, Composition, and Visual Language

Remember, this activity will evoke stereotypes as it engages students in the struggle to use props with which the audience will be immediately familiar.

- Discuss the issue of artistic license with students. How much leeway do they think an illustrator should have in interpreting a story? What are the implications of this for multicultural childrens literature? If the book conveys the spirit of the story, period, or culture, does it matter if it also contains historical inaccuracy such as clothing or artifacts?

## Panels, Pages, Spreads, and Vignettes

The organization, distribution, and layout of illustrations in a book contribute to both the flow of the narrative and, in some cases, to the actual meaning and impact of the illustrations. In the first double-page spread of *There's a Nightmare in My Closet* (Mayer 1968), for example, the layout contributes to the meaning. The boy occupies the right page and the gutter separates him from the threat of the closet. "The mystery of that closet is reinforced not only by its separation but by the text, which occurs on the right page with the boy" (Arakelian 1985, 123). The gutter is also used for separation and psychological significance in *Jack and the Bean Tree* (Haley 1986). The illustrator was fully aware of Bettelheim's reading of the text, which sees Jack in early adolescence, asserting his independence and breaking from his mother. "The end of childhood . . . is reached when childish dreams of glory are given up, and self-assertion, even against a parent, becomes the order of the day. Instead of approving of Jack's first act of independence and initiative . . . his mother ridicules what he has done" (Bettelheim 1977, 188–89). In depicting this moment, Haley breaks from the spreads that characterized all the earlier illustrations. Instead, she employs three vertical panels that immediately allude to the bean tree that is about to grow. The angry mother is isolated on the far left of the double page, her hand breaking out of the border to cast the seeds towards the right. She and her son are separated both by text and by the gutter. In an interesting image that implies the relationship among the seeds, mother's milk, Milky White the cow, and what Bettelheim calls "the magic phallic powers as symbolized by the huge beanstalk" (1977, 189), Haley shows Jack's body fluids in the form of his tears, watering the seeds that then begin to grow in the final panel to the right of the page. Although children do not need to be introduced to the psychological or sexual nature of the picture or text, many of them may be able to understand why the artist has employed the panels and why the text and gutter are used to separate mother and child.

The only other time in the book when the illustrator breaks what Stewig calls "the page orientation" (1992, 20) is toward the end of the story, when the giant pursues Jack down the bean tree. Dramatically, Haley abandons the horizontal spreads that were consistently used throughout the book. Suddenly, readers must turn the book to explore the vertical vision, which is further strengthened by the tilt up technique. "What Haley and others who have used this visual device appear to be doing is sending the viewer a larger message, not about WHAT but about HOW. . . . The artists are asserting their right to break convention when it suits their purposes. That's a valuable, albeit subliminal, message for child viewers" (Stewig 1992, 20).

*The Green Man* (Haley 1979) provides several examples of the use of panels. Whereas most of the book features the artist's characteristic double-page spread, using a horizontal design, panels are employed on four occasions. In three of these, the artist uses the panels to show the passage of time or a sequential series of events. We see the bony hands reach out from the bushes to steal Claude's clothes. Young children familiar with comic strips can clearly see the development of the action. Later, in a more elaborate series of panels, we see Claude as gatherer and preserver harvesting the grains, fruit, and crops. Each panel shows a different activity, and the presence of the sun and moon again allude to the passage of time. Finally, on the last page of story text, the artist creates three panels to show the various stages of Claude's return from Green Man to squire's son. The panels enable the illustration to present a sequence that is not possible in a single image.

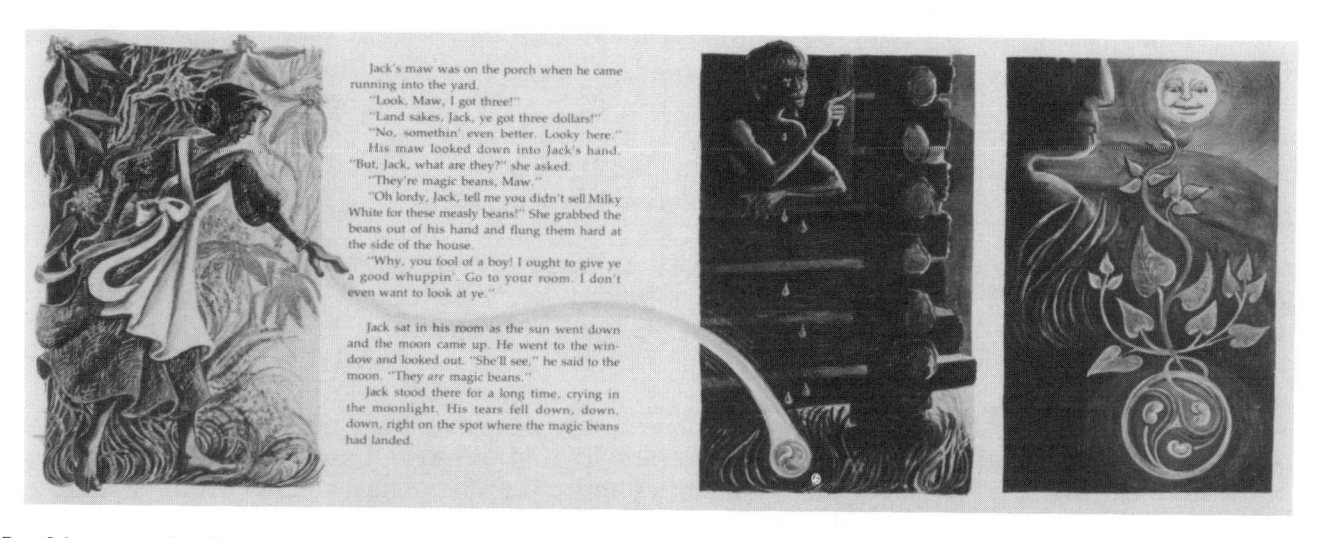

In this example, the artist employs panels, separated by text and the gutter, to represent the emotional and psychological separation that comes between Jack and his mother. (From *Jack and the Bean Tree,* retold and illustrated by Gail E. Haley.)

*Sea Tale* (Haley 1990) also employs panels to show the passage of time. Until this point in the book, the layout has consisted of spreads running across two-thirds of a double page, or full-page illustrations balanced on the other side by text and a small vignette. The panels are introduced to help children see the transformation in Tom. In the earlier sequences, Tom is shown wearing his captain's uniform, but in the panel sequences the uniform has been removed. As the economical text does not refer to this, the artist employs the panels to show him changing and the passage of time. In the first panel on the left, the sun is low in the sky. In each subsequent panel, the sun climbs higher. In essence, the panels enable the illustrator to use the sun as a prop to deal with the unfolding of the day.

Peter Spier's *Noah's Ark* (1977), a wordless picture book, relies heavily on the use of panels to build the stages of the narrative. As Haley uses the sun to indicate the time of day, Spier uses the level of the water to mark the passage of time. On one page, he employs four vertical panels to achieve this. In the first panel at the left of the page, the ark is still on dry land. In the three subsequent panels, the water rises, carrying the ark higher in each frame. In the sequence when Noah releases the dove, Spier uses three panels and a full-page illustration again dealing with the passage of time, covering the release, the waiting, and the return of the bird.

Other books that use panels include *The Golden Deer* (Hodges and San Souci 1992), *Strega Nona* (dePaola 1975), *Lon Po Po* (Young 1989), *Good Morning, Maxine* (Cazet 1989), and Sendak's *In the Night Kitchen* (1970). *The Fortune Tellers* (Alexander and Hyman 1992) consists mainly of double-page spreads, but late in the story, when the fortune teller falls from the balcony and is pursued by a lion, the illustrator employs panels in a cinematic way to convey the movement of the fall and the chase.

As we have noted, panels and vignettes can be interspersed throughout books, integrated into double-page spreads, or balanced with text against single full-page illustrations that appear opposite. These panels and vignettes provide visual variety, balance a page when the text is limited, and depict sequences which cannot be shown in a single picture. For many

## 76  Design, Composition, and Visual Language

illustrators, however, a more uniform look is preferred. Visual continuity, in which the organization and layout of the illustrations consistently remain the same, is very evident in the work of Van Allsburg. *The Garden of Abdul Gasazi* (1979) and *Jumanji* (1981) are remarkably consistent in design. Each black-and-white illustration occupies the right-hand side of the double page, with the text on the left. Each illustration is within a formal border, with no bleeds or overlaps and no panels or vignettes. Similarly, with the exception of the vignette of the wolf on the title page and the sleigh bell on the last page, *The Polar Express* (1985) consists of 14 three-quarter-page spreads, though this time there is some variation in the positioning and distribution of the art and text. Visual consistency and continuity can be found in *Mirandy and Brother Wind* (McKissak and Pinkney 1988), *The Talking Eggs* (San Souci and Pinkney 1989), *Shadow* (Brown 1982), *Tree of Cranes* (Say 1991), *Tar Beach* (Ringgold 1991), and *Follow the Drinking Gourd* (Winter 1988).

Although some illustrators repeatedly use a particular format and design in the layout and organization of their books, others vary their compositions. *Free Fall* (Wiesner 1988) and *Hurricane* (Wiesner 1990) are similar in design and reminiscent of Van Allsburg. But by the time David Wiesner worked on *Tuesday* (1991), his composition displayed much greater variety. The same can be said for *Go Away, Stay Away* (Haley 1977) and *Jack and the Fire Dragon* (Haley 1988). Although they were written almost a decade apart, and released by different publishers, there is a remarkable similarity between their organization and layout. In 1993, however, Haley's *Dream Peddler* demonstrated a marked departure from her traditional book design. A similar break in design can be found in the books of Audrey and Don Wood. *The Napping House* (1984) and *King Bidgood's in the Bathtub* (1985) both contain 14 full double-page spreads, with no white space, and the text is integrated into the art. *Heckedy Peg* (1987) totally abandons this look, providing a cornucopia of design. Ostensibly a vertically formatted book, this assumption is immediately shattered by a half-page horizontal landscape on the title page. The book features no less than eight different visual designs or compositions. These include six single full-page vertical illustrations, several double-page spreads with limited text at the bottom of the pages, numerous vignettes, a series of cameo portraits of the seven children, and various other designs.

- Introduce children to various design formats such as panels, vignettes, spreads, and single pages. Discuss possible reasons why an illustrator would select one of these formats.

- Once students have been introduced to these elements, assign them the task of locating one or more such elements in other books. This can be done as individual work or in cooperative learning groups, with each group working on a different element.

- Assign students the task of exploring the composition and design style of a single illustrator, such as Van Allsburg, Brown, Pinkney, Haley, Say, Wood, or Wisniewski. What design techniques characterize the look of this illustrator's books?

- When children make their own illustrated books for programs like book fairs or Young Author Conferences, help them make sure their books reflect an understanding of the variety of display and design formats that are possible.

# On the Border

Finally, in describing the design and organization of picture books, some consideration should also be given to the use of borders and frames. These borders vary from formal lines completely enclosing the art, to ornate decorative borders, to informal frames with characters and objects spilling over the edge, to books in which the only frame is the edge of the page. The books of Leo Dillon and Diane Dillon are among the most formal in the use of borders or frames. Although the art in their earlier books, such as *Why Mosquitoes Buzz in People's Ears* (Aardema, Dillon. and Dillon 1975) and *Who's in Rabbit's House?* (Aardema, Dillon, and Dillon 1977), is constrained only by the physical edges of the pages (what technically is called a *bleed edge*), their later books are much more formal. *Ashanti to Zulu* (Musgrove, Dillon, and Dillon 1976), *Aïda* (Price, Dillon, and Dillon 1990), and *Pish, Posh, Said Hieronymous Bosch* (Willard, Dillon, and Dillon 1991) all feature formal frames, often enclosed within ornate and elaborate borders, whether the kano knot in the African book or the silver, bronze, and brass sculpted frame employed in *Pish, Posh*.

Formal frames are often employed in books that try to evoke a sense of the golden age of children's books and the illustrations of Walter Crane or Kay Nielsen, for example. Typically, they are found in retellings of classic fairy tales. *Hansel and Gretel* (Lesser and Zelinsky 1984), *Rumpelstiltskin* (Zelinsky 1986), *Saint George and the Dragon* (Hodges and Hyman 1984), and *Puss in Boots* (Marcellino 1990) are all examples of this. But formal frames can also be used to create a sense of elegance or composure for folktales and contemporary stories. Van Allsburg's pictures are always formally enclosed. The formal frame of *Tree of Cranes* (Say 1991) is perfectly suited to the formality of Japanese society and the ritual the story depicts. Sometimes, as in the work of the Dillons, the formal frames may include decorative borders and other ornate designs. The book of the Chinese tale *Everyone Knows What a Dragon Looks Like* (Williams and Mayer 1976) contains such a border. The *Sleeping Bread* (Czernecki and Rhodes 1992) uses designs inspired by the Guatemalan story, fusing folk art with folktale. Ethnic designs are also evident in the decorative borders in *Marushka's Egg* (Rael and Wezyk 1993). The artist in *Little Red Riding Hood* (Hyman 1983) carefully constructed decorative borders to complement the story. The artist "wanted text, story and design to vigorously reinforce each other and combine to create a total graphic effect. . . . [T]he borders reflect motifs of Pennsylvania Dutch folk art, common garden plants, insects and quaint wallpaper" (May 1985, 130). The following year, Hyman employed an even more formal design for *Saint George and the Dragon* (Hodges and Hyman 1984). Although the book won the Caldecott medal, the artist herself admitted that what she intended the design to represent was often misunderstood. At the beginning of her Caldecott acceptance speech, Hyman noted the tendency of some people to read more into an illustration than she ever consciously intended. Later, she specifically referred to the number of people who believed the design of the frame in *Saint George and the Dragon* was intended to represent a window pane. In reality, the design was a device, "a visual trick" used like a matte to isolate the action and make the eye focus on it. What Hyman was also attempting to do was to develop the red cross of Saint George in the four corners of each page. Nonetheless, her intentions were widely misunderstood, and the book is frequently described in terms of the window-pane effect. Though it does not detract from the visual appeal of the book, it should nonetheless be noted that the border designs include tulips, which had not actually been introduced to England at the time the book is set.

**78** Design, Composition, and Visual Language

Decorative borders inspired by Guatemalan folkart. (From *The Sleeping Bread*, by Stefan Czernecki and Timothy Rhodes. Illustration copyright © by Stefan Czernecki. Reprinted with permission of Hyperion Books for Children, a division of Disney Publishing Group.).

Between the formal border and the bleed comes what might be termed the informal or semiformal border. Typically, such books employ a frame, though the lines are less rigid and usually not as dark as those of a formal frame. It is also quite common for figures, environment, or artifacts to spill over or pop out of the frame. Examples of the informal border can be found in *Sea Tale* (Haley 1990), *Hey, Al* (Yorinks and Egielski 1986), *On Market Street* (Lobel and Lobel 1981), *Fables* (Lobel 1980), and *Tom Thumb* (Watson 1989).

The frameless illustration, or *bleed*, is evident when the pictures extend to the very edge of the frame and appear to continue beyond it. On the first page of *The Girl Who Loved Wild Horses* (Goble 1978), for example, the buffalo are pursued from right to left across the double page. It seems apparent that there are buffalo ahead of the herd and buffalo and Indians yet to come into view. Though Trina Schart Hyman has skillfully used frames and decorative borders, she has also used the frameless approach, as evidenced in *Hershel and the Hanukkah Goblins* (Kimmel and Hyman 1989). The following books are all frameless, though they represent strikingly different stories, different artistic techniques, and a variety of shapes: *Tar Beach* (Ringgold 1991), *Elfwyn's Saga* (Wisniewski 1990), *Owl Moon* (Yolen and Schoenherr 1987), *The Legend of the Bluebonnet* (dePaola 1983), *Shadow* (Brown 1982), and *The Fool of the World and the Flying Ship* (Ransome and Shulevitz 1968).

It is also possible to find books that employ more than one of these techniques of framing. In *Anancy and Mr. Dry-Bone* (French 1991), the cover of the book provides the first evidence of this. Employing a wraparound design, the book opens out, revealing a formal border design extending vertically the entire length of the far right of the page, while another border extends horizontally across the entire bottom of the double-page opened cover. The left of the picture and the top of the picture bleed straight to the edge of the page. Variations on this border design occur throughout the book, which refuses to conform to a single format. *The Sign of the Seahorse* (Base 1992) also combines formal partial borders with edges that bleed.

- Introduce children to the three types of frames described in this section. Using specific examples, discuss why an illustrator might have selected a particular frame and how it might relate to the mood, theme, or period of the story. After students have seen examples of each type of frame, have them locate and identify other examples.

- When children make their own illustrations or design pictures for a book, encourage them to experiment with different types of frames.

# References

Aardema, Verna, Leo Dillon, and Diane Dillon (1975). *Why Mosquitoes Buzz in People's Ears*. New York: Dial.

—— (1977). *Who's in Rabbit's House?* New York: Dial Books for Young Readers.

Ackerman, Karen, and Stephen Gammell (1988). *Song and Dance Man*. New York: Alfred A. Knopf.

Alexander, Lloyd, and Trina Schart Hyman (1992). *The Fortune Tellers*. New York: Dutton.

Arakelian, Paul (1985). Text and Illustration: A Stylistic Analysis of Books by Sendak and Mayer. *Children's Literature Association Quarterly* 10 (3): 122–26.

Base, Graeme (1992). *The Sign of the Seahorse*. New York: Harry N. Abrams.

Benedict, Susan, and Lenore Carlisle (1992). *Beyond Words: Picture Books for Older Readers and Writers.* Portsmouth, NH: Heinemann.

Bettelheim, Bruno (1977). *The Uses of Enchantment: The Meaning and Importance of Fairy Tales.* New York: Vintage.

Brown, Lyvia Morgan (1975). Sexism in Western Art. In *Women: A Feminist Perspective*, edited by Jo Freeman. Palo Alto, CA: Mayfield.

Brown, Marcia (1982). *Shadow.* New York: Charles Scribner's Sons.

——— (1986). *Lotus Seeds: Children, Pictures and Books.* New York: Scribners.

Cazet, Denys (1989). *Good Morning, Maxine.* New York: Bradbury.

Considine, David M. (1986). Visual Literacy and Children's Books: An Integrated Approach. *School Library Journal* 33 (1): 38–42.

Considine, David M., and Gail E. Haley (1992). *Visual Messages: Integrating Imagery into Instruction.* Englewood, CO: Teacher Ideas Press.

Czernecki, Stefan, and Timothy Rhodes (1992). *The Sleeping Bread.* New York: Hyperion Books.

dePaola, Tomie (1975). *Strega Nona.* Englewood Cliffs, NJ: Prentice-Hall.

——— (1983). *The Legend of the Bluebonnet.* New York: Putnam.

French, Fiona (1991). *Anancy and Mr. Dry-Bone.* Boston: Little, Brown.

Friedman, H. S., et al. (1980). Perceived Bias in the Facial Expressions of Television News Broadcasters. *Journal of Communication* 30 (4): 103–11.

Gianetti, Louis (1976). *Understanding the Movies.* Englewood Cliffs, NJ: Prentice-Hall.

Goble, Paul (1978). *The Girl Who Loved Wild Horses.* New York: Macmillan.

Haley, Gail E. (1976). *The Post Office Cat.* New York: Scribners.

——— (1977). *Go Away, Stay Away.* New York: Scribners.

——— (1979). *The Green Man.* New York: Scribners.

——— (1984). *Birdsong.* New York: Crown.

——— (1986a). From the Ananse Stories to the Jack Tales: My Work with Folktales. *Children's Literature Association Quarterly* 11 (3): 118–21.

——— (1986b). *Jack and the Bean Tree.* New York: Crown.

———(1988). *Jack and the Fire Dragon.* New York: Crown.

——— (1990). *Sea Tale.* New York: Dutton.

——— (1991). *Puss in Boots*. New York: Dutton.

——— (1992). *Mountain Jack Tales*. New York: Dutton.

——— (1993). *Dream Peddler*. New York: Dutton.

Heyer, Marilee (1986). *The Weaving of a Dream*. New York: Viking.

Hodges, Betty (1990). Dismiss These Books as "Kiddy Lit" at Peril of Passing Up Worthwhile Tales. *Durham Morning Herald*, August 26, F3.

Hodges, Margaret, and Trina Schart Hyman (1984). *Saint George and the Dragon*. Boston: Little, Brown.

Hodges, Margaret, and Daniel San Souci (1992). *The Golden Deer*. New York: Charles Scribner's Sons.

*Horn Book* (1991). Review of *The Boy of the Three Year Nap*. November/December: 722.

Hyman, Trina Schart (1983). *Little Red Riding Hood*. New York: Holiday House.

Jameson, Cynthia, and Arnold Lobel (1973). *The Claypot Boy*. New York: Coward.

Kimmel, Eric, and Trina Schart Hyman (1989). *Hershel and the Hanukkah Goblins*. New York: Holiday House.

Lacy, Lyn Ellen (1986). *Art and Design in Children's Picture Books*. Chicago: American Library Association.

Lesser, Rika, and Paul O. Zelinsky (1984). *Hansel and Gretel*. New York: Dodd, Mead.

Lobel, Arnold (1980). *Fables*. New York: Harper & Row.

Lobel, Arnold, and Anita Lobel (1981). *On Market Street*. New York: William Morrow.

Marcellino, Fred (1990). *Puss in Boots*. New York: Farrar, Straus & Giroux.

Martin, Jr., Bill, John Archambault, and Ted Rand (1987). *Knots on a Counting Rope*. New York: Henry Holt.

May, Jill P. (1985). Illustration as Interpretation: Trina Schart Hyman's Folktales. *Children's Literature Association Quarterly*, Fall: 127–31.

Mayer, Mercer (1968). *There's a Nightmare in My Closet*. New York: Dial Books for Young Readers.

McCully, Emily Arnold (1992). *Mirette on the High Wire*. New York: Dutton.

McKissack, Patricia, and Jerry Pinkney (1988). *Mirandy and Brother Wind*. New York: Alfred A. Knopf.

Melmed, Laura Krauss, and Jim La Marche (1992). *The Rainbabies*. New York: Lothrop, Lee & Shepard.

## 82 Design, Composition, and Visual Language

Morimoto, Junko (1986). *The Inch Boy*. New York: Viking Kestrel.

Moss, Ruth (1986). Candidate Camera. *Psychology Today,* December: 20.

Musgrove, Margaret, Leo Dillon, and Diane Dillon (1976). *Ashanti to Zulu: African Traditions*. New York: Dial.

Nodelman, Perry (1988). *Words About Pictures: The Narrative Art of Children's Picture Books*. Athens, GA: University of Georgia Press.

Price, Leontyne, Leo Dillon, and Diane Dillon (1990). *Aïda*. San Diego, CA: Harcourt Brace Jovanovich.

Rael, Elsa, and Goenni Wezyk (1993). *Marushka's Egg*. New York: Macmillan.

Rice, Tamara Talbot (1963). *A Concise History of Russian Art*. London: Methuen.

Ringgold, Faith (1991). *Tar Beach*. New York: Scholastic.

San Souci, Robert, and Jerry Pinkney (1989). *The Talking Eggs*. New York: Dial

Say, Allen (1991). *Tree of Cranes*. Boston: Houghton Mifflin.

Seidman, Steven A. (1984). What's in a Face? Facial Expression as a Key Variable in Visual Literacy. *Visual Literacy Newsletter* 13 (3): 1.

Sendak, Maurice (1963). *Where the Wild Things Are*. New York: Harper & Row.

——— (1970). *In the Night Kitchen*. New York: Harper & Row.

Shannon, George (1989). *Arnold Lobel*. Boston: Twayne.

Snyder, Dianne, and Allen Say (1988). *The Boy of the Three Year Nap*. Boston: Houghton Mifflin.

Spier, Peter (1977). *Noah's Ark*. Garden City, NY: Doubleday.

Steptoe, John (1987). *Mufaro's Beautiful Daughters: An African Tale*. New York: Lothrop, Lee & Shepard.

Stewig, John Warren (1992). Reading Pictures, Reading Texts: Some Similarities. *The New Advocate* 55 (1): 11–22.

Van Allsburg, Chris (1979). *The Garden of Abdul Gasazi*. Boston: Houghton Mifflin.

——— (1981). *Jumanji*. Boston: Houghton Mifflin.

——— (1985). *The Polar Express*. Boston: Houghton Mifflin.

Watson, Richard Jesse (1989). *Tom Thumb*. San Diego, CA: Harcourt Brace Jovanovich.

Wiesner, David (1988). *Free Fall*. New York: Clarion.

——— (1990). *Hurricane*. New York: Clarion.

—— (1991). *Tuesday*. New York: Clarion.

Willard, Nancy, Leo Dillon, and Diane Dillon (1991). *Pish, Posh, Said Hieronymous Bosch*. San Diego, CA: Harcourt Brace Jovanovich.

Williams, Jay, and Mercer Mayer (1976). *Everyone Knows What a Dragon Looks Like*. New York: Four Winds.

Winter, Jeanette (1988). *Follow the Drinking Gourd*. New York: Dragonfly Books.

Winter, Paula (1980). *Sir Andrew*. New York: Crown.

—— (1981). *The Bear and the Fly*. New York: Crown.

Wisniewski, David (1989). *The Warrior and the Wise Man*. New York: Lothrop, Lee & Shepard.

—— (1990). *Elfwyn's Saga*. New York: Lothrop, Lee & Shepard.

Wood, Don, and Audrey Wood (1984). *The Napping House*. San Diego, CA: Harcourt Brace Jovanovich.

—— (1985). *King Bidgood's in the Bathtub*. San Diego, CA: Harcourt Brace Jovanovich.

—— (1987). *Heckedy Peg*. San Diego, CA: Harcourt Brace Jovanovich.

Yolen, Jane, and John Schoenherr (1987). *Owl Moon*. New York: Philomel.

Yolen, Jane, and David Shannon (1992). *Encounter*. San Diego, CA: Harcourt Brace Jovanovich.

Yorinks, Arthur, and Richard Egielski (1986). *Hey, Al*. New York: Farrar, Straus & Giroux.

Young, Ed (1989). *Lon Po Po*. New York: Philomel.

Zelinsky, Paul (1986). *Rumpelstiltskin*. New York: Dutton.

Chapter 5

# Illustrating as Art: Media, Method, and Message

> One of the nicest things about being an artist
> is to see things a little differently, a little more
> carefully perhaps, and a little more imaginatively
> than most people do.
>
> —Trina Schart Hyman, Caldecott
> medal acceptance speech (1985)

## Introduction

Chapter 1 documented the paucity of art information research found in picture-book reviews (Busbin and Steinfirst 1989; Stewig 1980; Stewig 1992). So although the artist may, as Trina Schart Hyman observed, see things differently, there is no guarantee that the artist's work will be seen, understood, or appreciated as intended. Maurice Sendak has been quite outspoken about the nature of the review process. This recipient of the Caldecott medal, the Hans Christian Andersen Medal, and the Laura Ingalls Wilder Award said, "I have not learned anything from reviews of other people's books that I thought did justice to a book's special qualities." For Sendak, most reviewers suffer from what he calls the limited vision of "Kiddiebooklanditis," which is an insult to both author and illustrator. "When you've worked a year on a book, when you've put your life into it, you expect the point of view of the professionals—editors, teachers, librarians—to be somewhat larger, more expansive" (1988, 191). Nor was Marcia Brown reluctant to speak out against "the blurb-quoting, shallow summaries of plots that often pass for reviews today" (Brown 1986, 199). For the meanest critics, Brown reminds us: "Vituperations tell a great deal more about those who utter them than the work attacked. Self-appointed experts are often people who are distinguished for their ignorance as well as for their arrogance" (p. 185–86). Such complaints may be considered by some as merely defensive posturing, but in reality, by voicing their concerns, the artists draw attention to the need for better reviewing, which can only come from devoting more attention to the art of the picture book in the education of teachers, librarians, and media specialists.

For those who lack this training, but not the interest, there are a growing number of sources that often provide significant insight into the artistic techniques employed in picture books. Lengthier, more academic analyses can be found in quality periodicals such as *Children's Literature in Education*, *The New Advocate*, *The Lion and the Unicorn*, and of course, that veritable institution of children's literature, *Horn Book*. In these journals, one finds first-person accounts of the creative process seen through the eyes and words of the author or artist; interviews with leading writers or illustrators; and thoughtful analyses of single titles or bodies of work. Earlier chapters alluded to the problem of just how widely disseminated these materials are among the professionals who work with children's books. A research project might benefit from studying the presence or absence of these and other journals in the collections and reading lists of colleges and universities that prepare our future teachers and librarians. The presence or absence of these journals in our public libraries and school library media centers should also be taken into account. Although *School Library Journal* and *Booklist* can be found in many libraries, and their reviews often affect purchasing decisions, these libraries also need journals and support materials to broaden the appreciation of children's books by both students and teachers.

In addition to the academic journals, there are also a growing number of biographies or autobiographies dealing with authors and illustrators, including Arnold Lobel (Shannon 1989), Trina Schart Hyman (1981), and many others. Reference collections can also access the *Something About the Author, Autobiography Series*, published by Gale Research. Finally, one cannot ignore the collection of Caldecott and Newbery acceptance speeches published about every 10 years by Horn Book. These collections allow the artists to describe their work in their own words. The collections also contain after-the-fact essays, providing an overview and comparative evaluation of each of the books. At times, these essays contain thoughtful, objective analysis. Unfortunately, however, too often their tone and tenor tend toward destructive rather than constructive criticism. *The Girl Who Loved Wild Horses* (Goble 1978) is dismissed, for example, as "stilted, arbitrarily stylized, art-modern absurdities" (Bader 1986, 292). *Saint George and the Dragon* (Hodges and Hyman 1984) fares even worse. "The border decorations on the text pages . . . are banal as motifs and vapid as picture forms." The book itself is derisively condemned as "a pretentious invocation of past illustrational glories, which it cheapens rather than enhances" (p. 309). Such criticism, we believe, contributes little to the understanding or appreciation of the art of picture books. The pungent prose, though entertaining, is less than enlightening. It also tends to operate from the elitist heights of adult aesthetic concerns, with little regard for the child for whom the book was intended. This head-on assault on Caldecott medal books is actually likely to do more damage than good. Although healthy debates about what does or does not constitute quality art is always welcome, the critical excesses evident in many of these comments may do nothing but confuse teachers. Lacking any substantial training in art themselves, many teachers and librarians would find it difficult to reconcile these comments with the fact that these books have won the Caldecott medal. This confusion might well drive many of them away from the relatively subjective world of art appreciation, turning them back to the literary aspects of the book where they feel on safer ground.

In recent years, however, there has been some evidence of greater attention to art in the review process. Significantly, many of these reviews are showing up in *School Library Journal*, which has enormous circulation in the libraries and media centers of U.S. schools. Reviewing *Mirette on the High Wire* (McCully 1992), the journal said "the impressionistic paintings, full of mottled, rough edges and bright colors, capture both the detail and the general milieu of Paris in the last century" (*School Library Journal* 1993, S8). In a brief sentence, the review manages to evoke the world of the Impressionist painters and to imply a rationale and relationship between the technique used and the setting of the story. *Orpheus* (Mikolaycak 1992) was another beneficiary of informed reviewing. Though the reviewer could not resist the clichéd "visually stunning," the rest of the analysis was detailed and thoughtful. The book was described as "a triumph of art and design" and specifics were provided to support the claim. "Dusky matte pages set off white type and white-edged illustrations. Both Maxfield Parrish and Caravaggio provide artistic precedents, while some unconventional color and composition underscore originality" (*School Library Journal* 1992, 286).

Popular art as well as fine art often inspires today's illustrators of children's books. The illustrations and posters of Maxfield Parrish reveal "a lasting interest in architecture" and "a fascination with geometric patterns" (Sendak 1988, 88). "Their photographic surrealism combines fact and fancy in a meticulously depicted dream world" (Sendak 1988, 87). Those familiar with the work of Chris Van Allsburg will recognize the description. As an artist, Van

Allsburg has shown himself to be "concerned with ways to imply depth through contrast and graduation of light and dark" and "strict geometrical principles of linear perspective" (Lacy 1986, 126). The title page of *The Garden of Abdul Gasazi* (Van Allsburg 1979), which shows the boy poised at the entrance to the garden, is reminiscent of Parrish's cover for *The Golden Age* (Grahame), first published in 1899. Our first glimpse of Gasazi's mansion further stirs memories of Parrish's house and landscaping. The inspiration for *In the Night Kitchen* (Sendak 1970) also owes much to popular art. "The flat comic book style" (Steig 1985, 146) and the composition of the books reflect the artist's admiration for Winsor McCay's *Little Nemo in Slumberland*, an early twentieth-century comic strip. According to Sendak, "McCay and I serve the same master, our child selves. We both draw, not on the literal memory of childhood, but on the emotional memory of its stress and urgency. And neither of us forgot our childhood dreams" (Sendak 1988, 78).

The fact that the illustrations with which we are concerned appear in books for children should not obscure or disguise the artistic merit with which they are executed, nor prevent teachers from using these images to build bridges to the study of fine art. This bridge is quite apparent in *Li'l Sis and Uncle Willie* (Everett 1991), a fictional story based on the life and paintings of William H. Johnson, whose African-American images are housed in the Smithsonian Institute and the National Museum of American Art. Marcia Brown believes that contemplation of the art of children's books can build a foundation to be carried over to adulthood. Though exposure to quality children's books does not guarantee "an adult taste capable of appreciating fine art . . . the child unconsciously forms an approach to his visual world of order, rhythm, and interesting arrangements of color from the books he sees. . . . [A] well designed page may start a chain-reaction that will continue into adulthood" (Brown 1986, 12). Like many illustrators, Brown believes the contemplation of picture books may provide a respite and "defense against the bombardment of visual material on his eyes in most of his waking hours" (p. 12). The issue of the well-designed page has already been addressed in this work. In this chapter we are concerned primarily with artistic technique or style and the decision-making process the artist uses in selecting a particular technique.

As the relationship to fine art has already been raised, it is not inappropriate to look at the way children's book illustrators have drawn on the content and traditions of the fine arts, whether in the decorative Chinese screens alluded to in the panels of *Lon Po Po* (Young 1989) or the Impressionist-inspired art of *Mirette on the High Wire* (McCully 1992). Books by Chris Van Allsburg and Mitsumasa Anno play with depth and perspective, often inviting comparison to the work of M. C. Escher. *Anno's Journey* (1978) actually contains visual references to the world of fine art, including *The Grain Sifters*, by Courbet; Millet's *The Gleaners*; and *The Bathers*, by Seurat. Perhaps nowhere is the link between children's literature and fine art more obviously stated than in *Pish, Posh, Said Heironymous Bosch* (Willard, Dillon, and Dillon 1991). Inspired by the work of the sixteenth-century Dutch painter, this intriguing book plays with the dark visions of a man whose work "reflected his pessimistic view of life" and whose "monsters and visual fantasy of the grotesque were personifications of the wickedness he felt existed in the world" (Cahan and Riley 1980, 9). The content, technique, and design of the book are all an homage to Bosch. The ornate frame that encloses each painting further enhances the art with references to individual Bosch works such as *The Adoration of the Magi*. Thomas Locker's *The Boy Who Held Back the Sea* (1987) also draws upon the traditions of the Dutch artists, including Vermeer and Rembrandt. But while the Dillons play with Bosch, creating a fantasy from his nightmare, a world that children can explore with each turn of the page, this is not true of Locker's work. Though his illustrations are, as reviewers noted, "visually stunning," they are also cold. The replication of an art style never intended for children, albeit technically competent and engaging to the adult eye, does not necessarily appeal to the child. Referring to *Hansel and Gretel* (Lesser and Zelinsky 1984), Barbara Bader addressed this concern. "Finished, old masterly paintings are perilous in picture books. . . . [E]nclosed, self contained, complete, they allow of no pictorial flow; coming one after another, they permit little of the variation in mood and tempo natural to narrative" (1986, 311). The absence of flow that Bader describes in *Hansel and Gretel* is in marked contrast to the dynamic, constantly shifting look of *Heckedy Peg* (Wood and Wood 1987).

Several of Gail Haley's books have been period pieces. In attempting to recreate another age, Haley tries to look through the eyes of the artist she would have been in this era and, whenever possible, keep in mind the reproduction techniques available at the time. For *Jack Jouett's Ride* (1973), set during the American Revolutionary War, she drew her inspiration from the wood engravings of Thomas Bewick, an eighteenth-century artist. Wanting a larger image to work with than was possible with expensive wood engraving blocks, Haley used linoleum cuts to create the effect she was looking for. *The Post Office Cat* (Haley 1976), set in Victorian England, reflected the visual expression of this period, lithograph. Toulouse Lautrec, Mucha, and many political cartoonists of the day drew on stone with crayon or liquid touche. Designs were bold—colors applied in brilliant, flat tones or predictable textures. Haley explored this art with the assistance of the staff at London's Victoria and Albert Museum. She did not own a lithograph press, but worked with an offset printer who understood stone lithography and was able, by separating colors and combining past and present techniques, to create a facsimile of these Victorian images. For her medieval story, *The Green Man* (1979), the artist drew on tapestries and the engravings of the sixteenth-century artist Pieter Brueghel. The village she creates for the hero owes much to the architecture, housing, and general milieu one can find in several Brueghel pieces, including *The Fair of St. George's Day* and *The Fair at Hoboken*. The Green Man himself shows up in Brueghel's *Play of the Death of the Wild Man*. Though Haley sets her story in England, the Green Man character could be found in European literature and art of the time, a fact that Haley documented in her Weston Woods filmstrip, *Tracing a Legend: The Story of the Green Man* (1980). Whether called the Green Man or the Wild Man, this "purely mythic creature was a literary and artistic invention of the medieval imagination" (Husband 1980). While Brueghel and other artists, both English and European, provided information about town and village life, Haley still needed to select a technique to bring the period to life. Nodelman (1988) has mistakenly suggested that the inspiration for the art came from British pub signs. Haley did first encounter the Green Man on a pub sign, but she explains in her filmstrip that the technique she used was actually chosen to evoke the feeling of a tapestry. As a result, she "used acrylic paint on rough canvas board to achieve a tapestry feeling. The colors are strong, the designs of figures and plans are bold and somewhat stylized" (Haley 1980).

After more than a decade away from England, Haley returned in the winter of 1992 in search of another legend that had long incubated in her imagination. *Dream Peddler* (1993) actually had its English origins in the fifteenth-century tale of the Peddler of Swaffham. Haley was familiar with the era but had already created this period for *The Green Man*.

Employing artistic license, she transplanted the story from its fifteenth-century setting to England in the eighteenth century. Haley's man of letters, her printer-Chapman, symbolized the growth of literacy in the eighteenth century. This expansion was fed by technological developments, which lead to the wider dissemination of the ideas that would later help to ignite both the French and American revolutions. The expansion of the press and the growth of literacy would radically change British society. The oral tradition would decline and the Chapman would disappear. For Haley, there seemed to be a parallel for today. The growth of television and visual technology in the twentieth century, threatens print, as print had threatened the oral tradition.

In bringing this era to life, the artist relied heavily on her research at the Victoria and Albert Museum, the National Gallery, the Museum of the History of the City of London, and the Printing Historical Society, where she examined old presses, plates, and chapbooks. The Tate Gallery had mounted a major exhibition called "Manners and Morals: Hogarth and British Painting 1700–1760." This catalog and her access to the work of Hogarth, Reynolds, and Gainsborough established the overall feel she wanted to convey in the illustrations. The formal family portraits of Gainsborough and Reynolds lent themselves to Haley's composition of the Chapman family. The London street scenes draw heavily on Hogarth's vision. The small boy in Hogarth's *The Graham Children* can be found on the lower right side of the book's cover.

The regiment of soldiers in the first London spread are derived from Hogarth's *March to Finchley*. The bagpiper and puppets in the same Haley spread can be located in Hogarth's *Southwark Fair*. Wherever possible, Haley tried to see the world through the eyes of the artists who inhabited it. Because Hogarth had a studio on London Bridge and some of his work depicts his view from its window, she was able to recreate this key location of her story with some sense of accuracy. She even "borrowed" Hogarth's clock, which she transplanted to the printing shop the hero buys.

In drawing upon the world of fine art, children's book illustrators do not seek to slavishly replicate the style or technique of these paintings, which were not intended for children. Rather, they seek to borrow the lens of another era to more accurately reflect the spirit, artifacts, and atmosphere of the day.

## Art and Multicultural Education

Sometimes illustrators must do more than set their story in a different time. Folktales in particular present the challenge of representing another culture, which often means researching and reproducing the art forms of that culture. In the process, the illustrator is often vulnerable to critics highly sensitive to the multicultural movement in education, who believe the final product misrepresents the culture or usurps its traditions for commercial gain. In the closing notes of *The Mouse Couple* (Malotki and Lacapa 1988) the author and illustrator complain about what they call the "often cartoonish illustrations" evident in many retellings of Native American stories. *Arrow to the Sun* (McDermott 1974) provoked the comment that its distortions and exaggerations "take on a comic (or horrific) aspect, to the detriment of a true perception of tribal art.... [I]n short, there is no basis in Pueblo art for this highly theatrical treatment (Bader 1975, 285). Despite the widespread popularity and success of Paul Goble's retellings, these too have been the object of attack." Native American art gains nothing by such misconceived and vacuous emulations" (Bader 1986, 292). The potential danger of such criticism is twofold. In the first place, it seems to be based on the notion that only exact duplication of the art forms of another culture are appropriate. This attitude denies the artist creative license to explore the art forms and to render them in a manner that is relevant to the modern child audience in a Western culture. Ashley Bryan, for one, said, "I am not copying any specific group. Just as in my retelling [of] African stories I want something in my art that reflects African art without necessarily being authentic" (1988, 175). The second danger of this criticism is the potential that, rather than increasing sensitivity to other cultures and consequently fostering wider dissemination of their traditions and stories, it may actually create a backlash among authors and illustrators who simply avoid these stories altogether rather than open themselves up to such attack.

A better avenue might be to ask whether the story and art capture, with dignity and respect, the customs and culture of the group represented. If the illustrations and text convey the spirit of the tale, surely no one has suffered even if they are not 100 percent faithful to the original. This is, of course, not to condone the "cartoonish" art described earlier or gross misrepresentation of a people's customs, traditions, and way of life.

In preparing *Shadow* (Brown 1982), Marcia Brown experienced some of these concerns and compromises. She had to reconcile "the images that formed in my head from reading the poem, with impressions gained from traveling in Africa, with records of anthropologists who had recently tried to record ways of life that are constantly changing and absorbing influences from other societies, and in some cases, disappearing altogether" (1986, 180). Inspired by African woodcuts, masks, and carvings, Brown believed "some cut medium might suggest the cleanness of line, subtlety of surface treatment and possibly some of the power" (p. 171) of the great works she had seen. Because she was having trouble with her hands, she avoided cutting the wood blocks, opting instead for cut paper shapes. Like so many great stories, Brown believed *Shadow* had universal themes and appeal. In creating it, she drew upon the Africa she knew, and the audience she was writing for, to create her own vision.

In the best retellings from other cultures, Western children are exposed to the customs and contributions of the peoples of the world. They find literary and mythic links in the legends and tales that pervade different cultures. They also are afforded the opportunity to explore the art forms of these cultures. In their first collaboration with Verna Aardema on *Behind the Back of the Mountain* (1973), Leo Dillon and Diane Dillon used African woodcuts and batik to create their human and animal figures in flat shapes. They built upon this style in *Who's in Rabbit's House?* (1977) and the Caldecott winner *Why Mosquitoes Buzz in People's Ears* (1975). For Western children accustomed to the perspective handed down from the Renaissance, these books offer a startlingly different way of looking at the world. "Unmodeled two dimensional figures are placed within a field of action that has little foreground, middle ground or background, to imply space in linear or aerial perspective" (Lacy 1986, 205). Similarly, the woodcut designs for *A Story, A Story* (Haley 1970) are characterized by "flat space in which shapes overlap in bold planes with no implied depth" (Lacy 1986, 213). In creating her vision of Africa, Haley studied African dance, music, and storytelling. In the motion picture *The Picture Book Animated* (Weston Woods 1978), the artist can be seen demonstrating Ananse's happy dance for the animator to reproduce. Haley chose woodcut because the shape, line, and grain it afforded suggested the African masks and carvings she had examined in researching the book. Africa is also brought to life in the beautiful images John Steptoe created for *Mufaro's Beautiful Daughters: An African Tale* (1987), which were based on a year's research of the flora, fauna, and environment he encountered in Zimbabwe.

In addition to exploring retellings of traditional folktales from other cultures, there is an increased opportunity to look at folktales told through the words and images of those native to the culture. The growth of the Australian children's book industry throughout the 1980s has resulted in a growing number of Aboriginal legends written and illustrated by artists and storytellers from this culture. Of particular interest are *The Rainbow Serpent* (Noonuccal and Noonuccal 1968), *Banana Bird and the Snake Man* (Tresize and Roughsey 1980), *Yulu's Coal* (Coulthard, Coulthard, McKenzie, and Heath 1987), *Platypus and Kookaburra* (Ingmells, Trezise, and Haginikitas 1987), and *Moon Man*, (Coulthard, Coulthard, McKenzie, and Heath 1987). These books not only expose American children to the authentic culture of a country with which they are generally fascinated, but they also present children with myths and art forms that can be usefully compared to Native American stories and art. The style and technique of these Australian artists draw upon natural materials. Raymond Meeks, for example, began painting on wood, making paint from clay mixed with berries, and creating brushes from his own hair. For Western eyes, and all the assumptions that go with them, the art of the Australian aboriginal often needs explaining. In the case of bark painting, for example, a picture is not intended "to be hung right way up on a wall and looked at straight on. It is painted on the ground and looked at on the ground by a circle of observers; thus some sections are drawn vertically, some parallel and some in reverse" (Parker and Drake-Brockman 1966, 11). Exploration of other forms of expression offers the children in our classrooms a wider vision of the world around them and the changing nature of their own society. For those interested in Australian children's books, *Horn Book* regularly features "News From Down Under."

As the population of the United States continues to take on a less European, more multicultural nature, it is natural to assume that the newcomers will contribute their own tales and traditions to our story pool. Already we find tales from Cameroon, Cambodia, Laos, and Nicaragua, among others, making their way into classrooms and libraries. Given the ever-important relationship between this country and Japan, it is not surprising also to find a growing number of tales coming from the East and the Pacific Rim. In the best of these books, as we have seen, skilled illustrators seek to bring a culture and life to share its traditions with a new audience. Such is the case with *The Warrior and the Wise Man* (Wisniewski 1989). In extensive notes at the back of the book, the artist explains that "details in many illustrations are derived from my research into Japanese decorative arts." Many patterns utilized in the papercuts "are taken from textile designs." The *shotoku* robe of the Emperor and his headdress "were copied from a twelfth century costume." Quality children's books like this do much more than provide teachers, librarians, and children with the opportunity to be exposed to stories from other cultures. Through the images they contain and the art forms created therein, they provide us with the chance to actually experience these cultures.

## Styles, Media, and Techniques

The world of film criticism has given us the idea of the director as author. In its broadest sense, author (auteur) theory argues that the so-called classic directors have their own inimitable techniques and distinguishing characteristics, which pervade their films in both theme and style. With such directors, their work is best understood not as single productions but as a body of work, each one building on and playing off the others. The westerns of John Ford, for example, are distinguished by the striking landscapes of Monument Valley and the recurrence of major motifs. The comedies of Frank Capra stress populist appeal, the triumph of good over evil, and rural values pitted against city cynicism. In more contemporary times, the films of Martin Scorsese reflect the director's fascination with New York. In the world of children's picture books, we might argue, some artists and illustrators have managed to create their own instantly recognizable techniques and styles. There is no mistaking the elaborate and beautiful papercuts of David Wisniewski. The haunting, surreal, black-and-white world evoked by the pencil art of Chris Van Allsburg is also unmistakable. Photorealism and fascination with depth and perspective have become characteristics of David Wiesner's intriguing fantasies. Paul Goble's art for his numerous Native American tales is instantly identifiable.

Sometimes, although an artists' techniques or styles may change from one book to another, they maintain a continuity and consistency in theme, genre, or character. Maurice Sendak's work reveals continuity of character. "Max has appeared in my other books, under different names: Kennie, Martin and Rosie. They all have the same need to master the uncontrollable and frightening aspects of their life and they all turn to fantasy to escape this" (Sendak 1988, 152). The books of Ezra Jack Keats also afford us the opportunity to progress with Peter, who "matures from a wide-eyed inquisitive pre-school child to a gangly adolescent" (Nikola-Lisa and Donaldson 1990, 76). The observant and the informed can see that some illustrators even project their own faces onto their characters in the time-honored tradition of Rackham, Hitchcock, and da Vinci. There is no mistaking the portraits of Trina Schart Hyman evident in many of her books. Steven Kellogg has confessed that his own characters often end up looking like himself, an experience shared by Amy Schwartz, who said that her "characters are usually rather rotund based on my own body image" (1987, 90). Whether by design or unconsciously, Gail Haley frequently assumes the persona of her characters. She may be found reliving her childhood, her head buried in books, as Edwardina in *The Abominable Swampman* (1975); sharing ice cream in the park with Clarence in *The Post Office Cat* (1976); or sitting at the feet of her grandmother, Poppyseed, in *Jack and the Bean Tree* (1986). The adult Haley appears as a mermaid, Jack's love interest, and Michael's princess in her later books. Though her faces may be familiar, her style and technique are constantly changing to meet the demands of each new story.

Although a handful of artists consistently work and excel in one format, most illustrators vary their techniques and styles to match the tales they have to tell. How the art for picture books is actually created might well be called "the great media mystery." Reviews and articles frequently speak of the illustrator's insight, vision, or imagination, but "mentioned less often is the physical process by which the images imagined by that unique eye come to life, and the role of the artist's medium in that process." Despite a history spanning more than half a

**92   Illustrating as Art: Media, Method, and Message**

century, "there has apparently been no systematic attempt to list the media used" in the Caldecott medal and honor books (Behrmann 1980, 198).

A striking example of the technique of papercut used to full effect in a series of books by an illustrator with a background in shadow puppetry. (From *Sundiata: Lion King of Mali*, by David Wisniewski. Copyright © 1992 by David Wisniewski. Reprinted with permission of Clarion Books, an imprint of Houghton Mifflin.)

The decision as to which medium (oil, watercolor, acrylic, pen and ink, pencil, and so on) to work in and which surface to work on (wood, linoleum, canvas, pressed board, rice paper) usually involves consideration of factors such as the feeling the artist is trying to convey and the technology available to create accurate reproductions. The relationship between the content of the story and the style of the artwork has already been addressed. An African tale might well be created from wood block to reinforce and represent folk art traditions of that country. A medieval story, seeking to recreate the feel of a tapestry from the period, might work on rough canvas to allow the grain to suggest the surface of the tapestry. For *Jack and the Bean Tree* (Haley 1986), which she described as her "first organic book," Gail Haley "actually used bits of the mountain, leaves, lichen, bark." This decision was again based on the plot and theme of the story. "Everything springs from the woods. That's why I decided this time around I had to paint on wood blocks. The wood was treated and then I applied a gesso covering because by using that, I could carve, and incise and inscribe other textures. The gesso allowed me to create a meaning beneath the surface, so that even after I applied the acrylic, there was something else going on beneath the surface, in the same way the story can be read on [more than] one level" (Considine 1986, 41). Singling out one image from the book, it is easy to see how the wooden surface contributed to the feel and flavor of the book, which after all centers around a tree. On the first page, when the text of the story begins, "It happened when Jack's paw and brothers were gone off to war," we see the interior of the mountain cabin, with the mother sitting by the hearth. By working on a wooden surface, Haley was able to create the surroundings, from the log in the fire, to the bare floor, the mantelpiece, and the butter churn. "The technique enabled me to stress the sparseness and bareboard existence" (Considine 1986, 41).

Trying to capture a watery surface's shimmer for *Sea Tale* (Haley 1990), Haley needed an altogether different medium and surface. Linoleum cuts lend themselves to the suggestion of movement; combined with the artist's experiences sketching and snorkeling in Bali, the Great Barrier Reef, and Hawaii, this medium enabled the pictures to convey the mood and movement of the seascape. "Haley's linocut illustrations are boldly assertive, yet hauntingly evocative of the magical sea of this master storyteller's fairytale setting" (Hodges 1990, F3). These results were specifically made possible by the use of linoleum cuts printed on rice paper and then colored. The printing employed black-and-white oil-based printer's ink. The figures and details above the water surface were printed in black, while the objects underwater were executed in white. Later they were colored with brilliant dyes, sometimes applied by brush and sometimes sprayed on the dampened surface of the paper to create a bleed or shimmering effect.

The dual black-and-white world above and below the ocean surface in *Sea Tale* is actually an extension of an earlier use of linoleum cut in *Go Away, Stay Away* (Haley 1977). Because this story dealt with earth and spirit worlds, the colors were used to distinguish between the inhabitants of each realm. "I wanted to give the reader special clues about the various characters. I printed Peter, his father and the villagers in black ink. The Bunshee and other mischief makers were printed in white ink" (Haley 1978). Whatever the technique, the production process is extremely difficult to describe in words alone, and teachers or librarians lacking any real background in art education are encouraged to explore these techniques visually through programs such as Weston Wood's *Wood and Linoleum Illustration* (1978) or Silver, Burdett, and Ginn's *On The Horizon* (1989), a videotape wherein Haley demonstrates this relationship between form and content.

In addition to the medium used and the surface worked on, the palette of an individual painting or series of illustrations also contributes to the overall statement of the art. For *Go Away, Stay Away,* as noted, the colors were coded to convey something about the characters. Working on the Indian story, *Once a Mouse* (1961), Marcia Brown used "the yellow-green of sun through leaves, of earth, the dark green of shadows, and the red that says India to me" (Brown 1986, 71). For the African setting of *Shadow* (1982), she used "the deep violetblue shadows I had seen at dusk in Africa to suggest actual shadows. I cut wood blocks and printed them in white on translucent paper to suggest memories, spirit-images and ghosts" (Brown 1986, 181–82).

Sometimes a palette progresses and changes throughout a story to support the action and mood. *Hey, Al* (Yorinks and Egielski 1986) begins with a drab palette, for the confined interiors of the apartment, only to explode across the pages in the exotic, brilliant hues of the tropical sequences. *Knots on a Counting Rope* (Martin, Archambault, and Rand 1987) is an excellent example of the progression of the palette. The story begins at night, as the small figures of the boy and his grandfather sit by the campfire dwarfed by the landscape. Throughout the early illustrations, the palette is dark, with just a glimmer of golden light from a lamp or the fire. In keeping with the text of the story, the palette brightens as the boy triumphs over his blindness. As the text says, "Yes, boy, you are learning to see through your darkness," the figure of the child fills a page for the first time, and the palette quickly changes to the brilliant blues, reds, and golds of the colorful costumes and the western sky and desert landscape.

Before moving to a quick consideration of various techniques and the awards given to picture books, it is necessary to remind ourselves again of the dual nature of the children's picture book as both an art form and a commercially manufactured product intended to meet the need of the children's book industry. At its best, this results in a cooperative and creative collaboration. At its worst, the book becomes a commercial compromise plagued by all the problems of creativity by committee, in which the author's and illustrator's visions may be watered down, altered, sometimes improved, and frequently misunderstood by editors, art directors, book designers, and all those along the way who have input into the finished form and content of the book. Nor is the problem unique to children's books. In *Sunday in the Park with George,* a musical based on the life of painter Georges Seurat, the song "Putting It Together" chronicles the constant struggle between economic viability and artistic vision. It is not difficult to find authors and illustrators to articulate this struggle in creating children's books. Gail Haley wrote, "In today's world, children's literature is marketed, packaged and sold like any other product in any other industry. Sometimes a beautiful idea or new approach never sees the light of day because the industry wants a safe, marketable product" (1992, 89). John Schoenherr, who won the Caldecott medal for his illustrations for *Owl Moon* (Yolen and Schoenherr 1987), said, "I wanted to make pictures in which everything—the subject, composition, edges, even painty texture, brushstrokes and size—was significant. I had a need to concentrate on the inner life of my subjects and their relationship to the world. Most publishers only understood economics and wanted something that sold easily" (1992, 177). Martin Provensen also articulated the clash that sometimes occurs between the artist and the industry. "Some editors, I am sorry to say, will look at a page like that and say, 'Well, who are all these people?' They don't always follow the sequence because they are trained to see the unity of the single illustration" (Willard 1983/84, 175). And, Provensen continues, sometimes an illustrator will encounter an editor or art director who simply cannot be made to understand what the artist is attempting to convey. In such a circumstance, the integrity of the art and the vision are inevitably compromised.

## *Collage*

The use of collage in the creation of children's books has recently been given a greater visibility. *Where the Forest Meets the Sea* (Baker 1988) and *Tar Beach* (Ringgold 1991) both use this multimedia style. The Australian story is depicted with a variety of materials, including sand, wood, and cloth. *Tar Beach*, which was a Caldecott honor book, represented a fusion of acrylic on canvas paper with a story quilt. Detailed notes explain the development of the art for this book. Collage is especially useful for conveying depth and texture, and this is an art form that children enjoy working with for their own creations. Another recent use of college appears in *7 Blind Mice* (Young 1992).

## Linoleum Cut

Unlike wood, which has its own natural grain, linoleum is man-made, with the artist cutting and creating his or her own grain, pattern, and design with sharp tools, usually when the linoleum has been slightly softened by a warming process. Linoleum cuts have a lengthy history; the technique was used by Picasso, Gauguin, and van Gogh, among others. Several of Gail Haley's books feature this technique, including *Go Away, Stay Away* (1977), *Jack and the Fire Dragon* (1988), and *Sea Tale* (1990). Once a set of black-and-white prints has been made from the cut, the artist colors the illustrations, sometimes using watercolors and other times employing colored inks.

## Painting

Generally, painting is the largest category accounting for the majority of children's book illustrations. Under this broad umbrella, however, a variety of techniques are possible. These include watercolor, which is transparent, used in *Hey, Al* (Yorinks and Egielski 1986); gouache, which works with opaque rather than transparent colors, as in *Fables* (Lobel 1980); oil, applied with a brush or palette knife and thinned with turpentine, used in *Rumpelstiltskin* (Zelinsky 1986); and acrylic, which is like oil except that it is water-soluble and dries faster than oil paint, used in *Ox-Cart Man* (Hall and Cooney 1979).

## Papercut

The use of papercut may be found in books with a collage technique, such as *Shadow* (Brown 1982) and *Fish Eyes* (Ehlert 1990), or in books based entirely on papercut. David Wisniewski specializes in this technique; his books, like *The Warrior and the Wise Man* (1989) and *Elfwyn's Saga* (1990), are excellent examples and provide clear descriptions of the technique. This is an important art form with roots deep in the folk art of many countries, including India, Japan, and Indonesia. Like collage, this is a medium that children enjoy working with (though, of course, care and supervision should always be provided when children work with sharp instruments like those required by this method).

## Pencil

In a world saturated by color, we often lose sight of the power of black-and-white pencil drawings. Whether working with graphite or conte pencil, striking effects have been created in a number of books that have achieved Caldecott success. These include *Moja Means One* (Feelings and Feelings 1971), *The Garden of Abdul Gasazi* (Van Allsburg 1979), and *The Story of Jumping Mouse* (Steptoe 1984). Of course, colored pencils are also available; this technique was used in *The Relatives Came* (Rylant and Gammell 1985).

## Woodcut

In woodcut, the images are cut on the side of a plank, utilizing the natural graduation and texture of the wood's grain. Images tend to be bold and frequently abstract, with broad lines because of the difficulty in carving the wood. The tools include chisels, gouges, and knives. The image is printed on paper. Illustrations consisting of more than one color require a separate block for each color. This technique can be found in the Caldecott medal winners *Once a Mouse* (Brown 1961) and *A Story, A Story* (Haley 1970).

## Wood Engraving

Unlike woodcut, wood engraving does lend itself to fine line and detail. The images are cut on the cross-grain, using blocks that are typically type-high (3/4 to 7/8 inches). The wood is hard and fine—often boxwood, fruit wood, or other dense and slow-growing wood. *Mountain Jack Tales* (Haley 1992b) was executed on lemon wood using gravers and multiple gravers to cut the fine lines. Whereas the image in woodcut actually consists of what is left uncut, the picture in wood engraving is created by the lines the artist graves (cuts) into the surface of the wood. This technique is becoming increasingly rare in the field of children's books because of several factors, including difficulty in locating wood, the cost of the raw material, and the time involved in the engraving process.

## Scratchboard

In the scratchboard technique, a surface like bristol board or illustration board is covered with a thin layer of plaster or gesso. India ink is applied to this surface in solid panels, lines, or shapes. Designs, forms, and shapes are then scraped, incised, or cut through the ink to expose the white undercoat. Gravers may be scooped, straight, or multiple. The images that are exposed after the scraping are then colored. This technique is used and explained in books by Brian Pinkney, including *Sukey and the Mermaid* (San Souci and Pinkney 1992). This technique can easily be demonstrated to children and incorporated into their own illustrations.

Wood engraving technique highlights fine lines and detail achieved by use of tiny gravers, in contrast to the bolder patterns achieved with a woodcut. (From *Mountain Jack Tales*, written and illustrated by Gail E. Haley.)

Styles, Media, and Techniques 97

This is an original woodcut. The black lines represent shapes and patterns left on the block, while the white represents areas that have been cut away. From *A Story, A Story*, retold and illustrated by Gail E. Haley.)

The technique of scratchboard, one of many styles with which children can be encouraged to experiment. (From *Sukey and the Mermaid*, by Robert San Souci and Brian Pinkney. Illustration copyright © 1992 Brian Pinkney. Reprinted with permission of Four Winds Press, and imprint of Macmillan.)

## "And the Winner Is...": Awards for Illustrating

No discussion of the art of the children's picture book would be complete without reference to the various awards given for illustration. Of all these awards, the most prestigious and the best-known in this country is the Caldecott medal. In considering books for this award, committee members (who change each year) discuss such things as "whether it is for children, what is the quality of the art as well as the entire book, how the book as a whole functions as a picture book, whether the book is accurate, how well the pictures communicate to children, what is the style of the art" (Peltola 1988, 154–55), and many other factors. In defining a *picture book*, the Caldecott rules indicate that a distinguished book "essentially provides the child with a visual experience" and "has a collective unity of story-line, theme or concept, developed through the series of pictures of which the book is comprised" (Peltola 1988, 157). Although many people think of the Caldecott medal as an award given to books for young children, in reality, by the conditions of the award, the subject books may be for persons up to the age of 14. Caldecott medal books are expected to display "respect for children's understanding, abilities and appreciations" (p. 157). Like the Academy Awards and so many other prizes, which attempt to single out one or two outstanding works from all that have been created in a single year, there is seldom unanimous agreement with the decisions of the Caldecott committee, and sometimes there is quite open disagreement about the final choices. Robert McCloskey said that "committees have sometimes ended up awarding medals for an author's or an illustrator's work in general rather than for a particular work" (Heins 1988, 188–89). Certainly, many teachers and librarians, lacking any real background in art, would have trouble reconciling such strikingly different choices as *Black and White* (Macaulay 1990) and *Saint George and the Dragon* (Hodges and Hyman 1984). One of the real dangers of lists of so-called best books is that they will be purchased and used without any real understanding of the design, composition, or media used in creating them. Another danger, of course, is that these books will be purchased and explored to the exclusion of other fine titles, which may not have won awards but still have much to offer young readers. These lists of quality picture books can certainly be expanded by widening teachers' knowledge of other awards in the field. The Caldecott choices, for example, can be compared to other American awards, which include the Boston Globe-Horn Book Award; the *New York Times* Best Illustrated Children's Book of the Year; the Parent's Choice Award Book for Illustration; and the Golden Kite Award, which, unlike most other prizes, is given by the practitioners, in this case the Society of Children's Book Writers. One interesting award given in the United States since 1974 is the Coretta Scott King Award, specifically designated for African-American illustrators whose work is inspirational and educational. Recipients include Jerry Pinkney, Ashley Bryan, Pat Cummings, and Tom Feelings.

The multicultural movement in education should also create some motivation for exploring what books win awards in other countries. In England, for example, the equivalent of the Caldecott medal is the Kate Greenaway Medal. To win this award, the book must have first been published in England. As a result, most books by American authors and illustrators are not eligible. One notable exception was *The Post Office Cat* (Haley 1976), an original story written and illustrated by Gail Haley while she was living in London. Haley remains the only person to have won both the British and the American award for the best picture book. If Caldecott choices can be controversial, so too can Greenaway selections; *Snow White in New York* (French 1987) certainly raised some eyebrows with its modern setting for a traditional fairy tale. The Canadian award for the most distinguished picture book is the Amelia-Frances Howard-Gibbon Medal, which can only be won by Canadian citizens. Australia has a Picture Book of the Year award. Over the years, many of these successful titles and their creators have achieved international recognition. These include Junko Morimoto, Graeme Base, Dick Roughsey, and Percy Trezise, and titles such as *John Brown Rose and the Midnight Cat* (Wagner and Brooks 1977) and *The Rainbow Serpent* (Roughsey 1976). Perhaps the highest distinction that can be won by an illustrator is the Hans Christian Andersen Award, an international prize given by the International Board on Books for Young People for lifetime contributions to children's literature. Given every two years, the award is truly international. Only one American illustrator, Maurice Sendak, has received the award; others include Robert Inkpen, an Australian illustrator.

Finally, most states have a Children's Choice Award. Introducing children and their parents to these awards is one way of involving the whole family in a love for children's literature and a recognition of the diversity of the field.

## *Caldecott Medal Winners Since 1960: Artistic Medium*

1960 Marie Hall Ets for *Nine Days to Christmas*. Aurora Labistida, author. Viking. PENCIL ON DINOBASE.

1961 Nicholas Sidjakov for *Baboushka and the Three Kings*. Ruth Robbins, author. Parnassus. TEMPERA AND FELT TIP.

1962 Marcia Brown for *Once a Mouse*. Charles Scribner's Sons. WOODCUT AND WATERCOLOR.

1963 Ezra Jack Keats for *A Snowy Day*. Viking. COLLAGE, INCLUDING PAPER AND PAINTS.

1964 Maurice Sendak for *Where the Wild Things Are*. Harper & Row. INDIA INK LINE OVER FULL COLOR TEMPERA.

1965 Beni Montresor for *May I Bring a Friend?* Beatrice Schenk de Regniers, author. Atheneum. PEN-AND-INK DRAWINGS.

1966 Nonny Hogrogian for *Always Room for One More*. Sorche Nic Leodhas, author. Henry Holt. THREE-COLOR, PRESEPARATED ART, INCLUDING PENS, PASTELS, AND WASH.

1967 Evaline Ness for *Sam, Bangs & Moonshine*. Henry Holt. THREE-COLOR, PRE-SEPARATED ART WITH PEN AND WASH.

1968 Ed Emberly for *Drummer Hoff*. Barbara Emberly, author. Prentice-Hall. WOODCUTS AND INK.

1969 Uri Shulevitz for *The Fool of the World and the Flying Ship*. Arthur Ransome, author. Farrar, Straus & Giroux. PEN AND BRUSH WITH BLACK AND COLORED INKS.

1970 William Steig for *Sylvester and the Magic Pebble*. Windmill. WATERCOLOR.

1971 Gail E. Haley for *A Story, A Story*. Atheneum. WOODCUT.

1972 Nonny Hogrogian for *One Fine Day*. Macmillan. ACRYLIC ON GESSO.

1973 Blair Lent for *The Funny Little Woman*. Arlene Mosel, author. Dutton. PEN AND INK WITH ACRYLIC.

1974 Margot Zemach for *Duffy and the Devil*. Harve Zemack, author. Farrar, Straus & Giroux. PEN AND INK WITH WATERCOLOR.

1975 Gerald McDermott for *Arrow to the Sun*. Viking. GOUACHE AND INK.

1976 Leo Dillon and Diane Dillon for *Why Mosquitoes Buzz in People's Ears*. Verna Aardema, author. Dial. INDIA INK, WATERCOLORS, AND PASTEL.

1977 Leo Dillon and Diane Dillon for *Ashanti to Zulu: African Traditions*. Margaret Musgrove, author. Dial. PASTELS, WATERCOLORS, AND ACRYLICS.

1978 Peter Spier for *Noah's Ark*. Doubleday. PENCIL AND WATERCOLOR.

1979 Paul Goble for *The Girl Who Loved Wild Horses*. Bradbury. FULL-COLOR PEN AND INK WITH WATERCOLORS.

1980 Barbara Cooney for *Ox-Cart Man*. Donald Hall, author. Viking. ACRYLICS ON GESSO.

1981 Arnold Lobel for *Fables*. Harper & Row. GOUACHE AND PENCIL.

1982 Chris Van Allsburg for *Jumanji*. Houghton Mifflin. CONTE PENCIL AND CONTE DUST.

1983 Marcia Brown for *Shadow*. Blaise Cendrars, author. Charles Scribner's Sons. COLLAGE: PAPER, WOODCUTS, AND ACRYLICS.

1984 Alice Provensen and Martin Provensen for *The Glorious Flight: Across the Channel with Louis Bleriot*. Viking. PEN AND INK WITH ACRYLIC.

1985 Trina Schart Hyman for *Saint George and the Dragon*. Margaret Hodges, author. Little, Brown. INDIA INK AND ACRYLIC.

1986 Chris Van Allsburg for *The Polar Express*. Houghton Mifflin. FULL-COLOR OIL PASTEL ON PASTEL PAPER.

1987 Richard Egielski for *Hey, Al*. Arthur Yorinks, author. Farrar, Straus & Giroux. WATERCOLOR.

1988 John Schoenherr for *Owl Moon*. Jane Yolen, author. Philomel. WATERCOLOR.

1989 Stephen Gammell for *Song and Dance Man*. Karen Ackerman, author. Alfred A. Knopf. COLORED PENCILS.

1990 Ed Young for *Lon Po Po*. Philomel. WATERCOLORS AND PASTELS.

1991 David Macaulay for *Black and White*. Houghton Mifflin. WATERCOLOR, PENCIL, PEN AND INK.

1992 David Wiesner for *Tuesday*. Houghton Mifflin. WATERCOLOR.

1993 Emily Arnold McCully for *Mirette on the High Wire*. Putnam. WATERCOLOR.

1994 Allen Say for *Grandfather's Journey*. Houghton Mifflin. WATERCOLOR.

# Strategies and Activities

- Identify biographies, autobiographies, and audiovisual programs exploring the life and work of well-known illustrators of children's books. Make sure these are housed in your library collections and that children and teachers have an opportunity to work with them.

- Major collections of art for children's books are housed at the De Grummond Collection (University of Southern Mississippi), the Kerlan Collection (University of Minnesota), and elsewhere. If these are in your area, arrange a field trip. If they are not in your area, contact the curators to see what traveling exhibits they offer and how this art might come to your school or library.

- In this chapter, we have seen how books like *Mirette on the High Wire* and *The Green Man* attempt to re-create a look or feel by using the form or style of fine artists and old masters. Select several of these books and examples of painting from various movements and artists. Help children explore the relationship between these past painters and today's picture books.

- Although the form or technique of an artist's style can be emulated, the content of paintings also provides historical evidence about the furniture, housing, architecture, fashion, and transportation of the age depicted. This is particularly evident in the recreation of eighteenth-century England in *Dream Peddler*. Using paintings or illustrations by Hogarth, Gainsborough, and others, help children understand how Haley used pictures from the past to recreate the period for her story.

- Folktales from other countries and cultures afford students the opportunity to explore folk art and the visual arts from these cultures. Select a series of tales like *Shadow*; *The Warrior and the Wise Man*; *The Girl Who Loved Wild Horses*; and *A Story, A Story*, and then explore African, Native American, and Japanese art forms with students.

- This chapter contains a list of Caldecott medal winners since 1960 and the media used for their art. Have students work individually or in cooperative learning groups, using this list, to explore the following issues: What technique is most commonly used? What relationship exists between the technique and genre or story/type? Have particular decades or periods been dominated by a particular look, style, or story-type? Look at the criteria for winning the Caldecott medal, as outlined in this chapter. Select several winners and see how students think the books succeed or fail in meeting the criteria. Can adults really select best picture books for children?

- Many states have a Children's Choice Award. In Missouri, this is called the Mark Twain Award. In Texas, it is the Bluebonnet Award. In Tennessee, it is the Volunteer State Book Award. The Ohio prize is called the Buckeye Children's Book Award, and Oklahoma designates its prize the Sequoyah Children's Book Award. Find out if your own state has an award (North Carolina, for example, does not). Familiarize students with the terms and criteria of their state award. Share this information with parents. Have your own class, school, or county schools vote for their favorite book, using criteria the children themselves have established. How do these results compare to Caldecott results? What accounts for the difference?

- We have had a chance to look at a variety of techniques used in the creation of children's books. Use picture books to introduce students to these styles. Then, whenever possible, provide students with hands-on experience in the creation of their own illustrations, using techniques such as collage, papercut, and linoleum cut.

# References

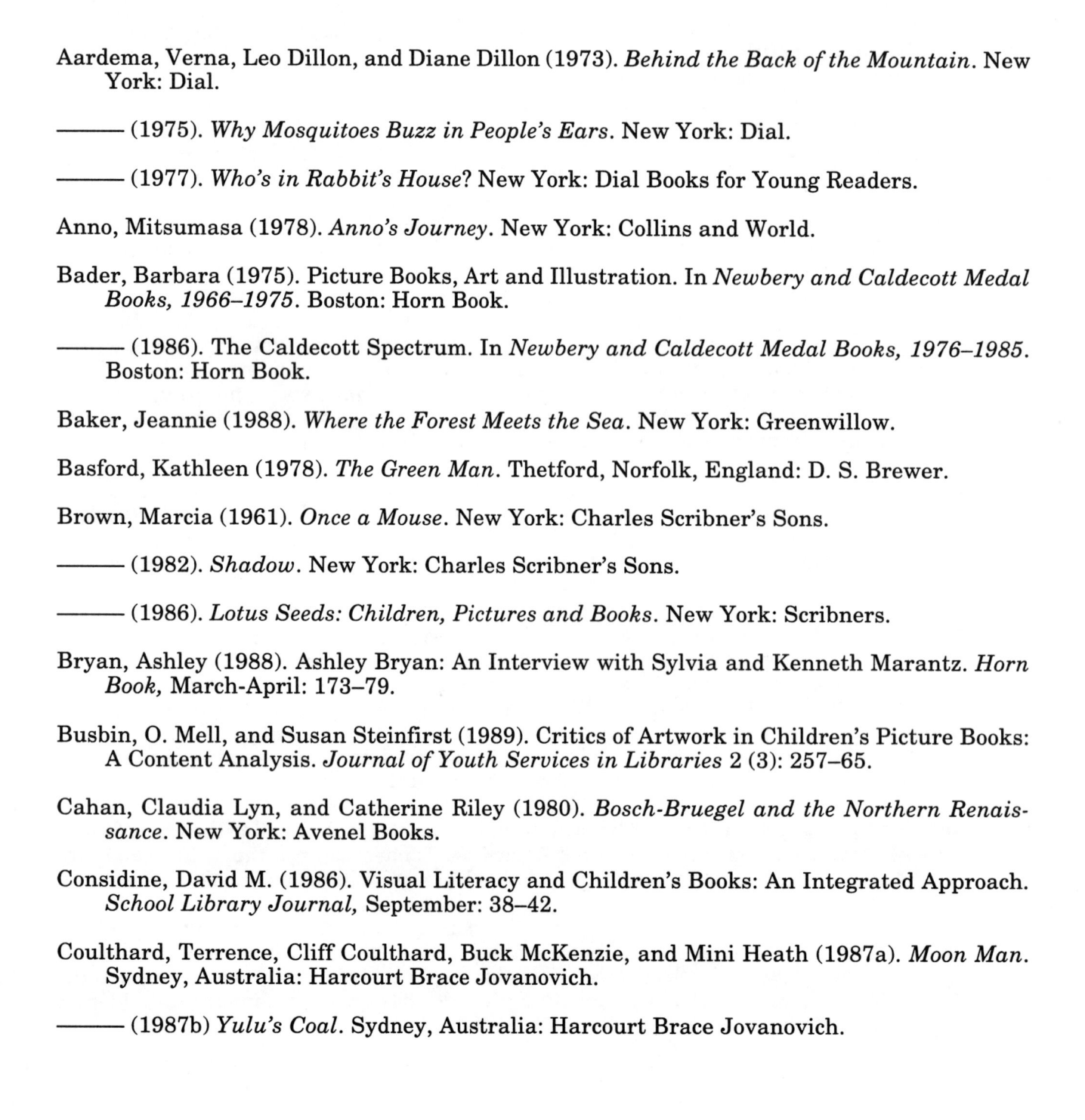

Aardema, Verna, Leo Dillon, and Diane Dillon (1973). *Behind the Back of the Mountain.* New York: Dial.

——— (1975). *Why Mosquitoes Buzz in People's Ears.* New York: Dial.

——— (1977). *Who's in Rabbit's House?* New York: Dial Books for Young Readers.

Anno, Mitsumasa (1978). *Anno's Journey.* New York: Collins and World.

Bader, Barbara (1975). Picture Books, Art and Illustration. In *Newbery and Caldecott Medal Books, 1966–1975.* Boston: Horn Book.

——— (1986). The Caldecott Spectrum. In *Newbery and Caldecott Medal Books, 1976–1985.* Boston: Horn Book.

Baker, Jeannie (1988). *Where the Forest Meets the Sea.* New York: Greenwillow.

Basford, Kathleen (1978). *The Green Man.* Thetford, Norfolk, England: D. S. Brewer.

Brown, Marcia (1961). *Once a Mouse.* New York: Charles Scribner's Sons.

——— (1982). *Shadow.* New York: Charles Scribner's Sons.

——— (1986). *Lotus Seeds: Children, Pictures and Books.* New York: Scribners.

Bryan, Ashley (1988). Ashley Bryan: An Interview with Sylvia and Kenneth Marantz. *Horn Book,* March-April: 173–79.

Busbin, O. Mell, and Susan Steinfirst (1989). Critics of Artwork in Children's Picture Books: A Content Analysis. *Journal of Youth Services in Libraries* 2 (3): 257–65.

Cahan, Claudia Lyn, and Catherine Riley (1980). *Bosch-Bruegel and the Northern Renaissance.* New York: Avenel Books.

Considine, David M. (1986). Visual Literacy and Children's Books: An Integrated Approach. *School Library Journal,* September: 38–42.

Coulthard, Terrence, Cliff Coulthard, Buck McKenzie, and Mini Heath (1987a). *Moon Man.* Sydney, Australia: Harcourt Brace Jovanovich.

——— (1987b) *Yulu's Coal.* Sydney, Australia: Harcourt Brace Jovanovich.

Ehlert, Lois (1990). *Fish Eyes! A Book You Can Count On*. San Diego, CA: Harcourt Brace Jovanovich.

Einberg, Elizabeth (1987). *Manners and Morals: Hogarth and British Painting, 1700–1760*. London: The Tate Gallery.

Everett, Gwen (1991). *Li'l Sis and Uncle Willie*. New York: Rizzoli.

Feelings, Muriel, and Tom Feelings (1971). *Moja Means One: A Swahili Counting Book*. New York: Dial.

French, Fiona (1987). *Snow White in New York*. New York: Oxford University Press.

Goble, Paul (1978). *The Girl Who Loved Wild Horses*. New York: Macmillan.

Grahame, Kenneth (1900). *The Golden Age*. London: John Lane.

Haley, Gail E. (1970). *A Story, A Story*. New York: Atheneum.

——— (1973). *Jack Jouett's Ride*. New York: Viking.

——— (1975). *The Abominable Swampman*. New York: Viking.

——— (1976). *The Post Office Cat*. New York: Scribners.

——— (1977). *Go Away, Stay Away*. New York: Scribners.

——— (1978). *Wood and Linoleum Illustration*. Weston, CT: Weston Woods Studios. Audiocassette and filmstrip.

——— (1979). *The Green Man*. New York: Scribners.

——— (1980). *Tracing a Legend: The Story of the Green Man*. Weston, CT: Weston Woods Studios. Audiocassette and filmstrip.

——— (1986). *Jack and the Bean Tree*. New York: Crown.

——— (1988). *Jack and the Fire Dragon*. New York: Crown.

——— (1990). *Sea Tale*. New York: Dutton.

——— (1992a). Gail E. Haley. In *Something About the Author, Autobiography Series*. Detroit, MI: Gale Research.

——— (1992b). *Mountain Jack Tales*. New York: Dutton.

——— (1993). *Dream Peddler*. New York: Dutton.

Hall, Donald, and Barbara Cooney (1979). *Ox-Cart Man*. New York: Viking.

Heins, Ethel (1988). From Mallards to Maine: A Conversation with Robert McCloskey. *Journey of Youth Services in Libraries* 1 (2): 187–93.

Hodges, Betty (1990). Dismiss These Books as "Kiddy Lit" at Peril of Passing Up Worthwhile Tales. *Durham Morning Herald*, August 26, F3.

Hodges, Margaret, and Trina Schart Hyman (1984). *Saint George and the Dragon*. Boston: Little, Brown.

Husband, Timothy (1980). *The Wild Man: Medieval Myth and Symbolism*. New York: Metropolitan Museum of Art.

Hyman, Trina Schart (1981). *Self-Portrait*. Reading, MA: Addison-Wesley.

Ingmells, Rex, Percy Tresize, and Mary Haginikitas (1987). *Platypus and Kookaburra*. North Ryde, New South Wales, Australia: Angus and Robertson.

Lacy, Lyn Ellen (1986). *Art and Design in Children's Picture Books*. Chicago: American Library Association.

Lesser, Rika, and Paul O. Zelinsky (1984). *Hansel and Gretel*. New York: Dodd, Mead.

Lobel, Arnold (1980). *Fables*. New York: Harper & Row.

Locker, Thomas (1987). *The Boy Who Held Back the Sea*. New York: Dial.

Macaulay, David (1990). *Black and White*. Boston: Houghton Mifflin.

Malotki, Ekkehart, and Michael Lacapa (1988). *The Mouse Couple*. Flagstaff, AZ: Northland Press.

Martin, Jr., Bill, John Archambault, and Ted Rand (1987). *Knots on a Counting Rope*. New York: Henry Holt.

McCully, Emily Arnold (1992). *Mirette on the High Wire*. New York: Dutton.

McDermott, Gerald (1974). *Arrow to the Sun*. New York: Viking.

Mikolaycak, Charles (1992). *Orpheus*. San Diego, CA: Harcourt Brace Jovanovich.

Nikola-Lisa, W., and O. Fred Donaldson (1990). Books with a Clear Heart: The Koans of Play and the Pictures of Ezra Jack Keats. *The Lion and the Unicorn* 13 (2): 75–89.

Nodelman, Perry (1988). *Words About Pictures: The Narrative Art of Children's Picture Books*. Athens, GA: University of Georgia Press.

Noonuccal, Ooderoo, and Kabul Noonuccal (1988). *The Rainbow Serpent*. Canberra: Australian Government Publishing Services.

*On the Horizons*. (1989). World of Reading videotape, Units 1 and 2. Columbus, OH: Silver, Burdett and Ginn.

Parker, K. Langloh, and H. Drake-Brockman (1966). *Australian Legendary Tales*. New York: Viking.

Peltola, Bette J. (1988). Choosing the Caldecott Medal Winner. *Journal of Youth Services in Libraries* 1 (2): 153–59.

*The Picture Book Animated* (1978). Weston, CT: Weston Woods Studios.

Ringgold, Faith (1991). *Tar Beach.* New York: Scholastic.

Roughsey, Dick (1976). *The Rainbow Serpent.* Sydney, Australia: Collins.

Rylant, Cynthia, and Stephen Gammell (1985). *The Relatives Came.* New York: Bradbury.

San Souci, Robert, and Brian Pinkney (1992). *Sukey and the Mermaid.* New York: Four Winds.

Schoenherr, John (1992). John Schoenherr. In *Something About the Author: Autobiography Series,* 13. Detroit, MI: Gale Research.

*School Library Journal* (1993). Review of *Mirette on the High Wire.* S8.

*School Library Journal* (1992). Review of *Orpheus.* September: 286.

Schwartz, Amy (1987). Mrs. Moskowitz and Yossell Zissel: The Making of Two Picture Books. *The Lion and the Unicorn* 11 (1): 88–97.

Sendak, Maurice (1970). *In the Night Kitchen.* New York: Harper & Row.

——— (1988). *Caldecott and Co.: Notes on Books and Pictures.* New York: Farrar, Straus & Giroux.

Shannon, George (1989). *Arnold Lobel.* Boston, MA: Twayne.

Steig, Michael (1985). "Reading *Outside Over There.*" *Children's Literature* 13: 139–53. New Haven, CT: Yale University Press.

Steptoe, John (1984). *The Story of Jumping Mouse.* New York: Mulberry.

——— (1987). *Mufaro's Beautiful Daughters: An African Tale.* New York: Lothrop, Lee & Shepard.

Stewig, John Warren (1980). What Do Reviews Really Review? *Top of the News* 37 (1): 83–84.

——— (1992). Reading Pictures, Reading Texts: Some Similarities. *The New Advocate* 55 (1): 11–22.

Trezise, Percy, and Dick Roughsey (1980). *Banana Bird and the Snake Man.* Sydney, Australia: Collins.

Van Allsburg, Chris (1979). *The Garden of Abdul Gasazi.* Boston: Houghton Mifflin.

Wagner, Jenny, and Ron Brooks (1977). *John Brown Ross and the Midnight Cat.* Sydney, Australia: Kestrel.

Willard, Nancy (1983/84). The Birds and the Beasts Were There: An Interview with Martin Provensen. *The Lion and the Unicorn* 7/8: 171–83.

Willard, Nancy, Leo Dillon, and Diane Dillon (1991). *Pish, Posh, Said Hieronymous Bosch.* San Diego, CA: Harcourt Brace Jovanovich.

Wisniewski, David (1989). *The Warrior and the Wise Man*. New York: Lothrop, Lee & Shepard.

——— (1990). *Elfwyn's Saga*. New York: Lothrop, Lee & Shepard.

——— (1992). *Sundiata: Lion King of Mali*. New York: Clarion.

Wood, Don, and Audrey Wood (1987). *Heckedy Peg*. San Diego, CA: Harcourt Brace Jovanovich.

Yolen, Jane, and John Schoenherr (1987). *Owl Moon*. New York: Philomel.

Yorinks, Arthur, and Richard Egielski (1986). *Hey, Al*. New York: Farrar, Straus & Giroux.

Young, Ed (1989). *Lon Po Po*. New York: Philomel.

——— (1992). *7 Blind Mice*. New York: Philomel.

Zelinsky, Paul (1986). *Rumpelstiltskin*. New York: Dutton.

## *Children's Literature Archives*

deGrummond Children's Literature Research Collection
McCain Library Archives
University of Southern Mississippi
Box 5148
Hattiesburg, MS 39406-5148
601-266-4349

The Kerlan Collection
Children's Literature Research Collection
109 Walter Library
University of Minnesota
117 Pleasant Street S.E.
Minneapolis, MN 55455
612-6244576

Chapter 6

# Playing with Pictures: Nontraditional Picture Books

> Meggendorfer never condescended to children. He granted them, as he granted himself, a lively intellect and cultivated visual taste. He knew that children observe life more cannily than adults, that they enjoy with a kind of sensual gusto the delights of color, shape and movement.
>
> —Maurice Sendak (1988)

## Introduction

So far, our discussion of illustrated children's books has concentrated on the codes and conventions of what might be termed traditional picture books. These books conform to unstated but apparent rules. Primary among them are that picture books 1) are static and two-dimensional; 2) have the same size pages bound inside covers; 3) are sequenced from left to right; and 4) are square or rectangular in shape. Although the vast majority of picture books on the market can be described in these terms, a growing number of books do not play by all these rules all the time. In recent years, many well-respected authors and illustrators have refused to observe these conventions and have increasingly experimented with both the form and the content of the picture book. These books, often mistakenly dismissed as toys or novelty items, afford children the opportunity to experience picture books in a completely new way, challenging their very assumptions about what constitutes a book.

One such book actually went on to win England's Kate Greenaway medal. *Haunted House* (Pienkowski 1979) consists of only six double-page spreads, but it is a multimechanical marvel, with a fully dimensional staircase that collapses flat, a monster with a spiral antenna that measures over a foot in length, a turning wheel that performs three actions at once, and a saw cutting across a board, which is not only seen but also heard. In the United States, these mechanical or moveable books have also won recognition. Eric Carle's *The Honeybee and the Robber* (1981) was a recipient of the A.I.G.A. certificate of excellence. *Sailing Ships* (van der Meer and McGowan 1985) was voted *Redbook*'s best children's picture book of 1985. Jonathan Miller and David Pelham won the Primero Graphico award for their startling *Human Body* (1983), a book of three-dimensional models the reader operates to make a heart beat, a muscle contract, and lungs breathe. The success of these books, both commercially and artistically, makes it clear that they deserve serious consideration in any discussion of the children's picture book.

## 108 Playing with Pictures: Nontraditional Picture Books

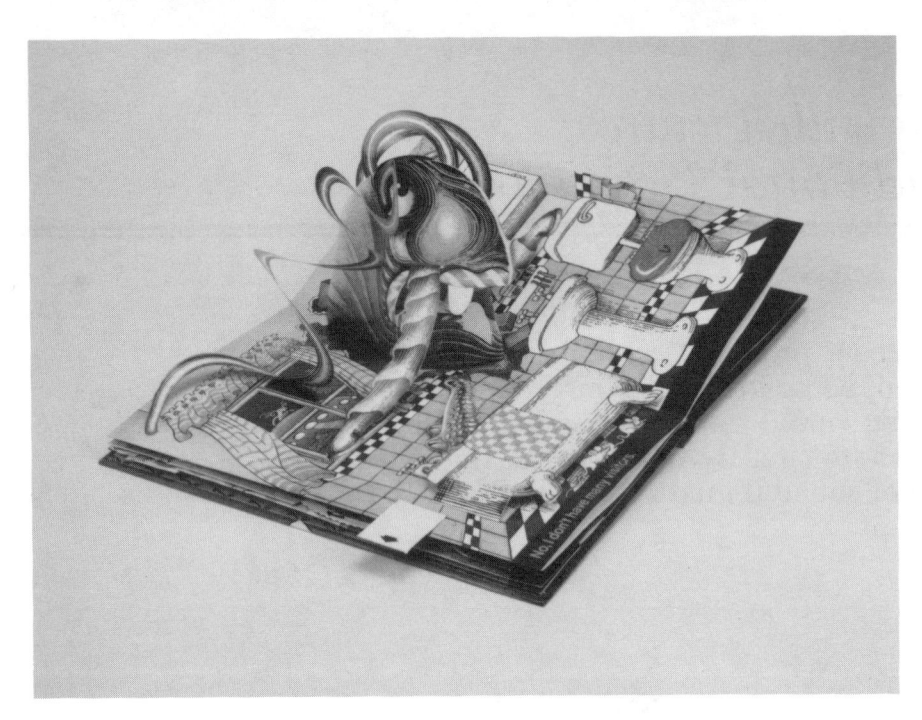

*Haunted House* by Jan Pienkowski received the Kate Greenaway medal in 1979. (From *Haunted House*, by Jan Pienkowski. Reprinted with permission of Intervisual Books, Inc.)

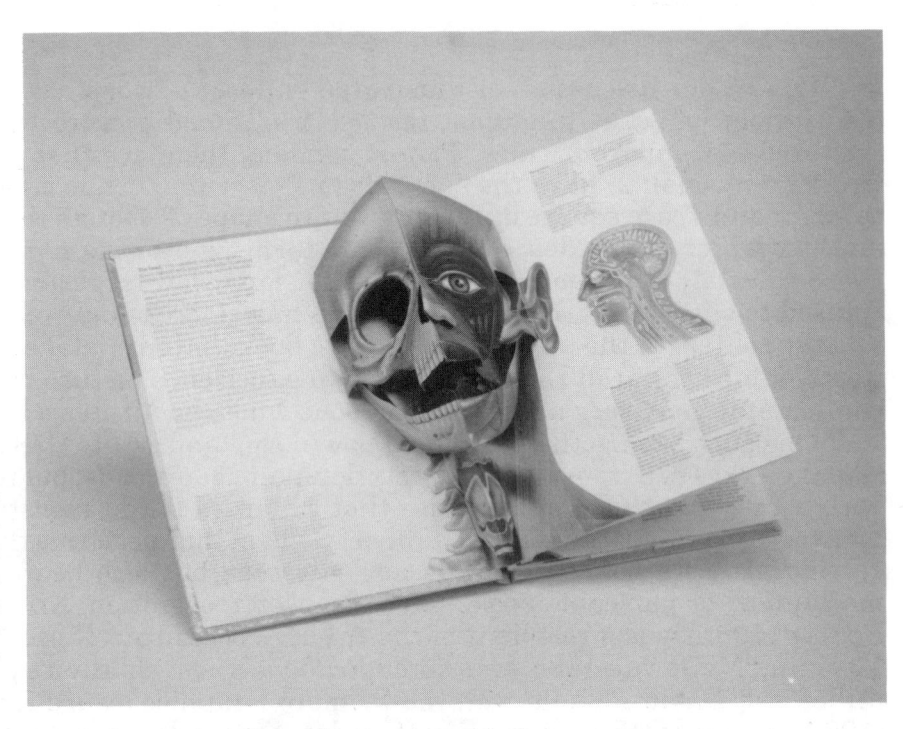

Extraordinary achievements are now evident in the paper engineering to be found in many of today's pop-up and moving books. (From *The Human Body*, by Jonathan Miller and David Pelham. Reprinted with permission of Intervisual Books, Inc.).

The range of these moveable books goes well beyond the old idea of the "pop-up." Today, in addition to the pop-up, books exist that fold up, turn sideways or upside down, have nonlinear narratives, and chirp like a cricket, though not all at the same time or in the same book. Once dismissed as fragile toys with limited play or novelty value, today's rule-breakers have increasingly achieved a status of quality. One reason for this is evident in the number of highly respected illustrators who have embraced these experimental forms. Among them are Tomie dePaola, Barbara Cooney, David Macaulay, and Alice and Martin Provensen, to mention just a few. In addition to the contributions made by noted illustrators, new technologies, assisted by computer design and the visions of creative paper engineers, are offering greater diversity and experimentation in the field of the moveable book.

Peter Seymour, creator of many contemporary pop-ups, wrote in the *Children's Book Council Calendar* that mechanicals have experienced a remarkable revival, and have become one of the most rapidly growing categories in the children's book industry. "If good children's books entertain as well as educate, and if they inspire a child's imagination, this new wave of pop-ups must be given high marks and bright prospects for the future" (Seymour 1981, 63–64). In a single chapter, it is not possible to do justice to all the variations found under the broad heading of what one might term books with special features. For our purposes, we will explore books that break the unwritten rules about picture books identified earlier. In particular, we will concentrate on the following six key variations:

1. Pop-up books

2. Lift-the-flap books

3. Partial pages

4. Panoramas

5. Nonlinear books

6. Wordless picture books.

Despite traditions that often date back several centuries, many of these formats have much to offer children of the late twentieth century, who are being raised amid the razzle-dazzle allure of a high-tech age. Many of these books have the power to entice and educate children accustomed to the special-effects wizardry of George Lucas and the compelling computer-generated imagery of video games. For many of these young people, close encounters with these books can be eye-opening experiences that force them to think about pictures, print, and books in entirely new ways.

By their very nature, books with special features meet many youngsters' needs to manipulate things, to be surprised, to have multisensory experiences, and to analyze dimensionality and movement firsthand and close up. In addition, their own experimentation with nontraditional book production offers children exciting interdisciplinary exercises in creative planning and problem-solving in science, mathematics, language arts, and visual discrimination.

Our desire that television-oriented children incorporate the enjoyment of traditional books more often into their daily lives does not mean they should not also be given opportunities to enjoy the special features these other books offer. Indeed, a constant diet of only one or the other, whether traditional or nontraditional, might be considered inappropriate fare because then there can be no appreciation for the rules that have been played with in the first place. What better way to lead children toward a definition for a picture book than to give them examples of what some adults still consider to be creative exceptions to that definition? For many children, a most effective way to seduce them away from television is to put a book with special features into their hands.

Older children in middle school and high school can also enjoy nontraditional books when they are presented as examples of performing paper or nonlinear thinking. Young people are often intrigued by the technical aspects, amused by the playfulness, or surprised by the unusual ways of telling a story or imparting factual information. As they are tempted to dissect the books—either literally or figuratively—to see what makes them work, older students learn quickly that such books are not just "kid stuff." They can be challenged to apply precepts from math and science to the creation of nontraditional pictures themselves.

# 110 Playing with Pictures: Nontraditional Picture Books

Adults have always enjoyed sharing interactive books with children and making attempts, to answer the inevitable question, "How do they *do* that?" Some books of nonfiction have even been published for adults, such as a family tree and keepsake volume called *Grandmother's Album* (1991), illustrated by Beshlie with pop-out figures. There is Nancy Lynch's *Old-Fashioned Garden* (1987), with Gill Tomblin's three-dimensional illustrations of flower garden designs for gardeners to adapt, complete with botanical advice in the text.

The best of the nontraditional books—those with well-engineered special features serving valid storytelling reasons—offer all of us unique opportunities to look at old things in new ways and to stretch our imaginations for experimentation with creating special pictures—playing with the rules—ourselves.

## Criteria for Form and Content

Many nontraditional books on the market today simply amuse or intrigue us for a moment, like a "pop-up" book that does nothing more than pop up, when the popping-up itself has not occurred for any genuinely enlightening reason. However, long-lasting pleasure can be found for adults and children alike in quality books in which truly contoured, three-dimensional figures may be animated to act out part of the story, or four stories have been ingeniously intertwined, or a hidden computer chip delightfully chirps like a real cricket.

As the best of these special-feature books have begun to play a more important role in the way we look at picture books in general, two important aspects about them should be analyzed—their content and their form—the same aspects of traditional picture book art. Among other things, appropriate content for books today is that which is gender-fair, exhibits multicultural sensitivity, and demonstrates respect not only for children's sensibilities but also for childhood's vulnerabilities. Appropriate form is a picturebook format and artistic style that is suited to the nature of the text; here, it additionally must include the technological aspect that achieves the paper engineering.

Some of the specific analytical questions listed here have been generously contributed by Kathy Piehl, Education Librarian at Mankato State University in Mankato, Minnesota, who has extensively researched books with special features.

*Content* (the story line, topic, or theme of the book).

1. Does the theme of the book suit the use of special features? Or would the story or topic be just as effective in a traditional format?

2. Is the story or topic suited to children? Or does content follow form? Does the special feature rely on such things as shock value or suspense to be effective, thus lending itself to horrific, scary, or violent stories or topics that merely titillate and prey on children's fears (as in stories about monsters that leap out at them)? Put another way, would you want a child looking at a book about this story or topic and/or with these illustrations if it weren't a book with special features?

3. Is the text well-written, pertinent, and of appropriate length, or is the text too wordy? Even worse, are the words merely labels for what is seen in the pictures? Still worse, do the words refer to things not even pictured? Regarding length of text, it is important to note that whereas most traditional picture books are up to 32 pages long, some nontraditional ones number only 6 to 8 pages because of the heavier paper and additional backing needed on each page to conceal the mechanics for the special features.

4. If the book is a retelling or repackaging of a familiar story, song, fairy tale, or nursery rhyme, is it an enhancement of the original, traditional version? Or does it miss the point and destroy an effect intended in the original?

*Form* (the design, art style, and special features in a book).

1. Are the illustrations themselves above the ordinary? Would they be outstanding in themselves if they did not have special features?

2. Do the book's special features have a valid visual reason for being there? Or are they just a gimmick, a fun diversion that really adds nothing to an understanding of the story line or content topic?

3. Do the features advance or change the visual action or otherwise enhance the story or topic? Or are they static, confusing, superfluous, and added clutter?

4. Have the special features been integrated with and given support by the entire visual environment in the illustration? Or does the special feature appear to be just an afterthought?

5. Have the special features been well-constructed, and are they easy to manipulate for potential heavy use by young children? Or are they confusing to figure out, work in too many ways, work awkwardly, or so complicated that they stop working altogether after a few uses?

This chapter cites many titles as a review of current work. For the majority, positive answers can be given to the preceding questions. A few, with text or illustrations considered less than remarkable, are included because they can fill a curriculum need, are the best (or only) example of a special feature, or because they break new ground entirely. Some favorite titles have surely been overlooked, but only selected examples could be included here. New books are published every day which are often even more exciting. Because of the fragile nature of many of these nontraditional books, libraries often do not invest in them for general circulation, so a trip to a children's bookstore is the best place to find other, equally ingenious books with special features. For librarians and media specialists concerned about excited young hands damaging such books, the video camera offers an opportunity to record and preserve these moving books.

## Playing with Dimensions and Movement

Pop-up books break the first unwritten rule, which says a picture book has flat, two-dimensional artwork. They are perhaps the most common and popular of the nontraditional picture books. The term is a misnomer, however, because popping-up is certainly not all these books usually do—at least not the best of them. The quality ones are better described variously as three dimensional, moveable, interactive, or mechanical books.

Paper engineers are the creative people who invent the moveable actions, make them work, and prepare a working model for a mechanical book. Paper engineering for a mechanical results in four basic types of what is called *paper performance:*

1. Figures and/or backgrounds go either in and out; more correctly called "popping out" in three-dimensions from the page, usually using a fold, hinge, or spring.

2. Figures go up and down; truly popping up toward the top of the page, usually using a fold, pull tab, sliding strip, or turning wheel.

3. Figures and/or backgrounds go to left and right or diagonally; popping over, usually using a fold, pull tabs, or flaps.

4. Figures and/or backgrounds go around; popping around, usually using a turning wheel, sliding slats, and/or a window.

Popping-out creates three-dimensionality. The other actions generally offer the book's creator opportunities to include surprises, answers, and changes of all kinds. Performing die-cut paper pieces can animate scenes in a most appealing way, bringing real action into an otherwise typically static, two-dimensional, picture book environment. Playing with movement and dimensionality seems to have attracted more picture book artists than any of the other possibilities for special features in nontraditional books. The fact that performing paper can create effects similar to that of animated cartoons makes it especially fun for young children.

## The Golden Age of Mechanical Books and Contemporary Classics

As we have noted, mechanical picture books are certainly nothing new. Linda Ellis Fishbeck, who has written extensively about the history of mechanicals, states that "the earliest known example is an astronomy text printed in 1540 in which elaborately engineered cardboard machinery revolves stars and planets through the clockwork heavens" (1985, 79). The scientific concerns of *Astronomicum Caesareum* were, of course, not for children. It would take all the technological advances and developments in the printing industry during the eighteenth century before this form could be applied to entertainment books for children. In this time, Robert Sawyer developed folding books, generally known as *Harlequinades*; these became the forerunners of what we describe today as moveable or mechanical books.

In the nineteenth century, these ideas were improved upon in England, particularly by the company of Dean and Sons, which dedicated its efforts to the toy book trade, developing concepts like dissolving scenes. Other English companies, such as Read and Company, explored the moveable book format with the panorama concept, used in stories like *Cowper's Diverting History of John Gilpin*, which stretched over nine feet when fully expanded.

But it was Germany that contributed the real geniuses and inspiration in the field of mechanical books; among them Raphael Tuck, Ernest Nister, and the incomparable Lothar Meggendorfer, "who was to mechanical books what Walt Disney was to cartoons" (Fishbeck 1984, 13). For serious students of this form, Peter Haining's lavishly illustrated history, *Movable Books* (1979) is highly recommended. It is also fortunate that many of the books of both Nister and Meggendorfer survive today and are widely available as reproductions. These titles include *The Doll's House* and *Surprise, Surprise* by Meggendorfer, and Nister's *We Visit the Seashore, Revolving Pictures, Mother Goose Favorites,* and *Magic Windows*. Teachers and librarians who introduce children to today's mechanicals like the Provensens' *Leonardo da Vinci: The Artist, Inventor, Scientist in Three-Dimensional Movable Pictures* (1984), might share with them something of the remarkable history of this art form by introducing them to the works of Meggendorfer and others.

Of today's pop-up books, there is certainly no shortage of recommended titles to demonstrate fine examples of paper engineering, while also providing children with a quality encounter and experience of both words and pictures. Original fantasy has resulted in the following exemplary mechanicals—our own contemporary classics.

*New at the Zoo*, Kees Moerbeek (1989). A variation on the mix-and-match format, in which tops and bottoms of different animals are paired up to create zany menageries.

*Dinner with Fox*, Stephen Wyllie (1990). Has a colorful style and humor and is good for action verbs, containing little notes to take out and read.

*In a Dark, Dark Wood,* David Carter (1991). An old tale with a new twist and a marvelous pop-out ghost.

*Pop-Up, Pull-Tab, Playtime House That Jack Built*, Nadine Westcott (1991). Has good pull tabs to make the television work and other features that contribute to the humor of the rhyme.

*It Was a Dark and Stormy Night: Mystery Whodunit*, Linda Birkinshaw (1991). Paper engineering by Keith Mosely and visual and mechanical clues that help readers solve the mystery of the stolen diamond.

Factual mechanical books are even more numerous than the fantasy titles. The following short list represents quality examples of such books, which are both entertaining and educational:

*Most Amazing Hide-and-Seek Alphabet Book*, Robert Crowther (1977).

*Most Amazing Pop-Up Book of Machines*, Robert Crowther (1988).

*Dinosaurs: A Lost World*, Tanner Otley Gay (1984).

*Weather Pop-Up Book*, Francis Wilson (1987).

*Anno's Sundial*, Mitsumasa Anno (1987).

*Pop-Up Book of Firefighters*, Peter Seymour (1990).

*Animals in Danger*, William McCay (1990).

*Big Creatures from the Past*, Clare Watson (1990).

*Castles*, Gillan Osband and Robert Andrew (1991).

## A Quick Glance at Lift-the-Flap Books

Whereas the structures, characters, and figures in pop-out books tend to do just that, reaching out from the page toward the viewer, lift-the-flap books ask the viewer to turn pages, panels, flaps, and other devices at their own pace and their own choice, to reveal the concealed element of the image. One of the most charming of these books is Norman Messenger's beautifully created *Annabel's House* (1989). This magical recreation of an Edwardian home comes complete with press-out figures, lift-up flaps, and numerous surprises behind doors, cupboards, and closets. The first page is largely blank save for a front door that opens out to reveal the maid who welcomes us to the family home. Each successive page takes young readers to a different room in the house, where they can delight in opening pantries, ovens, clocks, doors, even the master's desk and safe. But the book does more than simply provide the reader with a chance to see what each box or drawer contains. Often it reveals only partial pictures behind these doors, leaving the child to complete the image. Readers can also explore beneath beds, under armchairs, and even down in the cellar. One room sure to please is the nursery, which is full of authentic toys and games from the period the book so faithfully recreates. In this respect, *Annabel's House* is a hands-on history lesson that brings the past to life.

Books with plots that rely heavily on the lift-the-flap or open-the-door interaction date back to those eighteenth-century metamorphoses played with in family parlors. They continue to remain popular because their mechanisms are not too fragile and they are therefore more durable than many of the more complicated pop-up books. Equally important, they are clearly distinguished from pop-up books because they continue to reveal more to the picture than initially meets the eye. In that sense, they hold the same anticipatory appeal of a well-wrapped present or even the common fortune cookie; for each reader, each opening promises a revelation, a surprise, a change. These changes make, reveal, or complete a picture, add or reduce the number of characters, show a scene from a different point of view or perspective, or change the expression, posture, or gesture of characters. Good examples of lift-the-flap books that fulfill these functions are the following:

*Dear Zoo*, Rod Campbell (1982).

*I Spy: The Lift-the-Flap ABC Book*, Colin Hawkins and Jacqui Hawkins (1989).

*What's In?* (series), Peter Seymour (1990b).

*Jessie* (series), Harriet Ziefert (1991).

*Look Out, Mog*, Judith Kerr (1991).

*Riddle Flap Book*, Betty Birney (1992).

*Funny Hats*, Ron van der Meer and Atie van der Meer (1992).

# Partial Pages and Panoramas

Books that work with holes, partial pictures, or mats offer the opportunity to develop visual discrimination skills in students, particularly in terms of seeing whether they can construct wholes from only partially revealed pictures. Anyone who has ever played with children as they look for shapes and patterns in clouds know that they love to play with the shapes and forms they see. In working with books that use partial pages, teachers can also encourage children to create their own partial pictures and illustrations and see how quickly other students recognize them. A simple technique for teachers involves cutting a variety of shapes, in a number of sizes, in black construction paper, and then placing the paper over pictures of objects that students might be familiar with, revealing more and more of the object until the children finally recognize it. There are a large number of books, many by award-winning illustrators, that teachers and librarians can use to introduce children to the design decisions made when creating books with partial pictures.

In 1970, author/illustrator Eric Carle published his now-classic, *The Very Hungry Caterpillar,* with holes in partial and full pages as the caterpillar "eats" its way through this counting book. The following year, Carle went on to create *Secret Birthday Message* with partial pages in many shapes—a rock, steps, and a door. In Carle's *The Grouchy Lady Bug* (1977), the artist employed partials of increasing size—the larger the page, the larger the animal and typeface. One page is actually shaped like a whale's tail. British artist John S. Goodall is also an expert at this form, whether in his original wordless titles or in retellings of traditional fairy tales, which use partial pages to advance the visual action.

Many books with partial pages play with the concept of holes, often teasing us with surprises about missing parts. *Hi Mom, I'm Home* (Moerbeek 1992) has three-dimensional pop-out characters appear on the next page. Sometimes the holes provide clues about mysteries underneath, as in Millicent Selsam's *Is This a Baby Dinosaur?* (1972). Caldecott medal winner Ed Emberley developed an ingenious format for *Go Away, Big Green Monster* (1992). Die-cut black pages reveal multicolored eyes, nose, mouth, hair, and head for a monster, which then can be made to disappear by turning the remaining colored pages. A different approach is evident in Lois Ehlert's *Color Zoo* (1989) and *Color Farm* (1990). Here die-cut geometric shapes form animal faces when placed one on top of the other. *Color Zoo*, which was a Caldecott Honor Book, is an intriguing visual experience for young readers. Brightly colored and cleverly designed, it introduces children to shapes like diamonds, octagons, and hexagons and to animals like snakes, monkeys, and deer, while challenging them to "make some new ones for your zoo." Another book with an animal theme is Stephen Savage's *Making Tracks* (1992), which reveals pictures of animals, their names, and the kind of tracks they make.

Sometimes books extend beyond the covers, folding out or up to create what are generally referred to as *panoramas*. These books were particularly popular in the middle of the nineteenth century. They "unfolded much like modern road maps and were just as cantankerous to close" (Fishbeck 1984, 12). Once again, Eric Carle is a contemporary illustrator who has worked in this historic format. *The Very Long Tail* (1972a) and *The Very Long Train* (1992b) are two examples. In *Papa, Please Get the Moon for Me* (Carle 1986), the pages extend beyond the top, bottom, and sides.

## Strategies and Activities

Fold-out panoramas appeal to children who don't know where to stop when they are telling a story. The concept of extending the pictures can be used for the following ideas:

- A "tall story" can be incorporated into a panorama format in which the design of the art unfolds as the story grows more and more out of control.

- A traditional tale with a journey motif also lends itself to the panorama format. *Jack and the Bean Tree* (Haley 1986) could be designed to open up, growing vertically as the tree takes root. *Jack and the Fire Dragon* (Haley 1988) could also work vertically to create the underground world of the giant. Even novels can be used to develop understanding of the panorama format. *Huckleberry Finn* could be retold using a stretch format to represent the Mississippi River.

- Students can also develop diaries of a trip or journey they have taken, with the organization and design of the panorama reflecting the travel.

## Nonlinear Storytelling

Artists Remy Charlip and Jerry Joyner, in *Thirteen* (1975), created an early example of a book with more than one plot: thirteen little vignettes illustrated in the same artistic style and occupying the same double spreads. The illustrated plots, most of them wordless, can all be enjoyed on each page until you reach the end, or the book can be opened and shut 13 times and enjoyed 1 vignette at a time. The plots are linear, all beginning on the first page and ending on the last, with one actually starting and ending on the front and back endpapers.

Author/illustrator David Macaulay toyed with the same premise found in *Thirteen*—multiple vignettes—but he turned the idea upside down, in on itself, sideways, and inside out to create *Black and White* (1990), resulting in a nonlinear tour de force that has delighted some book lovers and bewildered other children and adults alike. Like Charlip's book, Macaulay's 1991 Caldecott Award winner has multiple vignettes occupying the same double spreads, in this case divided into quadrants. Each vignette has its own linear plot; one is a boy's adventures on a train; one is about two children and their rambunctious parents; one is about bored commuters at a train station; one is about an escaped convict hiding in a herd of Holsteins. Similar to *Thirteen*, one story begins on the title page and two others cleverly conclude together on the copyright page at the end.

Unlike *Thirteen*, however, *Black and White*'s vignettes are each illustrated in a different style, and no one story can be truly understood until all four are finished. No plot stands alone, as they are all imaginatively intertwined, coming together on different pages within the book. Sometimes one flips backward to establish where a character in one vignette enters another vignette. Befuddled linear thinkers have struggled to straighten out the story, satisfied at last that the vignettes actually form one plot, however convoluted it may be: After a convict and some cows delay arrival of a boy's train at a station, two frustrated commuters get home late and in a silly mood that mystifies their children. Cows, the convict, and even the train appeared in Macaulay's *Why the Chicken Crossed the Road* (1987), so flipping back to a previous picture book can be also involved in full interpretation of the artist's award winner.

*Black and White* appeals to nonlinear thinkers as a holistic, nonsequential creation that for the most part succeeds admirably in playing with fundamental concepts of time, space, and viewpoint. It has been compared to flipping television channels with a remote control, except here actors appear in each other's shows. In his Caldecott Award acceptance speech, its creator gave us food for thought when he explained that the "subject of the book *is* the book. It is designed to be viewed in its entirety, its surface read all over. . . . It is essential to see, not merely to look. . . . [W]ords and pictures can support each other. . . . [I]t isn't necessary to think in a straight line to make sense" (Macaulay 1991, 419–23).

What Macaulay neglected to mention was just how much fun he was having in *Black and White*, for it is a very funny book. Macaulay himself is a very funny man, as demonstrated in some of his other books and also in Betsy Hearne and Marilyn Kaye's edited essays on children's literature, *Celebrating Children's Books* (1981). There this creator of a well-known nonfiction book on architecture painted a word picture of the kind of illustrator he was determined not to be: the kind who "sees little faces on all the pansies and bluebells . . . imagines neighborhood pets to be clothed in specially adapted grown-up attire . . . tells children what they already know or shows them how to make things they already know how to make . . . and at no time considers the book as a whole" (Hearne and Kaye 1981, 98–103).

Other commendable nonlinear creations are author/illustrator Paul Goble's *Iktomi* series, picture books of legendary Dakota trickster stories. Excellent for beginning storytellers or for those who would like to learn a Native American way of storytelling, the text in these books corresponds to the oral tradition and is not intended to be read aloud in a left-to-right, sequential manner. Three typefaces for text serve three purposes and are included as help for the reader: narrative prose and dialogue are in large bold type; Iktomi's thoughts are in small print within the illustrations (and are upside down if Iktomi himself is shown upside down); conversational asides or questions to the audience are in gray italics, as encouragement for "listeners to express their own thoughts about Iktomi's foolishness. It is customary for all present, young and old, to engage in considerable witticisms," as Goble explains in his preface to *Iktomi and the Buffalo Skull* (1991).

Before we begin to share nonsequential books with children, many youngsters need first to be given experiences in the areas Macaulay mentioned in his speech: visual perception, visual/verbal connections, and holistic thinking. Even the most untrained of young artists benefits greatly from nonlinear thinking and playing with visual storytelling that is not left-to-right, as in the following activities.

## *Strategies and Activities*

- Experience in visual perception, or exploring the way in which "seeing" is more important than merely "looking," can be gained from "I Spy" games about objects in the room or on an outing. Children can also note details in Martin Handford's popular *Where's Waldo?* (1987) or in numerous detailed picture books by Anno.

- Visual/verbal connections can be made by studying words and images that support each other, as in traditional picture books or in magazine ads, or by studying how images replace words, as in body language, pantomime, dance, and sports.

- Experiences for children in holistic, nonlinear thinking can be provided through "concept webbing," making collages, and creating original jigsaw puzzles.

- Different children can be assigned the writing and illustrating of a number of different viewpoints about the same event (but starting at different times and ending in different places, as the four viewpoints do in *Black and White*). Combine these into a group book before children try this complicated exercise on their own.

- After practicing using Goble's three kinds of text in the *Iktomi* books, children can have fun telling stories themselves in three ways simultaneously, especially for stories already familiar to them, like "The Gingerbread Boy."

# Wordless Picture Books

No definition of picture books states that they must have words. In fact, author/illustrator Uri Shulevitz, in *Writing with Pictures,* stresses that "a true picture book tells a story mainly or entirely with pictures. When words are used, they have an auxiliary role" (Shulevitz 1985, 15). Therefore, wordless books have certainly not broken any rules, but they are mentioned in this chapter because they are still often considered a novelty and are usually critiqued separately from picture books with words—as if a lack of text were a special feature and requires specialized skill.

Wordless books bear a strong resemblance to, and seem to have the same appeal as, silent movies, those without even any dialogue printed on the screen. They also resemble rebuses for children, and perhaps that is how they began. Many very popular ones today include a few words, similar to a rebus: sometimes just as beginning or ending narrative or dialogue, sometimes within illustrations as signs ("Danger! Deep Water!"), as dialogue in speech balloons ("Oops!") or as sound effects ("Splash!"). These near-wordless books are not fooling anybody; it is plain that the words exist only to set a stage or as an inside joke and that their creators' primary delight is having pictures tell a story. Some artists reveal that they imagine music accompanying their pictures, as Maurice Sendak does for his three wordless "wild rumpus" double-spreads in *Where the Wild Things Are* (1963).

Several traditional picture-book illustrators have devoted much of their careers to wordless books and some of their titles are now classics, like Raymond Briggs's *Snowman* (1978), Tomie dePaola's *Pancakes for Breakfast* (1978), Peter Spier's Caldecott winner *Noah's Ark* (1977), and Lynd Ward's *Silver Pony* (1973), to name only a few. Two of the most imaginative wordless artists working today are Molly Bang, whose figure/ground transformations in Caldecott Honor Book *Grey Lady and the Strawberry Snatcher* (1980) are some of the most challenging illustrations seen anywhere, and Donald Crews, the master of illusionary movement in such books as *Freight Train* (1978) and *Truck* (1980), both also Honor Book selections.

Artist David Wiesner's ambitious exploration into wordless storytelling resulted in a 1989 Caldecott Honor Book, *Free Fall* (1988), in which words would not only be superfluous but intrusive. The 1992 Caldecott Medal winner, *Tuesday* (1991), allows more fun imagining what scenes might sound like than to be told in a text what is going on. A sleeping boy's fantastic dream adventures breathtakingly unfold in *Free Fall* through metamorphosing illustrations in seamless progression, as in a mural. The genesis for the book was indeed a 10-foot-long mural about transformations that Wiesner submitted as an art student years before. *Free Fall* is reminiscent of the surrealism of Salvador Dali, fantasy by turn-of-the-century illustrator Charles Robinson, and the figure/ground illusions of M. C. Escher, in which the subject becomes the background and background becomes the subject. As Wiesner said in his Caldecott acceptance speech, it "was the culmination of many ideas about an impressionistic kind of storytelling that I had been forming since art school" (Wiesner 1992, 418).

Wiesner also "longed to do a book that was wildly humorous, almost slapstick," as he further explained in his speech. That book turned out to be the near-wordless, hilarious *Tuesday*, with its "soft, round, lumpy, and really goofy-looking" frogs who "looked pretty silly, yet up in the air they clearly felt dignified, noble, and a bit smug." Perhaps they were so confident because they had already made their in-flight debut on the cover of the March 1989 *Cricket* magazine (Weisner 1992, 419). Just like the boy in *Free Fall*, the frogs have fantastic nighttime adventures, even "free falling" when their squadron of flying lily pads loses supernatural powers. *Free Fall*'s curious fish and smiling pigs also show up again in the second book, but there the likenesses between the two titles end. *Tuesday* is markedly different in design (the artist uses panels in a cinematic technique), in inspiration (among other things, animated cartoons, flying saucers from science fiction movies, and superhero comic books), and in intent, which was "to make people laugh; all that matters is that the pictures are funny" (Wiesner 1992, 421). Needless to say, Wiesner's imaginative pictures are much more than that. Indeed, they may signal a new trend in picture books that "challenges the perception of the wordless book as a novelty" (p. 422).

## *Strategies and Activities: Playing with Ideas from David Wiesner*

Quoted here are some remarks from David Wiesner's 1992 Caldecott speech that offer excellent insight into fostering children's appreciation of the wordless format. They additionally suggest ways, some of which are expanded upon, to involve them in the creative process itself. Wordless books, says Wiesner, "have become springboards for all kinds of writing, bookmaking, and even drama classes," and he offers some additional ideas for teachers to play around with (all quotations are from Wiesner 1992, 417–22):

- "One first-grade class wrote their own book, *Wednesday*. In it, their school is subjected to some interesting revenge fantasies involving scissors and math papers."

- "Teachers of English as a second language tell me that wordless books are particularly useful in helping students express their thoughts in English. The students aren't inhibited by the burden of having to translate literally."

- To understand and experience what Wiesner means when he says, "I began to understand the process by which a story is distilled, and the essential information presented in visual terms," children can study a variety of wordless books, discussing possible reasons behind similarities or changes in the settings, characters, and details. They may then try creating wordless stories themselves.

- Children can create picture versions of stories read aloud, to practice making a series of illustrations that demonstrate the need to be "very carefully plotted, and details developed in ways that move the story forward as logically as possible."

- To "fit the particular mood and tone you have in mind," children can begin by selecting paper of different colors and sizes, and unusual media such as chalk or fluorescent pens. Then they can create compositions with expressive uses of color, directional lines, interesting perspectives, and a variety of sizes and shapes. Finally, they can end by demonstrating aloud what their wordless pictures "sound like."

- In addition to Wiesner's idea of a "perfect assignment: do anything you want to do," children who are stumped can also be given "food for thought," such as a list of animals that would make interesting characters. They can also be encouraged to ask themselves a question like Wiesner's own, "Okay, if I were a frog, and I had discovered I could fly, where would I go? What would I do?" They can be shown a picture and encouraged to create "what happened before and after the image."

## References

Anno, Mitsumasa (1987). *Anno's Sundial*. New York: Putnam.

Bang, Molly (1980). *Grey Lady and the Strawberry Snatcher*. New York: Macmillan.

Beshlie (1991). *Grandmother's Album*. New York: Viking.

Birkinshaw, Linda (1991). *It Was a Dark and Stormy Night: Mystery Whodunit*. New York: Dial.

Birney, Betty (1992). *Riddle Flap Book*. New York: Simon & Schuster.

Briggs, Raymond (1978). *Snowman*. New York: Random House.

Campbell, Rod (1982). *Dear Zoo*. New York: Dutton.

Carle, Eric (1970). *The Very Hungry Caterpillar*. New York: World.

——— (1971). *Secret Birthday Message*. New York: HarperCollins.

——— (1972a). *The Very Long Tail*. New York: Crowell.

——— (1972b). *The Very Long Train*. New York: Crowell.

——— (1977). *The Grouchy Lady Bug*. New York: HarperCollins.

——— (1981). *The Honeybee and the Robber*. New York: Putnam.

——— (1986). *Papa, Please Get the Moon for Me*. Saxonville, MA: Picture Book Studio.

Carter, David A. (1991). *In a Dark, Dark Wood*. New York: Simon & Schuster.

Charlip, Remy, and Jerry Joyner (1975). *Thirteen*. New York: Macmillan.

Crews, Donald (1978). *Freight Train*. New York: William Morrow.

——— (1980). *Truck*. New York: William Morrow.

Crowther, Robert (1977). *Most Amazing Hide-and-Seek Alphabet Book*. New York: Viking.

——— (1988). *Most Amazing Pop-Up Book of Machines*. New York: Viking.

dePaola, Tomie (1978). *Pancakes for Breakfast*. New York: Harcourt Brace Jovanovich.

Ehlert, Lois (1989). *Color Zoo*. New York: HarperCollins.

——— (1990). *Color Farm*. New York: HarperCollins.

Emberley, Ed (1992). *Go Away, Big Green Monster*. Boston: Little, Brown.

Fishbeck, Linda Ellis (1984) Pop-Up Books. *Franklin Mint Almanac,* November/December: 12–13.

——— (1985). Pop-Up Picture Books: The Paper Pranks of a Victorian Childhood. *Country Home,* December: 79.

Gay, Tanner Otley (1984). *Dinosaurs: A Lost World.* New York: Putnam.

Goble, Paul (1988). *Iktomi and the Boulder.* New York: Franklin Watts.

——— (1989). *Iktomi and the Berries.* New York: Franklin Watts.

——— (1991). *Iktomi and the Buffalo Skull.* New York: Franklin Watts.

Haining, Peter (1979). *Movable Books: An Illustrated History.* London: New English Library.

Haley, Gail (1986). *Jack and the Bean Tree.* New York: Crown.

——— (1988). *Jack and the Fire Dragon.* New York: Crown.

Handford, Martin (1987). *Where's Waldo?* Boston: Little, Brown.

Hawkins, Colin, and Jacqui Hawkins (1989). *I Spy.* Boston: Little, Brown.

Hearne, Betsy, and Marilyn Kaye, eds. (1981). *Celebrating Children's Books: Essays on Children's Literature in Honor of Zena Sutherland.* New York: Lothrop, Lee & Shepard.

Kerr, Judith (1991). *Look Out, Mog.* New York: Random House.

Lynch, Nancy (1987). *Old-Fashioned Garden.* New York: Rizzoli.

Macaulay, David (1987). *Why the Chicken Crossed the Road.* Boston: Houghton Mifflin.

——— (1990). *Black and White.* Boston: Houghton Mifflin.

——— (1991). Caldecott Medal Acceptance Speech. *Horn Book*, July-August: 419–23.

McCay, William (1990). *Animals in Danger.* New York: Macmillan.

Messenger, Norman (1989). *Annabel's House.* New York: Orchard.

Miller, Jonathan, and David Pelham (1983). *The Human Body.* New York: Viking.

Moerbeek, Kees (1989). *New at the Zoo.* New York: Random House.

——— (1992). *Hi Mom! I'm Home.* Los Angeles: Price Stern Sloan.

Osband, Gillan, and Robert Andrew (1991). *Castles.* New York: Franklin Watts.

Pienkowski, Jan (1979). *Haunted House.* New York: Dutton.

Provensen, Alice, and Martin Provensen (1984). *Leonardo da Vinci: The Artist, Inventor, Scientist in Three-Dimensional Movable Pictures.* New York: Viking.

Richey, Virginia H., and Katharyn Puckett (1992). *Wordless/Almost Wordless Picture Books: A Guide.* Englewood, CO: Libraries Unlimited, Inc.

Savage, Stephen (1992). *Making Tracks.* New York: Dutton.

Selsam, Millicent (1972). *Is This a Baby Dinosaur?* New York: Harper & Row.

Sendak, Maurice (1963). *Where the Wild Things Are.* New York: Harper & Row.

——— (1988). *Caldecott and Co.: Notes on Books and Pictures.* New York: Farrar, Straus & Giroux.

Seymour, Peter (1981a). Pop-Up Books: Where They Come From, How They're Made. *Children's Book Council Calendar*, March-October: 63–64.

——— (1981b). The Resurrection of the Pop-Up Book. *Publishers Weekly*, February 27: 1–2.

——— (1990a). *Pop-Up Book of Firefighters.* New York: Dutton.

——— (1990b). *What's In?* New York: Henry Holt.

Shulevitz, Uri (1985). *Writing with Pictures: How to Write and Illustrate Children's Books.* New York: Watson Guptill.

Spier, Peter (1977). *Noah's Ark.* Garden City, NY: Doubleday.

Tuten-Puckett, Katharyn, and Virginia H. Richey (1993). *Using Wordless Picture Books: Authors and Activities.* Englewood, CO: Teacher Ideas Press.

van der Meer, Ron, and Alan McGowan (1985). *Sailing Ships.* New York: Henry Holt.

van der Meer, Ron, and Atie van der Meer (1992). *Funny Hats.* New York: Random House.

Ward, Lynd (1973). *Silver Pony: A Story in Pictures.* Boston: Houghton Mifflin.

Watson, Clare (1990). *Big Creatures from the Past.* New York: Putnam.

Westcott, Nadine (1991). *Pop-Up, Pull-Tab, Playtime House That Jack Built,* Boston: Little, Brown.

Wiesner, David (1988). *Free Fall.* New York: Clarion.

——— (1991). *Tuesday,* New York: Clarion.

——— (1992). Caldecott Medal Acceptance Speech. *Horn Book*, July-August: 417–22.

Wilson, Francis (1987). *Weather Pop-Up Book.* New York: Simon & Schuster.

Wyllie, Stephen (1990). *Dinner with Fox.* New York: Dial.

Ziefert, Harriet (1991). *Come Out, Jessie.* New York: Harper & Row.

Chapter 7

# *Painting with Words: Writing with Pictures*

> There are two views of a picture book. The first is
> that it is a palette with words. The second is that it is
> a story with illustrations. People who subscribe to the
> first view are artists. Most writers subscribe to the second.
> Both are correct.
> —Jane Yolen, *Writing Books for Children* (1976)

## Introduction

In chapter 6, we explored the way in which the form, design, and look of a book could be employed to advance the story. Chapter 4 and chapter 6 demonstrated how the artistic technique and visual composition in quality picture books relate to the content, mood, period, and setting of the story. To fully appreciate and understand the picture book, it is essential that children, and those who teach them, understand the integral relationship between image and text. The pictures are much more than decoration. In the best picture books, they enhance, explain, elaborate, and expand the information provided by the words. Steven Kellogg lucidly described the relationship between words and image and the power of this union as a teaching tool and an art form. The strength, he says, "is derived from the fact that it communicates in two voices, verbal and visual." In the best picture books, "these components do not rehash the same material, but rather reinforce and enhance each other, like two dissimilar but related melodies in a duet that is eloquently sung by different instruments" (1990, 705).

Recognizing this delicate balance requires that we accept the idea that "reading is produced by more than words on the page" (Tatar 1992, xv). As *School Library Journal* wrote, "if reading is image-making, viewing is image reading." Young readers "both bring meaning to and take meaning from the symbol system in which the story is encoded" (Vandergrift and Hannigan 1993, 20). In short, by teaching children to read the pictures, we give them the potential of understanding the story on a deeper level. Certainly this involves an awareness and appreciation of the aesthetic aspects of the book, but comprehension of the pictures must be related to the narrative role they play, not just their artistic contribution. In fact, a successful picture book need not contain award-winning art. "It does not matter that not one picture from the book is suitable for framing. Each picture should best function in concert with all other pictures in the book." The real art of the picture book lies in "how well it tells the story, how well it interacts picture to picture, and how well it supports and extends the text" (Lorraine 1977, 146). In *Words About Pictures: The Narrative Art of Children's Picture Books* (1988), Perry Nodelman articulates the two-way traffic between reading words and pictures. "Reading a picture for narrative meaning is a matter of applying our understanding of words.... [W]e are engaged in an act of turning visual information into verbal" (p. 211). For Nodelman, the relationship between the picture and words is ironic because "each speaks about matters on which the other is silent" (p. 221). Two good examples of this can be seen in books by Gail Haley and Chris Van Allsburg. In *Jumanji* (Van Allsburg 1981), the words tell us that Peter is bitten by a tsetse fly and falls asleep. This event from the story is not represented in the illustrations for the simple reason that the subject matter lacks action and drama. The pictures have nothing to say about this incident described by the words. Author Jane Yolen put it very well, stating that "what you write must be illustratable. This means action is the most important thing; not the thoughts in your characters' heads" (1976, 73). Gail Haley's *Puss in Boots* (1992b) demonstrates how much pictures can tell us that is never described in the text. The front matter of the book consists of three images, all providing information about characters and events only alluded to in the opening line, "On the day the miller was buried his will was read." The half-title page shows the miller making out his will as the cat watches. It is night, a fact clearly indicated by the moon and the candle by which the miller writes. The quill and the costume both provide a clear indication that this is not a contemporary story. Though it is not yet recognizable, the interior scene is located inside the mill, and we can see a partial blade of the windmill passing in front of the window. The title page is even more elaborate and full of detail. The cat sits on the right of the double-page spread, next to the sealed will and the miller's hat. He looks down at the coffin and the family members gathered there. The interior of the mill is now clearly visible, depicting the mechanism for grinding wheat into flour. Through a window we see one monk preparing the wagon that will take the coffin to the cemetery, while the interior shows another entering a door about to take the casket. A third monk stands among the mourners reading from a Bible. The copyright/dedication page depicts the funeral procession, but it also does much more. It tells us that the day was wet, windswept, and overcast. It locates the story in a village with a rural surrounding, evidenced by the shepherd tending his flock on the nearby hill. It gives readers the first external view of the mill, and finally it employs proportion to show the now greatly diminished cat, watching as his master's coffin moves up the hill. Of course, all this information could have been expressed in words, but the 32-page limitation of the picture book requires an economy of text, which means that the best picture books skillfully balance words and images so that each plays a unique and complementary role in the telling of the tale.

Children can be helped to comprehend and construct the meanings contained in such pictures. In fact, their ability to process pictures contributes to their overall understanding of any story. Exploring illustrations involves investigating concepts such as cause and effect, sequencing, anticipation, inference, projection, and other key aspects of narrative structure. *The Reading Teacher* said, "[W]hen the capacity for interpreting imagery is weak, comprehension is at best superficial. . . . Quality picture books can create understanding and use of metaphor. However, this can only occur when the child has developed visual awareness to interpret, evaluate and creatively construct meaning from image" (Goldstone 1989, 594).

In reality, all stories commence as images; pictures in the mind struggling to take shape, to be set free, to be given expression. Before words ever find their way to the daunting open spaces of the blank page, they have formed in the imagination and insight of the writer. In his 1986 Caldecott medal acceptance speech, Chris Van Allsburg said: "As I consider a story, I see it quite clearly. Illustrating is simply a matter of drawing something I've already experienced in my mind's eye" (1982, 348). For Gail Haley, the front matter of her books is often treated cinematically, in a series of establishing shots that introduce us to her cast, set, and period, in the same way that many films introduce us to characters as the title and credits roll. It is hardly surprising that Haley draws upon the convention of the movies, for they themselves grew out of the theatrical traditions of the stage, a world that is familiar to Haley. As a puppeteer, she draws freely on its forms to advance the stories she tells through what she calls her "little ambassadors of the subconscious." Writing in *The Puppetry Journal*, she described a visit to the home of Ashley Bryant and the interest both share in puppetry as a form of storytelling. The interest she noted is also shared by Marcia Brown, Natalie Babbit, Katherine Patterson, and others. "This really does not surprise me, since the pages of a picture book could well be compared to the proscenium of a puppet stage, with its receding layers of scenery, painted and cut out to simulate depth and perspective. Foreground details in both are often executed in trompe l'oeil detail. Stage design and page design both use implications of meaning derived from the placement and posture of the actors. . . . Both are direct descendants of storytelling in which all visuals were created internally by the imagination of the audience" (1992a, 11).

Nor is Haley alone in recognizing the role the visual arts play in constructing story and carrying narrative. Caldecott medal winner Uri Shulevitz initially struggled to communicate. "My fear that I could not write was based on a preconception . . . that writing was strictly related to words and the spoken language." He overcame his fear through visualizing the action. Describing the development of *The Moon in My Room* (1963), he said: "The story unfolded in my head like a movie. I was the camera seeing the action conveyed by pictures. The few words necessary to communicate the story fell into place on their own" (Shulevitz 1982, 19). Chris Van Allsburg also linked the picture book to motion pictures. "It is a unique medium that allows an artist-author to deal with the passage of time, the unfolding of events, in the same way film does" (1982, 381). A recent example that clearly demonstrates this is the Caldecott medal winner *Mirette on the High Wire* (McCully 1992). The title page introduces the young heroine Mirette, her raised foot clearly conveying a sense of movement. Over the page to the copyright/dedication, the scene pulls back for an establishing shot of Paris in the 1890s, as the young girl moves across the crowded street. Later, when she first attempts to walk the tightrope, the artist uses a series of panels in a montage effect, using tilt ups and tilt downs to show the various stages of Mirette's progress. When Bellini's identity is revealed, the book presents a series of flashbacks recalling his triumphs and exploits. The visual language or vocabulary evident in this book clearly employs techniques also found in television and cinema, which, like it or not, are today's storytellers for most American children. Teachers and librarians who lament this should understand that many of today's leading authors and illustrators acknowledge the impact of mass media on their own work and the relationship between the picture book and electronic storytelling. Don Wood, for example, described the picture book as "a spectacular marriage of image and text. As such it is probably as close to drama or a thirty two page movie as it is to either literature or art" (Wood 1986, 557). For Charles Mikolaycak, motion pictures were extremely influential in his formative years. "Movies intrigued me as a child. . . [T]hey stimulated a curiosity in me about ways of life different from my own" (Mikolaycak 1986, 169).

Young readers should also be taught to be astute observers of the world created for them in the pages of picture books. They can recognize the content and the construction of the illustrations and how these relate to the language and forms of the mass media that surround them. Children may also listen to the words and visualize based on what they hear. The value of these mental imaging activities is well documented (Fredericks 1986). The images can also be experiential, providing sensory stimulation. "Can a picture be noisy?" Gail Haley asks the children she visits in libraries and classrooms all over the country. She is not talking about today's chirping, creaking, singing, talking, computer-chip picture books. She is asking children to step into the picture, unfreeze the frame, and listen. It is as if the artist has become director, calling "Lights, camera, action!" With the copyright page of *The Green Man* (Haley 1979) open in front of them, the children bring the sounds of the medieval street scene to life. The blows of the blacksmith's hammer on the anvil ring out. The sheep bleat and baa as they wander through the village. A woman cries out as a dog steals the butcher's sausages. Children's voices fill the air as they play their simple games, and the river babbles and gurgles as it winds its way beneath the bridge leading to the tavern. The vision is given voice, and its words are eloquent.

Over a dozen different activities never referred to in the text bring this medieval village to life. (From *The Green Man*, written and illustrated by Gail E. Haley.)

If the illustrator can talk to us, the author's words often paint pictures, using language to bring a character, location, or event to life. The skillful use of vocabulary and the careful selection of language create worlds young readers can both see and hear. In *Song and Dance Man* (Ackerman and Gammell 1988), the author's words bring the grandfather to life. "His tap shoes make soft, slippery sounds like rain on a tin roof." In *Owl Moon* (Yolen and Schoenherr 1987), we are told that the train whistle blew "like a sad, sad song." The use of alliteration and simile clearly contribute to the way children experience the story, especially when it is being read to them, and they derive their impressions more from words than pictures. Selecting small passages like these from quality pictures books is a useful way of helping children recognize literary techniques so that they can incorporate them into their own creative writing.

Both *Song and Dance Man* and *Owl Moon* represent a collaboration between an author who writes the story and an artist who is contracted to illustrate the story. That relationship inevitably poses problems of integrity and unity. Marcia Brown believes that the illustrator is "the performer of the spirit of the book" (1986, 62). The creative partnership between the author and the illustrator also involves collaboration with the publisher and printer. The end result, says Brown, necessitates a "certain amount of personal compromise and mutual understanding of each others' needs and problems, so the production of a picture book entails concessions." The triple Caldecott medal winner concedes "that it is conceivable that other artists could provide better illustrators than those of the author," but believes, ultimately, "when the artist is also the author, the chance for unity between text and pictures is usually greater" (p. 5).

Much depends on the balance between image and text. A wordy text often contains a great deal of detail that helps the child picture the story. Although these words provide cues and clues about characters and events, if they are too detailed, they limit artistic license or expression. In *Saint George and the Dragon* (Hodges and Hyman 1984), for example, almost a full page of text describes in detail the appearance of the dragon. The tail, we are told, is huge and long, speckled red and black with 100 scaly folds. The dragon's wings billow and stretch like two giant sails. At the end of the tail are two sharp, cruel claws. From tip to tail, the author's words both create the character and constrain the illustrator, who can do little more, however skillfully, than bring the writer's vision to life. Rather than adding a dimension of its own, this beautiful illustration does no more than repeat what we have already been told by the words. In contrast, *Jack and the Fire Dragon* (Haley 1988), a product of an author who was also the illustrator, used words sparingly, allowing the pictures to tell part of the story. Haley's words provide only sketchy glimpses of her villain. The dragon, we are told, has a scaly head, sharp claws, and a spiky tail. It is for the pictures to tell us how the metamorphosis from man to dragon occurred, the size of the dragon in relation to Jack, and the details of the battle.

*Mirandy and Brother Wind* (McKissack and Pinkney 1988) offers a fine balance between image and text. As the story begins, author Patricia McKissack writes: "Swish! Swish! It was spring and Brother Wind was back. He come high steppin' through Ridgetop dressed in his finest and trailing that long, silvery wind cape behind him. Swoosh! Swoosh! Swoosh!" The writer provides only a partial picture. Though she does tell us that Brother Wind wears a cape, the rest of his costume is left to the imagination of illustrator Jerry Pinkney. The cane, the top hat, the tie—these are all products of the artist's vision. The environment is also left to the imagination and contribution of the illustrator, who uses a double-page spread to embody Ridgetop, with its flowers, pastures, barn, livestock, and cabin. The "Swish!" and the "Swoosh!" are well conveyed by the line and the movement in the artwork.

*Hey, Al* (Yorinks and Egielski 1986) is another good example of a successful collaboration between author and artist in which less is more. The text tells us that Al and Eddie live in a one-room apartment on the West side and that Al is a janitor. Beyond that, all detail and description are provided by the pictures. Even when Eddie complains that the apartment is a dump, the disgruntled dog is denied the words to more fully articulate his discontent. Again, this is a task best left to the illustrator, who tells us what the words do not. Later, when Al is visited by what the text simply refers to as "a large bird," the artist once again contributes to the overall meaning of the event. Children to whom this section of the story is read, without benefit of the picture, are given no framework in which to conceptualize the size, color, or species of the bird. Nor, in fact, apart from being told that Al is confused, are they given words to understand that he is quite startled. His posture and expression are used to tell us that. When the bird carries the two friends to the island in the sky, the author begins to use vocabulary to direct the artist and inform the reader. Now we learn that the island has "lush trees, rolling hills, gorgeous grass," and cascading waterfalls, but when we next turn the page, a wordless double-page spread shows Al and Eddie stuck up in a tree, surrounded by exotic birds—an incident not even referred to in the text.

Several stories with multicultural themes also rely heavily upon the illustrations not only to advance the narrative, but also to bring the culture to life. *Sundiata: Lion King of Mali* (Wisniewski, 1992) uses palette and picture to re-create the time and place of this thirteenth-century African story. As the story begins, we are told that one day two hunters approached the throne of the king. In half a page of text, we are told what happened and who was involved, but given little description. It is the illustrations that recreate the court, the climate, the costumes, and the characters (based, as is this illustrator's habit, on extensive research). When the author is also the illustrator, he or she is are able to visualize the story as he or she works through it. It has its own meaning, which they see. But an author's words, given to an illustrator who does not know the culture or the context of the story, would be very difficult to depict meaningfully. The West African nation of Cameroon is the setting for *The Fortune Tellers* (Alexander and Hyman 1992), but the text is totally bereft of any cultural reference to this country; the multicultural nature of the book is entirely created and conveyed by Hyman's illustrations, not Alexander's words. *A Story, A Story* (Haley 1970) is another African tale by an author who also illustrated the book. Like *Sundiata*, this book uses images to provide description. Nyame the Sky God is introduced in the briefest of terms. We are simply told that he keeps all the stories in a golden box by his royal throne. Information about his age, physique, personality, costume, and kingdom can be derived only from observing the illustrations. Similarly, Ananse's village is never described in words, though the cover of the book and the last double-page spread provide great detail about the lodging, landscape, and lifestyle. Neither Haley nor Wisniewski feel the need to employ words to tell us what the pictures so clearly say. As Haley says to the students in her writing and illustrating classes, "Show me, don't tell me."

Of course, within the space limitations of a picture book, it is not possible for an illustrator to depict every event from a story or even to visually represent everything the author has described. The words in *Jumanji* (Van Allsburg 1981) tell us that there were "a dozen monkeys tearing the room apart." When we inspect the picture, however, the artist has decided to imply most of the monkeys. Two are clearly visible. Another two are suggested by their tails, and another is evident in the pantry knocking food from the shelf. *The Talking Eggs* (San Souci and Pinkney 1989) seems to suggest that some choices about what to illustrate depend upon what is considered appropriate for the young reader. Most of the earlier fantasy adventures are depicted. Children get to see the two-headed cow with its corkscrew horns. They are shown the chickens of every color and the singing, dancing rabbits. In each of these incidents, the illustrations depict what the text tells us. But when the words casually tell us, "[T]he old woman sat down near the fireplace and took off her head. She set it on her knees like a pumpkin," the artist does not illustrate the event. Whether Pinkney regarded the scene as too graphic and potentially disturbing for young readers, or decided that it was best to leave this to the child's imagination, we do not know. What we are presented with is an ambiguous image—one must look at it very carefully to note the gap between the old woman's head and her neck.

For some stories, the real role of the illustrator is not simply to depict what happened, but to show what it felt like; the mood, the atmosphere, and the emotions of the experience. *The Wretched Stone* (Van Allsburg 1991) often ignores the obvious events to concentrate more on the detail. The text describes the effort involved in getting the stone on board the ship, but the event is not depicted. The color; the mood; the ominous, eerie overtones of the island with its sickly palette and sweet overpowering scent: these are the elements of the tale the art strives to convey. *The Polar Express* (Van Allsburg 1985) contains similar minimalist text with illustrations that convey mood more than action. Two images from the book clearly reveal Van Allsburg's aversion to the obvious. "'Look,' shouted one of the children, 'the elves,'" the text begins as the train draws closer to the North Pole. Rather than playing with these figures, firmly rooted in the imagination of most children, Van Allsburg opts to depict a crowded street scene that resembles the real world but obviously is not. It is this constant emphasis on the border between fantasy and reality that pervades so much of this author/artist's work. Later in *The Polar Express*, when the young boy loses the silver bell from Santa's sleigh, the picture is used to depict not the event, but the response and reaction to it. The art here works emotionally, embellishing the words and narrative, which convey what happened but not what the experience felt like.

Feelings also infuse the illustrations for *Owl Moon* (Yolen and Schoenherr 1987). When he agreed to do the book, John Schoenherr had never heard of Jane Yolen. But he had snow, woods, and owls around his property, which meant he would not have to leave home to work on the book. The artist knew that the mood of the book would rely on the pictures. He walked in the woods on snowy nights and began to establish his palette. "I had to interpret the color very freely. There was no other way to make the pictures interesting, but the main interest of the story was in the feelings of the little girl, and that feeling of meeting wildness . . . I treasured" (Schoenherr 1992, 178).

David Wiesner is also capable of using art to depict the feeling of an event. How the two brothers react to the storm, and the oscillation from fear to fantasy, are the subject matter of *Hurricane* (Wiesner 1990). As the family gathers in front of the fireplace, Wiesner uses image and text to convey the storm raging outside the sanctuary of the living room. "They had supper by the fireplace that evening. It felt safe with everybody together, even though there were creaks and groans and sometimes great roaring sounds coming from outside. The hurricane was in full force." The triangulated composition of the mother, father, and two brothers in front of the warm light of the fire brings unity and contentment to the scene. As an event, there is little of importance in this picture. It is the mood of the art, rather than its content, however, that really contributes to the meaning of the moment. Later, when the storm has abated and the boys explore the damage, Wiesner significantly reduces the length of his text, presenting three double-page spreads, each with just one sentence. The jungle, ocean, and space sequences do not require words. The artist chooses to show us what the author need not tell us.

This sudden reduction of words is also evident in two Caldecott medal winners. *Where the Wild Things Are* (Sendak 1963), as noted earlier, employs artwork that progressively grows, the frame of the scene expanding from Max's small room to the double-page jungle sequences. Max provides the cues and clues for the expanding art and diminishing text. When he proclaims, "Let the wild rumpus start!" the illustrations expand to occupy three full double-page spreads, and there is no text at all. When Max says, "Now stop!" the size of the illustrations grows gradually smaller, and the book ends on a blank page with no art and the words "and it was still hot." *Arrow to the Sun* (McDermott 1974) also provides a strong example of the balance between words and images. The text is used to tell readers that the boy must undergo the trials represented by the four chambers of ceremony. Once the boy has agreed that he will "endure these trials," the art is used to carry the narrative, and the words disappear for several pages as the illustrations show the boy's encounter with the lions, serpents, bees, and lightning. For any who doubt the ability of pictures to tell a tale without the support of words, perhaps no better example can be found than the front matter for *Anno's Alphabet* (1975). In six charming illustrations, the artist depicts the development of a book, starting with an image of a tree, then a chopped tree, to a block of wood, followed by pictures of the tools the artist uses to cut and carve the wood block, and finally an image of the book itself.

Triangulated composition and lighting create a mood of safety and solidity while the storm rages. (From *Hurricane*, by David Wiesner. Illustrations copyright © 1990 by David Wiesner. Reprinted with permission of Clarion Books, an imprint of Houghton Mifflin.)

Most of the time, the illustrations in picture books affirm or correspond to the text, providing more information or content about what happened to whom and where. These images may also provide context, extending our understanding of the mood or emotional circumstances, so that we better appreciate not just what happened, but also what that experience felt like. It is also possible for text and image to be juxtaposed; to actually present two different points of view of a given story. *The Green Man* (Haley 1979) deliberately employs this technique, with the illustrator using visual cues to contradict one of her characters.

Claude, the squire's son, is arrogant and aloof, disdainful of the peasants and his servants. On a hunting trip, he complains, "Those beaters are incompetent. I haven't seen an animal all day!" If this story is read to children without benefit of the picture that accompanies this text, they will accept Claude's account of events. The picture, however, presents a different interpretation. The haughty young man is so preoccupied with himself that he literally cannot see the forest for the trees. While he complains that his servants have failed to flush out animals for the hunt, illustrator Haley makes it clear that there are animals all around him. Deer, boar, squirrels, rabbits, and raccoons are just some of the creatures to be found peering out from the woods.

An interesting example of the visual contradicting the text. Claude complains that his beaters are lazy and he has seen no animals. Observant young readers, however, can see at least seven animals this arrogant squire is too aloof to notice. (From *The Green Man*, written and illustrated by Gail E. Haley.)

The deliberate design decision to use images to contradict text is not the only reason why pictures occasionally do not correspond to words. Sometimes the illustrator simply makes a mistake. One of the best-known examples of this appears in Ludwig Bemelmans's *Madeline* (1939). Despite the fact that the text clearly tells us that one of the twelve girls is in the hospital, the picture at the dinner table still shows twelve girls. *Jack and the Bean Tree* (Haley 1986) contains another example. Author Haley tells us that Jack and his mother groomed and prepared old Milky White the cow for sale. The words make it clear that "They hung her bell around her neck." When we look at the pictures of Milky White, though, the bell is nowhere in sight. Finally, images sometimes lack authenticity or validity. The decorative borders of *Saint George and the Dragon* (Hodges and Hyman 1984) contain tulips, though in reality these flowers were not present in England during the period in which the story is set. In *The Legend of the Bluebonnet* (dePaola 1988), the illustrator depicts Indians wearing blankets during the summer, which at the very least seems unlikely in Texas heat.

For the most part, however, quality picture books, written and illustrated by leading authors and artists, represent an outstanding union of storytelling through the creative fusion of picture and print. This fusion is not infrequently the result of detailed and exhaustive research, which merits far more than the condescension of "kiddy lit" and often reflects great scholarship. When children ask these writers and artists, as they often do, "Where do the stories come from?" it is important that the process behind the product be made known to them.

## Strategies and Activities

- *Jumanji* (Van Allsburg 1981) and other picture books refer to incidents and events in the texts that are not pictured. Share this example with students and have them locate other examples. Help students begin to develop awareness of what is shown, what is left out, and *why*.

- The concept of front matter has been discussed several times in this book. Haley's *Sea Tale* (1990) and *Birdsong* (1984) use poems as a preface to the text and illustrations, whereas *Puss in Boots* (1992b) uses several pictures before the text begins. Introduce students to the concept of front matter and prologue and have them find examples of other books where words or images set the scene before the story actually begins.

An opening vignette, the first of three images in the front matter that appear before any text. The image introduces Puss and the miller, who is preparing his will. It establishes the time of day and the exterior of the mill with the passing blade. (From *Puss in Boots*, retold and illustrated by Gail E. Haley.)

132  Painting with Words: Writing with Pictures

The second illustration from the front matter uses props like the will and miller's cap, along with the tilt down on the casket and the interior of the mill, to continue a visual narrative that is never addressed in the text. (From *Puss in Boots*, retold and illustrated by Gail E. Haley.)

- *Mirette on the High Wire* (McCully 1992) has been noted as containing several cinematic devices. The off-screen gaze and progressive panels that simulate continuous movement can also be found in *The Fortune Tellers* (Alexander and Hyman 1992). Introduce students to these examples and have them locate other picture-book images that use techniques from film and television.

- This chapter mentioned several books in which the words and text complement (but do not duplicate) each other. These include *Hey, Al* (Yorinks and Egielski 1986) and *Mirandy and Brother Wind* (McKissack and Pinkney 1988). Share these with students and have them find their own examples.

- Pictures are particularly useful in multicultural stories, conveying information about landscape, lodging, and lifestyle. Select a series of books depicting different cultures, and before reading the story have children make notes about the type of life the people in these stories lead. Students must be able to connect their responses to cues and clues in the images.

- Van Allsburg, Wiesner, and others often use illustration not simply to tell us what happened, but to let us know what it felt like. Use examples of pictures that convey mood and feeling with students. Discuss the way that palette, lighting, shadow, and tone affect our response. Have students locate pictures from other books which they think tell us more about *how* something felt than *what* happened. Students must be able to explain their selections.

- *Hurricane* (Wiesner 1990), *Song and Dance Man* (Ackerman and Gammell 1988), and *Owl Moon* (Yolen and Schoenherr 1987) all use words to paint pictures, describing characters and climate. Without using the images in these books, read selected passages to students and have them visualize, and then paint, draw, or otherwise illustrate, images to match the scenes you have described for them. Have students find examples from other books where the words graphically create a scene for readers.

# The Write Stuff

Creating stories for children is an experience fraught with ambivalence. Although the final product is very public, the creative process is intensely personal and private. No two authors or illustrators go about their work, or came to their profession, in exactly the same way. What they have in common, however, is insight, creativity, and the need to share their stories. For Susan Cooper, the stories fulfill an important function. They "teach us how to survive and understand and enjoy the lives we live. To keep the stars going round in our heads" (Cooper 1991, 50). Many of today's leading authors and illustrators of children's books grew up in their own fantasy worlds. Though teachers and librarians admire these people today, they might not have admired them so much if they had taught them. In her autobiography, *Self Portrait* (1981), Trina Schart Hyman says, "I was a terrible student. I couldn't ever concentrate on what I was supposed to be learning about.... [A]ll I wanted to do was to be left alone to read books.... or draw pictures of witches and princesses." For teachers with such daydreamers in their classes, the challenge is to see the value of their imagination and harness it. Maurice Sendak came upon his love of children's literature as a child. At a young age, he said, he felt "that books were holy objects to be caressed, rapturously sniffed and devotedly provided for" (1970). Cynthia Rylant, on the other hand, grew up in rural West Virginia, where books were unknown to her. "I did not read many books. I did not *see* many books. There was no library in our little town. No bookstore.... I read comics by the hundreds. ... All I wanted to do was read *Archie* and play the Beatles" (1992, 158).

Parents and teachers who frequently fret about the negative impact television, comics, and the mass media have on children's willingness to read or desire to write may take heart from Rylant's experience. Exposure to popular culture is not incompatible with a love of either reading or writing, and certainly does not doom a child to enter adulthood as a reluctant writer or reader. Fostering their interest in writing does, however, require patience. It also necessitates understanding that they will pass through phases, and that they can be successfully nurtured through these stages by nonjudgmental teachers who encourage the storyteller in each child.

Gail Haley participates in many Young Author Conferences every year and visits schools across the country as part of author/artist school visits. She is very familiar with the frustration many teachers experience in trying to get children to write. She is also aware that initial and tentative writing should be encouraged as a process, not rejected because of its content. In her initial contact with children, the stories they tell inevitably emulate or mimic her own stories, which the children have dutifully studied in preparation for the visit. This "variation on a theme" approach may lack creativity and originality in terms of plot, but it does give the child a chance to structure a narrative and to develop a protagonist, an antagonist, a dilemma, and, of course, a solution. Another phase that Haley sees, especially among young boys, is the tendency to write stories filled with violence. Given the degree of violence in Saturday morning cartoons, video games, action figures, and movies, all aimed at this young audience, it is hardly surprising that it finds its way into their stories. Although teachers are often dismayed by this, rejecting these young writers' products because of content, this discouragement risks making them retreat within themselves and not pursue the writing process. It also ignores the obvious fact that violence has been a staple ingredient of fairy tales and children's literature for centuries. Exploring the nature of the violence, and discussing its dramatic contribution and its viability as a solution, offers a more constructive way of helping children see a relationship between the themes in literature and mass media. Telling them they cannot inject violence into their stories is likely to turn many of them off. Telling them they cannot use violence gratuitously—that it must be creative, well written, and dramatically feasible—offers a framework and guidelines that encourage them to grow without rejecting a subject matter in which they express natural interest. After working with such students, Haley finds that peer review frequently serves as an effective screening process to guide these young writers.

Another way to stimulate children's interest in writing and reading is to focus on the value of the tale and the willingness to tell or share it. Keeping a journal, jotting notes on index cards, or making entries into a computer diary can act as building blocks for recording the stories of students' own lives. Jane Yolen uses such fragments as inspiration for her own stories. The ideas, she says, come from "the scrap basket of your brain, the sum total of all your experiences . . . the connection made between the was and the could be" (Yolen 1976, 14–15). First, however, children must be encouraged to believe that they live stories everyday and that the world around them is full of characters that might fill the pages of a book. At the 1993 Young Writers Conference, hosted by Eastern Washington University, participants were given a bookmark signed by the guest authors and illustrators. The inscriptions included small encouragements to foster a love of literature. Patricia McKillip told them to "always be in the middle of a book or the middle of a story." Gail Haley said that "anyone who ever was or ever could be, can be met in a book."

The technical skills of writing, such as grammar, syntax, and punctuation, are, of course, important. Nevertheless, care should be taken to ensure that this technical structure does not subvert or inhibit the story it contains. If children are to tell their own stories, they must not only be exposed to quality children's literature, but must also be taught to be observers and recorders of life. For some, this is a matter of artistic insight. Susan Cooper said, "[W]e live in the same world as the rest of you. Its realities are the same. But we perceive them differently. We don't quite see what you see" (Cooper 1991, 44). For Gail Haley, stories sometimes spring from observation and reflection on the world around her. "More than one idea has come to me while sitting in a train depot, airport lounge or dock, watching the world pass by. Good storytellers take time to look, listen and learn. That's one of the real secrets to good writing and it helps turn the mundane into the marvelous" (Haley 1992c, 103). Cynthia Rylant attributes her skills as an author to what she calls "sensitivity." Those who have it, she says, "can see into things more deeply than other people and can write or paint or sing what they saw in a way that moves people profoundly" (Rylant 1992, 158).

Along with this insight, there is also insecurity and uncertainty. Children who stare in fear at the blank pages confronting them might be comforted to know that writer's block does exist, and even successful authors struggle with their own inner fears and uncertainties. For Rylant, it is "the fear that there won't be a next book at all. Or that I'll just keep repeating myself, stuck writing the same kind of book over and over" (1992, 162).

Whatever the source of inspiration, most artists and authors agree that the process itself involves work, which is perhaps the least understood aspect of creating for children. Occasionally, there is a breakthrough, a fluke, a burst of brilliance and creativity that explodes on the scene already perfect in form. Such was the case with *When I Was Young in the Mountains* (Rylant and Goode 1982). This first attempt by the young author was written in bed, in one hour, and mailed, typed but unrevised, to the publishers, who accepted it immediately. Rejection and revision, however, are much more common, and children need to be aware of this. Even a hugely successful book like *The True Story of the Three Little Pigs* (Scieszka and Smith 1989) made the rounds of publishers and was repeatedly rejected before Viking finally accepted it. Marilyn Singer's first attempts at writing for children drew on a character she had invented as an eight-year-old. Although these stories were rejected by the publishers she sent them to, she knew enough to persevere. "I was not discouraged. I had heard that it took a long time to get a book accepted, and I told myself I had to be patient" (Singer 1992, 192). Accounts like these are well documented in the Gale Research *Something About the Author, Autobiography Series,* and they play an important role in helping children understand just what is involved in becoming a successful author or illustrator.

Research plays an increasingly important role in the development of picture books. Once again, because these books are for children and are often dismissed as "kiddy lit," many adults and children alike are unaware of just how much time and effort an author or illustrator may put into making sure that the language and the look of a book are authentic. "The painstaking research that artists undertake to accurately represent the story is often overlooked. Children need to be made aware of this visual information and encouraged to look carefully at what may seem to be an effortless piece of work (Evans 1990, 832). John Steptoe spent a year in Africa researching *Mufaro's Beautiful Daughters: An African Tale* (Steptoe 1987) and another 18 months writing and illustrating the book. Jerry Pinkney developed a detailed dummy for *The Talking Eggs* (San Souci and Pinkney 1989) and explored libraries to find authentic fenceposts specific to Louisiana to lend to the accuracy of this Creole folktale. *Sea Tale* (Haley 1990), *Puss in Boots* (Haley 1992b), and *Dream Peddler* (Haley 1993) all involved intensive research. Haley's mermaid has two tails, a phenomenon she was able to document in period paintings, sculpture, and silverwork. The preparation of the ocean sequences included snorkeling in Hawaii and visits to Australia's Great Barrier Reef. For her seventeenth-century French classic, she explored the world of the Sun King, Louis XIV. She was particularly interested in the ornate art of the period, which was dominated by baroque and rococo styles. *Dream Peddler* required a trip to England and a visit to Swaffham where the story was actually set. In addition to sketching John Chapman's church and his home, she also videotaped the entire trip, including various visits to printing museums throughout the country. The videotape not only provided a record of the research process, but also added invaluable footage for the videotape she made of the development of the art. As a result, the entire history of the book was documented in videotape, so a viewer could see her working on an illustration of the church in one sequence and actually walking through that church in the next scene.

Jane Yolen believes the best research transforms data into information. "It can be the journalist's who-what-when-where-how. But the truly creative researcher is the one who asks not only how did it happen, but *how did it affect other things*" (Yolen 1976, 71). Her notes at the back of *Sky Dogs* (Yolen and Moser 1990) demonstrate how she employs research and embellishes it with artistic license. Haley's *Dream Peddler* (1993) also provides notes that tell of the author's belief that, even though the story is set in the eighteenth century, it has meaning today, as visual means of communication challenge print literacy. For Haley, like Yolen, the emphasis is not just on what the story is about, but on what it means and what implications or value it has. Robert San Souci also used extensive research in preparing *Sukey and the Mermaid* (San Souci and Pinkney 1992), which offers an excellent comparison and contrast to *Sea Tale*. The research notes contained in *Sukey and the Mermaid, Sundiata: Lion King of Mali* (Wisniewski 1992), and an increasing number of other quality picture books can be used to help children understand the process involved in developing one of these stories. As a result, they will not only recognize the work involved in creating a picture book, but some of them will also understand how they might employ such techniques when researching a topic they are interested in.

Part of this process includes the editing, writing, and revision that come once the inspiration or idea for the story has taken root. This process also varies from one author to another. Shirley Hughes conceives ideas while puttering around the house or doing the dishes. She describes writing as "onion-like," noting that "the ideal finished text should be rounded and lucidly simple, but it is the result of many layers of rigorous editing" (Hughes 1991, 18). Jane Yolen labored over and fretted about her text for *Owl Moon* (Yolen and Schoenherr 1987). "Did the text read well aloud; was the relationship between the child and father clear; was I being too arty and poetic?" (Yolen 1989, 200).

In addition to this self-criticism, authors and illustrators are, of course, subject to the scrutiny of critics and reviewers, who at times can seem poisonous. Imagine the reaction, for example, of the authors whose work was condemned in a piece called "Betraying the Young" in *Education*. This critic complained that adolescents are bombarded by "authors who are an embarrassment to cultivated readers. Immediate examples are Judy Blume, S. E. Hinton, Robert Cormier and Paul Zindel, but others come to mind" (Kramer and Moore 1986). The mention of "cultivated readers" immediately suggests elitist standards that reflect adult sensibilities rather than an understanding of how such stories might be appropriate to the nature and needs of young readers. Such decisions "are more a reflection of the judge's own class and age biases and prejudices than a reflection of an understanding of the reading behavior of the young" (Saxby 1991).

Despite the obvious awards and prizes, such competitions inevitably spawn lists of "good" titles, to the detriment of equally fine books that do not win prizes. It is not difficult to find award-winning authors and illustrators who question the validity of these decisions. Jane Yolen noted that award-losing books are "often the better stories" (1976, x). Marcia Brown said that an artist often "receives recognition for work inferior to what he has done previously" (1986, 15). The pain and hurt of losing an award can be very real. Although such moments are usually kept private, Australia's Mem Fox was quite open about the dismay she felt when two of her books, *Possum Magic* (1987) and *Wilfred Gordon McDonald Partridge* (1984) failed to garner the award from the Australian Children's Book Council (1991). In fact, she confessed to having cried for days.

For many creative people, there is something of a parental relationship with their books. In fact, the book itself is a labor of love, a child they carry, often for longer than nine months. They nurture it and refine it as a parent raises a child. *Koala Lou* (Fox 1989) actually went through 43 drafts before it hit the bookstores. Although thick skin might be necessary armor against critics, in reality, like most parents, authors and artists do not enjoy having their children criticized. Teachers whose work involves nurturing young writers should likewise be careful that their criticism is constructive. They should also expose children to a variety of reviews of children's books and help them evaluate the validity of these comments.

Perhaps most importantly, they should help children distinguish between the internal and external rewards of writing. Although winning prizes is enjoyable, awards are not always based on either artistic or literary merit. Sometimes a flashy book that has been heavily promoted by a publisher will beat out a superior book from a smaller press. In the end, children need to value their own writing for what it said and how it said it. If they told their story in a way that was meaningful to them and those they told it to, they have fulfilled the real function of writing, which is to enhance human experience and understanding through communication.

## Planning an Author/Artist Visit: Guidelines by Gail E. Haley

For two decades now, I have been working in schools and libraries throughout the United States, as well as in Canada, England, and Australia. Sometimes I travel alone to a single school, or a whole school district, as part of an author/artist-in-the-school program. Sometimes my visit is the culmination of a long Young Author Program in which I meet the children, their parents, and their teachers, often awarding prizes for outstanding writing. These visits might also see me arrive as part of a group of authors and illustrators, who spend a day or two working with children at the end of their writing projects. Over the years, I have come to develop a set of guidelines that I think are useful in helping plan successful visits. Although these ideas are based on my own experiences, I have had many chances to discuss such visits with other writers and illustrators, and the ideas suggested here reflect their concerns and comments as well as my own.

1. Plan early, especially for a leading author or illustrator. Usually that means approaching the individual anywhere from 6 to 18 months ahead of time. It also helps to have some alternative dates. Keep in mind that April and November are usually very busy months.

2. Have a list of two or three people you would like to invite, rather than relying just on one individual who may already be booked or busy.

Gail Haley is a regular visitor to classrooms around the country.

3. In selecting an author or artist, remember you cannot just rely on the fact that you or your children like the person's books. Does the person like children? Is the person good at working with children? Word-of-mouth can be a good source here, but the best way to make a decision is from direct experience and observation. Many of my invitations, for example, begin by someone writing, "I heard you at Ohio State" or "I saw you in such-and-such." I feel good about that because I know they have a sense of what they're buying.

4. Contacting authors can usually be done through agents or publishers. The publishers can often tell you, when you call or write, if the author you have selected does school visits, and they may even able to tell you the fee. Various publishers have different titles for departments and it may take some time to track down the right place. Generally, if you ask for Children's Marketing or the Author Appearance Coordinator, you should find the right person.

138 Painting with Words: Writing with Pictures

Artist Gail Haley brings her characters to life in quick sketches for the children she visits.

5. The fee will vary quite a lot depending on the individual, the number of days you want their services, and, of course, the distance they travel. The honorarium could be anywhere from $500 to $1,500 or even more per day, plus expenses. Think about airline tickets and the advantages and disadvantages, for example, of a Saturday stayover. Make sure you and the author have a clear, written understanding about travel, meals, and lodging reimbursement and limitations. You do not want any surprises, like receiving a bill for a first-class airline ticket when you didn't expect it. You should also be clear on when payment is due and make sure your local bureaucracy agrees to it. I take the honorarium on the day of the presentation and everything else is reimbursed within a reasonable time frame.

6. Where is the money coming from? Sometimes schools cover costs through funding from local arts or reading councils, whereas others apply for and get small grants. In some cases, my appearances have been funded by Title IV money. I always encourage planners to explore sources of funding. One obvious source is book sales and autograph sessions. Most authors are happy to sign books you sell as part of the visit. If you add a small price increase to the discount publishers provide, this can

go a long way toward covering costs, depending on the size of the school and the socioeconomic composition of the population.

7. Who pays the piper? Sometimes parent groups put up the money for the visit. Though this is generous, it often means that the parents want all children to see the author, even though this may not be the most instructionally effective use of time. The quality of the contact time must be measured against the quantity. This is a delicate issue that can make a big difference in the success of a visit, and it needs to be discussed in the early planning stages.

8. When your author or illustrator has accepted your invitation, make sure your agreement is in writing and you have a clear understanding about what you want and what your guest wants. For example, if your author is coming for a day, will these be four 45-minute sessions? Will your author work with all grade levels? Will your author have lunch with the children, breakfast with the teachers, or present an after-school workshop for parents and teachers? Are you allowed to videotape the sessions? Whatever you have in mind, make sure these ideas are discussed early, so there are no surprises.

9. Will your visitor need audiovisual material? Do you have it? In part, this may depend upon how well you describe the working conditions to the author. For example, will you want all of the program to be in an auditorium or gymnasium? Do you want the author to visit classrooms? Will the presentations to be in the media center? How are the acoustics in these locations? Do you have a lapel or lavaliere microphone that enables the author to move around? If you are in an auditorium, can the children ask questions? Can they be heard? Could questions be submitted ahead of time on index cards? There is a great need to plan for this level of interaction. I work with kindergarten through high school students, often spending time with the older students in their art or journalism classes, but my favorite time is close-up contact with fourth-graders, developing their writing skills and working through peer critiques. Find out the presentation preferences of your author and plan the visit around these.

10. Who's in charge? Often I find that the person who makes the initial contact with me disappears after the agreement has been reached. One of the problems with this is that initial discussions or understandings do not get passed on. A successful visit requires continuity and clarity of communication. Sometimes a centralized coordinator can work for a multiple-site visit. This does cut down on the amount of correspondence. It can, however, result in top-down management, which is resented at the classroom level by teachers who did not feel involved in the decision making. As much as possible, I like to have direct contact with at least one coordinator at each site. This gives me the best opportunity to make sure that teachers have been provided with biographical materials, lesson plans, and so on. The coordinator of your visit should let the author/artist know how the communication will work.

11. Planning for the personality or the process. Meeting "a real live author," as the children put it, can be a thrill, but educationally, the most effective visits are ones where writing and/or illustrating activities are integrated into the curriculum. Literature-based learning, multicultural education, and visual literacy offer diverse areas of the curriculum for writers and illustrators to supplement. If this is going to happen, a curriculum committee or curriculum coordinator should be involved with the planning committee from the start, so that there is a lead-up to, and a follow-up on, the visit; as a result, the children will be involved for much more than a single day. When I send schools support materials, I also ask for a list of the number of students in each session, their ages or grade levels, and what books they have read

and studied in preparing for my visit. Teachers can then ask me to cover certain themes or genres, such as folktales, with their own classes. It can also be very useful for authors to know if they will be working with students with disabilities, gifted and talented students, or various minorities. This gives us a chance to think about what we might do with each group before we leave home and not suddenly have to improvise on the spot.

12. Autographing and book sales. With a popular author or illustrator, this can take up a lot of time, and you do not want it to eat into the instructional time. I usually send schools a list of my current titles in print and refer to books that I tend to stress. Sometimes a school will ask me to design a bookmark or bookplate for them, and I sign these ahead of time. I may also sign in the evening, in my hotel room, or even after the event. Presales work well when parents are involved and have been provided with a list of books and prices. If this is done several weeks ahead of the visit, schools often send me bookplates to be personally autographed for each student who has purchased a book. In my experience, schools typically underestimate sales and the time it takes to sign. Ask your visitors if they will do autographs and what format they want to work with.

13. Creature comforts and killing with kindness. Life on the road can be grueling. I like to be able to relax at the end of the day, which sometimes means turning down dinners and socializing. This is not aloofness; it's just a question of recouping my energy so I can do a good program the next day. Although planners are understandably concerned primarily with the school program, do not ignore the after-school needs of your visitors. Some people like to go out to dinner and socialize with their hosts. Increasingly, I tend to need peace and quiet, so I like to request a quiet room away from the pool, the elevator, and the drink and ice machines. I like a restaurant in the hotel. Some authors like solitude; others cringe at finding themselves in a hotel in the boonies with no mall, shops, or restaurants in sight. If I have time, I like to be escorted to local museums. All of these minor considerations can make an enormous difference as to how comfortable your guests are, which can affect the type of program they present, so do not leave this out of your planning.

Finally, remember that these are suggestions and guidelines. Their application will vary from program to program and person to person, but they should provide a useful framework for thinking about a visit and planning one, once your invitation has been accepted.

# References

Ackerman, Karen, and Stephen Gammell (1988). *Song and Dance Man*. New York: Alfred A. Knopf.

Alexander, Lloyd, and Trina Schart Hyman (1992). *The Fortune Tellers*. New York: Dutton.

Anno, Mitsumasa (1974). *Anno's Alphabet*. New York: Harper & Row.

Bemelmans, Ludwig (1939). *Madeleine*. New York: Simon & Schuster.

Brown, Marcia (1986). *Lotus Seeds: Children, Pictures and Books*. New York: Scribners.

Cooper, Susan (1991). Stars in Our Heads! The Writing of Fantasy. In *On Writing for Children: Nine Papers from the Annual Lecture Series in Children's Literature*, edited by Kerg Mallan. Brisbane, Australia: Queensland University of Technology, 43–51.

dePaola, Tomie (1988). *The Legend of the Bluebonnet*. New York: G. P. Putnam.

Evans, Dilys (1990). Literacy Through Art. *Book Links*, December 15: 832–37.

Fox, Mem (1991). Writers as Human Beings. In *On Writing for Children: Nine Papers from the Annual Lecture Series in Children's Literature*, edited by Kerg Mallan. Brisbane, Australia: Queensland University of Technology, 29–34.

Fox, Mem, and Pamela Lofts (1989). *Koala Lou*. San Diego, CA: Harcourt Brace Jovanovich.

Fox, Mem, and Julie Vivas (1984). *Wilfred Gordon McDonald Partridge*. Sydney, Australia: Omnibus.

——— (1987). *Possum Magic*. Nashville, TN: Abingdon Press.

Fredericks, Anthony (1986). Mental Imagery Activities to Improve Comprehension. *The Reading Teacher*, October: 78–81.

Goldstone, Bette (1989). Visual Interpretation of Children's Books. *The Reading Teacher* 42 (8): 592–95.

Haley, Gail E. (1970). *A Story, A Story*. New York: Atheneum.

——— (1979). *The Green Man*. New York: Scribners.

——— (1984). *Birdsong*. New York: Crown.

——— (1986). *Jack and the Bean Tree*. New York: Crown.

——— (1988). *Jack and the Fire Dragon*. New York: Crown.

——— (1990). *Sea Tale*. New York: Dutton.

——— (1992a). Puppetry as Illustration, Part 1. *The Puppetry Journal* 43 (3): 11–14.

——— (1992b). *Puss in Boots*. New York: Dutton.

——— (1992c). Gail E. Haley. In *Something About the Author, Autobiography Series*. Detroit, MI: Gale Research.

——— (1993). *Dream Peddler*. New York: Dutton.

Hodges, Margaret, and Trina Schart Hyman (1984). *Saint George and the Dragon*. Boston: Little, Brown.

Hughes, Shirley (1991). Word and Image. In *On Writing for Children: Nine Papers from the Annual Lecture Series in Children's Literature*. Brisbane, Australia: Queensland University of Technology, 17–19.

Hyman, Trina Schart (1981). *Self Portrait*. Reading, MA: Addison-Wesley.

Kellogg, Steven (1990). Colleagues and Co-conspirators, *Horn Book*. November-December: 704.

Kramer, Leonie, and Susan Moore (1986). Betraying the Young. *Education* Sydney, Australia. New South Wales Teachers Federation, August: pages not available.

Lorraine, Walter (1977). The Art of the Picture Book. *Wilson Library Bulletin* 52 (2): 145–47.

McCully, Emily Arnold (1992). *Mirette on the High Wire*. New York: Dutton.

McDermott, Gerald (1974). *Arrow to the Sun*. New York: Viking.

McKissack, Patricia, and Jerry Pinkney (1988). *Mirandy and Brother Wind*. New York: Alfred A. Knopf.

Mikolaycak, Charles (1986). The Artist at Work: The Challenge of the Picture Book. *Horn Book,* March/April: 167–73.

Nodelman, Perry (1988). *Words About Pictures: The Narrative Art of Children's Picture Books*. Athens, GA: University of Georgia Press.

Rylant, Cynthia (1992). "Cynthia Rylant." In *Something About the Author, Autobiography Series*. Detroit, MI: Gale Research.

Rylant, Cynthia, and Diane Goode (1982). *When I Was Young in the Mountains*. New York: Dutton.

San Souci, Robert, and Brian Pinkney (1992). *Sukey and the Mermaid*. New York: Four Winds.

San Souci, Robert, and Jerry Pinkney (1989). *The Talking Eggs*. New York: Dial.

Saxby, Maurice (1991). Matters of Judgement. In *On Writing for Children: Nine Papers from the Annual Lecture Series in Children's Literature*, edited by Kerg Mallan. Brisbane, Australia: Queensland University of Technology, 35–42.

Schoenherr, John (1992). John Schoenherr. In *Something About the Author, Autobiography Series*. Detroit, MI: Gale Research.

Scieszka, Jon, and Lane Smith (1989). *The True Story of the Three Little Pigs*. New York: Viking.

Sendak, Maurice (1963). *Where the Wild Things Are*. New York: Harper & Row.

——— (1970). Hans Christian Andersen Medal Acceptance Speech. Bologna, Italy.

——— (1988). Hans Christian Andersen Medal Acceptance Speech. In *Caldecott and Co: Notes on Books and Pictures*. New York: Farrar, Straus & Giroux.

Shulevitz, Uri (1963). *The Moon in My Room*. New York: Harper & Row.

——— (1982). Writing with Pictures. *Horn Book,* February: 17–22.

Singer, Marilyn (1992). Marylin Singer. In *Something About the Author, Autobiography Series*. Detroit, MI: Gale Research.

Steptoe, John (1987). *Mufaro's Beautiful Daughters: An African Tale*. New York: Lothrop, Lee & Shepard.

Tatar, Maria (1992). *Off with Their Heads: Fairy Tales and the Culture of Childhood*. Princeton, NJ: Princeton University Press.

Van Allsburg, Chris (1981). *Jumanji*. Boston: Houghton Mifflin.

——— (1982). Caldecott Medal Acceptance Speech. *Top of the News* 38 (4): 347–50.

——— (1985). *The Polar Express*. Boston: Houghton Mifflin.

——— (1991). *The Wretched Stone*. Boston: Houghton Mifflin.

Vandergrift, Kay, and Jane Anne Hannigan (1993). Reading the Image. *School Library Journal,* January: 20–25.

Wiesner, David (1990). *Hurricane*. New York: Clarion.

Wisniewski, David (1992). *Sundiata: Lion King of Mali*. New York: Clarion.

Wood, Don (1986). The Artist at Work: Where Ideas Come From. *Horn Book,* September/October: 556–65.

Yolen, Jane (1976). *Writing Books for Children*. Boston: The Writer.

——— (1989). On Silent Wings: The Marketing of *Owl Moon*. *The New Advocate* 2 (4): 199–211.

Yolen, Jane, and Barry Moser (1990). *Sky Dogs*. San Diego, CA: Harcourt Brace Jovanovich.

Yolen, Jane, and John Schoenherr (1987). *Owl Moon*. New York: Philomel.

Yorinks, Arthur, and Richard Egielski (1986). *Hey, Al*. New York: Farrar, Straus & Giroux.

## Chapter 8

# Windows on the World: Picture Books as Social Construction and Representation

If we can see the present clearly enough,
we shall ask the right questions about the past.
—John Berger, *Ways of Seeing* (1972)

## Demographics Is Destiny

For most of this book, we have concerned ourselves with analysis of the relationship between image and text in children's picture books. We have explored aesthetic elements and the question of composition and design. We have outlined strategies and activities that teachers and librarians can use when working with these books to foster critical viewing and thinking skills. But those who regularly work with the art of the children's picture book do not isolate their interest or understanding merely to an internal reading of the frame. Recognizing what technique an illustrator has employed, or how page design and layout facilitate the telling of a tale, is not as meaningful an exercise unless that story and the world it constructs and communicates are connected to the world in which our children live. Joel Taxel, the editor of *The New Advocate,* has noticed that some people are reluctant to deal with children's books as more than art or literature. The preeminent concern of critics, he says, "remains with the selection of best books, with best being defined in terms of literary and aesthetic value," and to deny that these books have "anything to do with politics, let alone ideology" (Taxel 1992, 9). Nevertheless, in an era when the classroom and the curriculum have become battlegrounds for various factions and interest groups, each with its own agenda, it is increasingly difficult to divorce children's picture books from their social, political, and cultural context. Questions of aesthetic value and literary worth, for example, do little to foster our understanding of Marcia Brown's controversial Caldecott medal winner, *Shadow* (Brown 1982). Despite her admiration for the illustrator as an artist, Lyn Lacy was critical of the social consequences of such imagery:

> Critics point out that by choosing to illustrate only primitive figures in an untamed environment, she presented denigrating and destructive pictures that foster stereotypic thinking and damage black children's racial image of themselves. *Shadow* is defended by others as but one picture book, depicting one aspect of an enormously broad African experience. This defense might have been acceptable, if it were not for implications from the text supporting the pictures . . . It implies that shadows are spiritual symbols of an ancestral past represented by masks and other powerful objects, evoked by dancers and musicians and other storytellers, and found in fire or

ghostly light or in ash and slithering darkness. Such sophisticated textual images are beyond the comprehensive of most young children, and the book is left to communicate primarily through Brown's visual images alone. These repeatedly use unrelenting darkness in pictures of Africa and its people (Lacy 1986, 138).

Faced by the decision of the Caldecott committee on the one hand, and social critics like Lacy on the other, it can be difficult for teachers and librarians to formulate an appropriate response to a book. In part, that decision is compounded by the attempt of the Caldecott committee to divorce art from social significance, as though such a thing were possible. To a large degree, though, the problem occurs because of overreliance upon lists of quality books and a near-absence of teacher training that addresses children's literature holistically. The lack of such training leads teachers and critics to place undue emphasis on the book as product rather than on the experience of the book as process. Asking whether *Shadow* is a good book or a bad book misses the point. An instructional process that enables children to see the book from many perspectives (literary, artistic, social) fosters a variety of viewpoints rather than forcing a single conclusion based upon a limited context. The *Horn Book* editors clearly articulated this at the time *Shadow* won the Caldecott medal. The mission for librarians and others who have the major responsibility of introducing children to quality literature, they said, was to build bridges and create connections that show children, through stories, the common humanity we all share. "*Shadow* cannot contribute what it could to the one world we all seek, if it is promoted primarily as an artistic and literary statement of American appreciation of things African" (Howard 1983, 622).

The same year that *Shadow* won the Caldecott medal, American schools received a less-than-glowing report card in the form of *A Nation at Risk*, a national study that warned of a rising tide of mediocrity in our schools (National Committee 1983). In the decade that has elapsed since that time, our schools have undergone significant changes toward improvement. Whole-language, literature-based learning, multicultural education, and the broad school reform and restructuring movement all represent a clear understanding that the old ways and "back to basics" will not address the changing nature and needs of today's students. Nowhere was this change more evident than in the portrait of the nation that emerged from the 1990 census. As the last decade of the twentieth century began, one in every four Americans defined themselves as Hispanic or nonwhite. By the end of the decade, based on current trends in immigration and birth rates, the Hispanic population will have increased by 21 percent, the Asian population by 22 percent, and the black population by some 12 percent; the white population is expected to total nearly 115 million. Commenting on these figures, *Time* magazine said we are approaching an age when "the average US resident, as defined by Census statistics, will trace his or her descent to Africa, Asia, the Hispanic world, the Pacific islands, Arabia—almost anywhere but Europe" (Henry 1990, 28). In New York State, more than 40 percent of students are already a minority. Those changes are already manifesting themselves in other states. In North Carolina, the 1990 census indicated that Asian-Americans represented the fastest growing segment of the population. For a state whose largest teacher training institution is located in a largely white, rural environment, this represents a major challenge. Can a university really prepare teachers to respond to the growing diversity of the classroom population if this training is isolated almost exclusively in a white, middle-class environment? Despite attempts to revamp the curriculum, the reality remains that no amount of changes in the content of the curriculum to which student teachers are exposed can serve as a credible alternative to experience that comes only from direct contact with people from other cultures. In fact, the cultural composition of the nation's teaching population is disturbingly unrepresentative of the nation as a whole. In 1992, the National Education Association reported that the number of minority teachers in elementary schools had declined from 18 percent in 1981 to just 12 percent a decade later. Commenting on the statistics, the association said, "[O]ur failure to attract and keep minority teachers threatens to deny minority students role models they need" (Orodovensky 1992, 1).

Direct experience with children of color and the experience of living in other cultures have had a major impact on Gail Haley. Working in a culturally diverse California school system, she has had the opportunity to employ a variety of techniques to get through to all students. One afternoon, while she was setting up her Asian shadow puppets on the overhead projector, she heard an excited group of youngsters whisper, "She's got puppets that look like us." Always aware of the impact of stories on the self-image and self-concept of her young audience, Gail Haley's picture books have repeatedly attempted to forge cultural links by showing how children from different countries and backgrounds often shared the same stories, myths, and legends. This was particularly evident in her Caldecott medal winner, *A Story, A Story* (1970). Haley came across the Ananse stories while living in the Caribbean. She was attracted to the trickster tales and particularly interested in telling a story that would "give black children in this country a chance to know that black is beautiful" (Haley 1992b, 96). Haley has also admitted that the book was a form of catharsis for the guilt she felt "about having been white in a segregated society" (1992b, 95). Not prepared to let the story stand on its own, she developed an introduction for the book that linked the Kwaku Ananse spider stories of Africa to the Anancy stories of the Caribbean islands and the Aunt Nancy tales of the southern United States. Before *Roots* made the search for black heritage fashionable, *A Story, A Story* traced cultural connections through the oral tradition. In winning the Caldecott medal, the book became the first in a number of black stories that would be similarly honored throughout the 1970s and 1980s. Yet the appeal of the story is more diverse than its African origins. The universal nature of the sky journey and the hero's quest is one reason why *A Story, A Story* has been successful in such different countries as Japan, Brazil, and Korea.

Haley's interest in tribal culture and the oral tradition also led to the creation of *Go Away, Stay Away* (1977), which anticipated her own movement into masking, storytelling, and puppetry. In the author notes to the story, which is set in Switzerland, she explores traditional rituals in Asia, Africa, Europe, and the United States in an attempt to demonstrate the common fears and ritual responses that pervade so many different cultures. Even after returning to her native South, after years of living in England, she continued to use her books as a way to build bridges between cultures. Immersing herself in Appalachian traditions, she began to trace the origin of the Jack stories which she documented in the Weston Woods program, *Tradition and Technique: Creating Jack and the Bean Tree* (Haley and Considine 1986). On the cover notes of *Jack and the Bean Tree* (Haley 1986), she linked the mountain tales to their origins in England, Ireland, Scotland, and elsewhere, noting that "all these tales from different lands twine like the bean tree up through the sky, where adventure awaits a hero brave enough to climb there." This message is repeated visually in the very first image of the book, which shows eight multicultural manifestations of Jack surrounding the poppyseed from which the stories spring. As one review noted, this image from the front matter of the book "impels study of national folk heroes, their similarities and differences in character" (*Perspectives* 1986, 4).

The challenge today, for those who work with children, is to use literature like this to build bridges instead of walls. Properly understood and used, these stories can celebrate diversity and difference while recognizing unity and continuity. In an ethnocentric culture, we too often fail to perceive that we are part of a universal process. The changing nature of society is not restricted to American shores or borders. German reunification has forced that nation to struggle to forge a new identity for itself. As is often the case, the growing pains that accompany this process have resulted in the search for a scapegoat, which in that country has meant the rise of neo-Nazis, attacks on foreigners, and, perhaps the most disturbing example, attacks on individuals with disabilities. England, too, has been traumatized by its changing self-image. Historically, culturally, and geographically isolated from the rest of Europe, the island nation that once ruled the seas has had to come to terms with the fact that its future depends on embracing European unity. Australia is also experiencing a major identity change. Until World War II, that country had been solidly tied to the future of the United Kingdom. The decline of the British Empire and the growing American presence in the Pacific forced the country to align itself more solidly with the United States, even to the extent of fighting alongside America in the Vietnam War and drafting young men to do so. Previously a white island in a brown sea, Australia now has a culturally diverse population. Despite the Australian stereotype of *Crocodile Dundee*, most immigrants are Asian, and the government anticipates that 25 percent of the population will be Asian-Australians sometime within the next fifty years. In April 1993, in a broad break from British heritage, Prime Minister Paul Keating established a commission to shape Australia's path to a republic. Keating said the nation was "undergoing a revolutionary change in its consciousness and its situation in the world." In each of these countries, the curriculum in general, and children's books in particular, can be useful teaching tools helping students understand who they are, where they have been, and where they are going.

There is little doubt, that children's books both show and shape the society they serve. Although they may reveal much about the past and the present, their mere existence makes them active agents in shaping the behavior and belief system of the children who encounter them. While they do in part, reflect society, by repeating particular themes, stories, and motifs, they also reinforce that culture. The Council on Interracial Books for Children has said that children's books "carry a message—a moral, a value or set of beliefs . . . and they mold minds" (1976, 1). *The American Journal of Sociology* has also articulated this role, stating that "children's books reflect cultural values and are an instrument for persuading children to accept those values" (Weitzman 1972, 1126). As American society continues to become more multiracial, more multicultural, those of us who work with children must increasingly focus our attention on the validity and value children's books offer young readers as a window on this world.

## Pictures of Pluralism

Almost two decades ago, as America celebrated the bicentennial, research from the field of children's literature indicated that not all children were fairly, accurately, or representatively pictured in the stories created for them. A content analysis of the value system in these books indicated that it was "very white, very contemptuous of females except in traditional roles, and very oriented to the needs of the upper classes" (Council on Interracial Books for Children 1976, 2). Not content to isolate the analysis to an internal reading of these books, the researchers addressed the social consequences of such storytelling. The production, publication, and dissemination of these stories, they suggested, serve to "keep people of color, poor people, women and other dominated groups in their place . . . because it makes children think this is the way that things should be" (p. 2).

In the time that has elapsed since then, there is little doubt that the publishing industry has responded to such criticism. Even a casual observer of children's books could not fail to note that the number of titles reflecting cultural diversity increases each year. In 1991, *Newsweek* said, "[P]ublishers have awakened to the complaints of parents, educators and booksellers" (Jones 1991, 64), though they added that multicultural titles represented only about 10 percent of all books published for children. By the following year, *USA Today* declared that "a new wave of multiculturalism, that politically charged buzzword of racial and ethnic inclusion, has swept the world of children's literature" (Donahue 1992, 1D).

Pictures of Pluralism 149

Multicultural children's literature offers an excellent opportunity to build bridges and stress commonalities among peoples, as shown here by following the character Anansi from the Ashanti culture to his depiction in this Nicaraguan version. (Used by permission of BookStop Literary Agency, Agent for Children's Book Press, from the book *Brother Anansi and the Cattle Ranch* told by James De Sauza, adapted by Harriet Rohmer, illustrated by Stephen Von Mason. Illustration copyright © 1989 by Stephen Von Mason.)

Whereas the 1970s saw a number of very successful titles based on African and Native American stories, the 1980s and 1990s showed much greater diversity. Titles during this time included stories from Persia, such as *Fortune* (Stanley 1990); Cambodia, such as *Silent Lotus* (Lee 1991); China, such as *The Weaving of a Dream* (Heyer 1986); *Lon Po Po*, (Young 1989); *Moon Lady*, (Tan and Schields 1992); and *How the Ox Star Fell from Heaven* (Troy 1991); Laos, such as *Nine-In-One* (Xiong, Spagnoli, and Hom 1989); Japan, such as *The Mandarin Ducks* (Paterson, Dillon, and Dillon 1990); and *Tree of Cranes* (Say 1991); and Nicaragua, such as *Brother Anansi and the Cattle Ranch* (De Sauza, Rohmer, and Von Mason 1989), among other countries. In many cases they were endeavors of the Children's Book Press in California, which specializes in traditional and contemporary stories from minority and new immigrant cultures in the United States. In some cases, these stories included both English and Spanish text, as was the case with *Abuela* (Dorros and Kleven 1991). The period also witnessed an increase in the number of contemporary, urban, or realistic stories about blacks, rather than depending upon folktales, as was so often the case in the 1970s. These books included *Amazing Grace* (Hoffman and Bich 1991), *Red Dancing Shoes* (Patrick and Ransom 1993), *Working Cotton* (Williams and Byard 1992), and the Caldecott Honor Book *Tar Beach* (Ringgold 1991). Reviews of books like these have emphasized the effect they can have on children's self-concept. *Publishers Weekly* called *Joshua's Massai Mask* a story "centering on real children with real feelings," adding that "children may well take pride in recognizing themselves in Rich's bold artwork" (*Publishers Weekly* 1993, 71). The praise was equally strong for *Amazing Grace* (Hoffman and Binch, 1991). *School Library Journal* said it portrayed "a determined talented child and her warm family" and called the story "a positive message of self-affirmation" (1991, 97). Interestingly enough, images of contemporary Native Americans are almost totally missing from the picture, while traditional folktales and celebrations of a previous age continue in *Love Flute* (Goble 1992b); *Thirteen Moons on Turtle's Back* (Bruchac, London, and Locker 1992); *Spotted Eagle and Black Crow* (Bernhard and Bernhard 1993); *Brother Eagle, Sister Sky* (Jeffers and Seattle 1991); and *Dreamcatcher* (Osofsky and Young 1992). Although many of these are wonderful stories featuring excellent art, and some, like the Seattle/Jeffers collaboration and *Keepers of the Earth* (Caduto and Bruchac 1988) have experienced enormous success, selling several hundred thousand copies, publishers, authors, and illustrators continue to create inappropriate images of Native Americans. Despite the popularity, for example, of *Ten Little Rabbits* (Grossman and Long 1991), the book violates a basic principle (Moore and Hirschfelder 1977) by depicting Native Americans as animals.

There are numerous reasons for the changing image of African-Americans in children's literature and the relatively stable representation of Native Americans. These reasons exist at both the production and the consumption ends of the children's book industry. In the case of African-Americans, there are quite clearly more prominent and successful black authors and illustrators than there are Native Americans. As a result, the black experience is more able and likely to be told through African-American eyes. In the dynamics of the marketplace, African-Americans also constitute a larger and more formidable presence in the population, particularly in large cities, where their presence affects major markets in film and television, for example, but also in the publishing industry as is evident in magazines like *Ebony* and *Jet*. For Native Americans, there are few comparable publications (*Native Peoples* is one example). The issue of mass media representation of blacks also has a long history, with roots in the civil rights movement. Major studies of how blacks have been depicted in film (Bogen 1974; Leab 1975) and television (U.S. Commission on Civil Rights 1989) all contributed to a heightened sensitivity to these images and their potential impact on the self-image of blacks as well as on the attitudes of white society. In the 1960s and 1970s, white authors and illustrators like Dayrell and Lent, in *Why the Sun and the Moon Live in the Sky* (1968), and Haley, in *A Story, A Story* (1970), brought African stories to the attention of the majority culture, in the same way that directors began to present film audiences with acceptable black images in movies like *Guess Who's Coming to Dinner* (Kramer 1967).

Although such stories acknowledged the heritage of African-Americans, and though they achieved both commercial and critical success, they did not recognize the contemporary condition of the culture they depicted. Nor was the success of these books representative of the industry as a whole. At the time the civil rights movement achieved its greatest success, with Dr. King's march on Washington and the passage of the Civil Rights Act, blacks were almost invisible in children's books. Of 5,206 books published between 1962 and 1964, only 6.7 percent had African-Americans in the titles or plots (Larrick 1965). "Publishers offered many excuses and rationales: their customers, i.e., white customers were not interested in books about African Americans . . . publishers would offend White Southern sensibilities and consequently lose long-standing customers, and few African-American authors and illustrators created works for children" (Harris 1992, 67). As a result, it was white authors and illustrators who brought black stories and images to the majority culture. Of course some did. Ezra Jack Keats made a major contribution with *A Snowy Day* (Keats 1962), which won the Caldecott medal and was proclaimed as "the first successful representation of the Black child" (Mikkelsen 1982, 117). In reality, however, and from the distance of hindsight, the child that Keats presents to us is more black in color than culture. Writing in *Interracial Books for Children,* Shepard has observed that Peter's "character might just as easily have been white" (1971, 2). At the beginning of her career, Gail Haley recalls publishers asking her to tone down the color of her characters; tan tones and Caucasian features were often requested rather than realistic illustrations of blacks. The image of blacks in the cinema changed as directors such as Spike Lee and John Singleton began to tell their own stories in their own words, through their own eyes. So, too, the image of blacks in children's literature has been transformed because of the contribution of black authors and illustrators like John Steptoe, Ashley Bryan, Patricia McKissack, Brian Pinkney, and numerous others. Though there are more titles available today to introduce children to the black heritage and experience, even in the midst of the multicultural education boom the figures are depressing. As the 1990s began, less than 2 percent, or only 51 titles of the 5,000 children's books published that year, were created by African-Americans (Harris 1992, 68). Given such statistics, it is no wonder that those who do create for children cannot separate their color or their culture from the work, which must consistently articulate their identity. Describing what it is like to be a black writer, Virginia Hamilton said it is "a constant in myself and my work. . . . [I]t is the imaginative use of language and ideas to illuminate a human condition, so that we are reminded again to care who these black people are, where they come from, how they dream, how they hunger, what they want" (1986, 17).

As our society becomes more racially and culturally diverse, those who are charged with the responsibility of raising our children must keep a vigilant eye on the children's book industry, monitoring the society that is modeled in the words and images of their products. There is little doubt that the industry has responded to the multicultural education movement and created an increasing number of titles that show the diversity of American society. The accuracy and authenticity of these representations now finds itself the subject of discussion in both reviews and journal articles. When Gerald McDermott created *Raven: A Trickster Tale of the Pacific Northwest* (1993), *School Library Journal* observed that the "traditional dress, furnishing and house construction are clearly depicted" (1993b, 100). Similarly, a review of *The Fortune Tellers* (Alexander and Hyman 1992) commented on "colors so rich and clear that they invite readers to touch the fabrics and breathe the air. Visual details—carved wooden stools, traditional cloth patterns, signs in French—add an authenticity to the story" (*School Library Journal* 1993a, S4). But whereas one of these books is an authentic tale from another culture, the other merely uses the culture as an exotic backdrop. We must be wary of confusing set decoration with substance, and stories set in a country with stories from that country. At the moment, though there are many signs of progress, those inside the children's book industry are also uncertain of what the signs really mean. Phoebe Yeh of Scholastic, for example, cautioned about mistaking quantity for quality. Merely having more multicultural stories available will bring very little improvement in our understanding of each other if they are not quality stories. Yeh also notes the fact that although there are many titles for young children,

**152 Windows on the World: Picture Books as Social Construction and Representation**

there are considerably fewer titles for the twelve-and-older group. Writing in *The Journal of Youth Services in Libraries,* she asked a question we must all address: "[A]re publishers genuinely trying to respond to a desperate need for books which serve to inform and entertain from a multicultural perspective, or is everyone jumping on the bandwagon?" (Yeh 1993, 157).

A visually stunning picture of Cameroon culture, rich in detail and flavor. But the text nor the story are from Cameroon. Is this multicultural children's literature, or simply set decoration? (From *The Fortune-Tellers* by Lloyd Alexander, illustrated by Trina Schart Hyman. Copyright © 1992 by Trina Schart Hyman, illustrations. Used by permission of Dutton Children's Books, a division of Penguin Books USA Inc.)

# Gender Fair?

In *The Beauty Myth*, Naomi Wolf argues that if women are to free themselves from the cultural controls imposed upon them, "it is not ballots or lobbyists or placards that women will need as much as a new way to see" (1990, 8). Like all issues related to media representation and construction, understanding the depiction of females in children's books involves three stages. The first stage involves recognizing the nature of these representations. The second stage moves from recognizing the message or ideology conveyed to realizing its potential impact on the child-consumer of these messages. The third and most liberating or empowering stage of the process comes when we act responsibly in responding to these images. This might involve supportive or critical letters to authors, illustrators, publishers, and bookstores, for instance. It might include helping others to recognize and realize the effect of these images. And, of course, it includes the decisions we make when we purchase books for ourselves or others.

Along with the civil rights movement, which focused attention on representations of blacks in the mass media, the women's movement addressed the way women were depicted in media. The film industry was scrutinized in *From Reverence to Rape* (Haskell 1973) and *Popcorn Venus* (Rosen 1974). Recently attention has shifted to the small screen, perhaps most noticeably with the publication of *Growing Up in Prime Time: An Analysis of Adolescent Girls on Television* (Steenland 1988). It is within this context, and against this broader background, that the depiction of females in children's books should be considered. In fact, scholarship suggests that, rather than being confined to the electronic or visual media, the representation of women in all media is related to the patriarchal nature of both society and the production process. One study of the recording industry, for example, found the "men have always done and still do most of the writing, directing, producing, reviewing and advertising of what reaches the public" (Reinartz 1975, 295). Evidence suggests that these trends were well established long before the mass media age. Analyzing the tradition of sexism in western art, Brown concluded that "the paintings that depict women as independent individuals can virtually be counted on one's fingers" (1975, 309).

*Sexism* can be defined as discrimination based upon gender and is often reflected in terms of a double standard. Far from being isolated to the pages of children's books, attitudes about gender pervade our entire culture. In September 1992, with the presidential election entering its final phase, *Time* declared that "to a large extent the controversy swirling around Hillary Clinton today reflects a profound ambivalence toward the changing role of women in American society" (Carlsdon 1992, 30). Part of that ambivalence centers on just what role women should play in society. At the Republican convention in August of that year, Marilyn Quayle and other speakers attempted to characterize Hillary Clinton and her views as out of touch with mainstream America. These attacks were simply part of an ongoing debate about the traditional and emerging role of women in this country. The issue, however, is more than a question of what roles or opportunities are open to women. Clearly there has been improvement in that area on both sides of the political spectrum. Beyond the question of what jobs women can or should be able to perform exists the whole issue of how our culture—particularly the male culture—perceives women, and how this affects behavior toward women.

One need do little more than pick up a newspaper or turn on the television to find examples of this. Typically, such stories take the form of reporting on sexual harassment charges. This may be a Minneapolis lawsuit filed by female employees of the Hooters chain of restaurants. Or it may be a major breach of appropriate behavior, such as the Tailhook scandal of 1992, which ultimately led to the resignation of the Secretary of the Navy and forced the armed services to begin training programs to sensitize males to the whole issue of sexual harassment. In 1991, the nomination of Clarence Thomas to the Supreme Court resulted in a sensationalized, nationally televised confirmation process, as Thomas battled allegations of sexual harassment made by law professor Anita Hill. In 1993, Congress once again had to confront the issue of sexual harassment when charges were made against Oregon's Republican Senator, Robert Packwood.

Rather than representing isolated (albeit sensational) cases, the issues embodied in these incidents reflect broad changes in American society as a whole. Social learning theory clearly suggests that our behaviors and attitudes about gender are, to a large degree, learned rather than innate. In part, they are learned by observing those with whom we are in immediate contact. For the child, that usually means observations of mother and father, but it also includes observations of teachers and the way they interact with students. *How Schools Shortchange Girls,* a 1992 study, documented clear bias and differences in the way teachers interact with male and female students (American Association of University Women 1992). Consciously or otherwise, teachers had higher expectations of male students and frequently directed their attention to males rather than females. The report prompted *Creative Classroom* to ask, "[A]re we as teachers adequately aware of our own gender biases and the way they surface in the classroom?" (1993, 57).

As suggested at the beginning of this section, the initial stage in developing gender-fair education requires recognizing the nature of the materials we use when working with children. In fact, a substantial body of research documents the bias inherent in children's literature. In the same year that legislation was introduced banning sex discrimination in public schools, Weitzman documented the pervasive bias in award-winning picture books. The study reported that "women are greatly underrepresented in their titles, central roles and illustrations" (1972, 1125). Four years later, *Sexism in Children's Books: Facts, Figures and Guidelines* argued, "[I]t would be impossible to discuss the image of females in children's books without noting, that, in fact, women are simply invisible" (Writers and Readers Publishing Group 1976, 8). Exploring both Caldecott and Newbery titles, researchers concluded that, despite their awards for literature and illustration, these books "are bound to give the impression that girls are not very important because no one has bothered to write books about them" (Weitzman et al. 1976, 9). The impact of this image-making, said an earlier report, is that our "children learn that boys are more highly valued than girls. And, regarding personality differences, they learn that boys are active and achieving, while girls are passive and emotional" (Weitzman 1972, 1125). Studies throughout this period explored gender representations both quantitatively and qualitatively. They documented the ratio of male characters to female characters and described the nature of these representations. Boys were typically shown engaged in a greater diversity of activities than girls. Male characters were also more likely to be shown outdoors, whereas female characters were typically more likely to be confined indoors. Boys tended to lead, whereas girls tended to follow. Only a few images of males suggested that it was appropriate for men or boys to engage in emotional or nurturing behavior. Years later, the further significance of these findings began to surface in studies of the depiction of mothers (Donovan 1983) and fathers (Stewig 1988) in children's literature. One of the most extensive studies of gender representations in children's books, conducted in the 1970s, actually indicated an increase rather than a decrease in sexist depictions. The report suggested that even when female characters were visually depicted, they were often not referred to in the text (Czaplinski 1976).

Throughout the 1980s, these earlier studies formed the benchmark against which changes in gender depiction were measured. A 1987 study that attempted to replicate Weitzman's work with award-winning books concluded that the Caldecott medal and award winners of the 1980s "represented a shift toward sex equality and provide some changing sex characteristics and roles," though the researchers also cautioned that "they are not enough" (Dougherty and Engel 1987, 398). Teachers and librarians who are interested in this issue could examine more recent titles, such as *Tar Beach* (Ringgold 1991) and *Mirette on the High Wire* (McCully 1992), to see how female characters are depicted today. Rather than restricting themselves to a simple description of the content of picture books, some studies added the significant elements of context and causes. The issue of gender representation cannot be separated from the context in which these depictions occur. This is particularly important in the case of folktales, which often spring from the oral traditions of tribal and patriarchal cultures. To impose a late-twentieth-century

American perspective upon these stories, expecting them to conform to contemporary standards—or worse still, to change the stories to address the concerns of our age—represents nothing less than cultural arrogance and imperialism, not to mention a total disregard for the context in which these traditional tales were created. The Dougherty and Engel study acknowledged this context in the case of what they classified as traditional literature. This, they said, was "a genre reflecting times past, when men did exciting deeds and women were often in the background. This was certainly true in *Saint George and the Dragon* (Hodges and Hyman 1984), which had a ratio of three males to one female." They suggested no such contextual excuse for the fantasy images in *Fables* (Lobel 1980). Here they documented a character count of 49 males to 17 females and an image count of 744 male and 217 female characters. "Male gender was given to the majority of the animal characters even though it usually had no bearing on the circumstances. This, we felt, was unfortunate" (Dougherty and Engel 1987, 397).

Another issue related to context concerns whether researchers focus on the whole picture or merely part of it. Some feminists were critical of *A Story, A Story* (Haley 1970) because its only female character, Mmoatia, was depicted as a bad-tempered fairy. In addition to the fact that she was retelling a traditional tale, the author felt that these critics failed to see the way in which other elements of the book promoted positive images. The depiction of the black deity represented a new image in American children's books. More importantly, however, the image of Ananse broke through stereotypes of the elderly by showing a mentally agile and physically capable character. Given research in this area, this remains an important achievement. Years later, for example, in a study of portraits of old people in children's books, Francelia Butler concluded that "stereotypical old people prevail in all stories, as perhaps they do in life: the silly and the addlepated, the obsessed, the pitiful, the overly genteel, the old notable mainly for their pathetic imitation of the young, the old and corrupt" (Butler 1987, 29). Images of the elderly as wise and thoughtful are, she concludes, in the minority.

One final aspect related to context shifts the focus of attention from the context of the story to the context of consumption. When researchers analyze the internal elements of a story, one must be careful about concluding that what they find is what the child perceives. Just because a book contains certain information does not mean that the information is necessarily communicated. How the child perceives and processes the information is as important as what information exists. Once again, this realization forces us to emphasize process as much as product. It forces us once again to accept a basic tenet of media literacy: that audiences negotiate their own meaning. In the case of the child's encounter with the picture book, clearly, different children will respond to the same book in different ways. This is partly the result of their nature and needs and partly the result of their age or developmental level. Much depends upon whether "one is reading the illustration as a young child would do, or reading the text, or reading the two in combination" (Dougherty and Engel 1987, 395–96).

The last area to consider in analyzing the content of picture books is the element of cause; that is, the forces and factors that contribute to the creation of these images. One of the most interesting studies of this appeared in *Top of the News*. Exploring the unequal treatment of females in children's picture books, Nilsen identified a series of reasons that contributed to the tradition. One factor was the male bias inherent in traditional education, as a result of which "the preference for male characters eventually spread through both trade and text divisions of publishing houses" (Nielsen 1978, 256). Another element was the sexist literary tradition. Looking at McDermott's *Anansi the Spider* (1972), for example, Nielsen wonders why the father is a male with six sons when, in reality, "a father spider is nowhere around when new spiders are hatched, and even if he were, it is highly unlikely that his offspring would be exclusively male" (p. 257). Looking at the sex of the illustrators of children's books, the author found both men and women more likely to draw male characters, largely as a result of their own social conditioning. This trend was more apparent in the male artists, and male artists outnumbered female illustrators. Finally, it was suggested that the sexuality of women's bodies has traditionally caused them to be presented as sex objects, which invariably means limiting the other roles in which they could be represented. Such image-making, of course, contributes cumulatively to the way men see women and the way women see themselves.

Although the content, context, and cause of these images must be understood, the real significance resides in the images' consequences. Irrespective of intent, children's picture books have often been a window on the world, which limited the options available to females. As such, they have been part of a visual environment that has conditioned and contained women's selfimage. "To be born a woman has been to be born, within an allotted and confined space, into the keeping of men" (Berger 1972, 46).

## Starting Safely

Sleeter said that "multicultural education can be defined broadly as any sort of process by which schools work with, rather than against, oppressed groups" (1992, 141). However well-meaning, such a definition employs the language of the left, which often alienates many who in actuality are sympathetic to the concept and concerns of multicultural education. To talk in terms of an oppressed group automatically suggests an oppressor; if some group has been victimized, then someone, or some other group, must be guilty of victimization. In such a context, polarization occurs, even though in many cases those engaged in ageism, sexism, or racism are not even consciously aware of it.

One way to defuse the issue is to place it in the context of information skills. A particular story or illustration may be looked at in terms of fairness, accuracy, balance, or bias. A body of works can be explored in terms of whether the works accurately represent the group depicted. When multicultural education becomes controversial in a school or a community, teachers can serve as agents of change, helping parents and others see the way the concept relates to information skills and to critical thinking. One successful approach focuses on the way local concerns have been addressed in the media. In Milwaukee, for example, community leaders expressed concern about the image of the city presented by the media during the grisly Jeffrey Daumer murder trial. In Los Angeles, many people were concerned about the distorted media coverage of the 1992 riots. In both cases, concern centered on the impact information, presented through pictures, would have on public perception. This concern is at the heart of multicultural education, which looks at the way knowledge about various groups has been filtered and constructed.

Because representations of gays, people of color, and women often provoke heated debate, other, safer avenues might better be used to approach this topic in schools and communities where multicultural education is a volatile issue. Finding a safe issue, for which there is likely to be widespread support, can often be a major catalyst for promoting the concept of multiculturalism. One potentially useful issue is the representation of persons with disabilities. Recent legislation, questions of wheelchair access, special parking facilities, and changes in popular vocabulary (from *handicapped* to *disabled* and *persons with disabilities*) all represent increasing social awareness of and sensitivity to this issue. There is also a growing body of research related to the way such persons are represented in literature (Sapon-Shevin 1982; Rubin and Watson 1987). One study reported that the range of representations included: 1) pitiable and pathetic individuals; 2) objects of violence; 3) laughable objects of humor; and 4) super cripples (Binklen and Bogden 1977). Clearly, this range of representations, which is ingrained in both literature and the mass media, is in no way representative of persons with disabilities.

Exploration of the family, particularly images of mothers and fathers, also seems to be a topic that can generate parental interest and support, and once again there is a growing body of research to draw on which looks at the reflection of these roles in literature (Donovan 1983) and mass media (Considine 1985b; Considine 1985a; Pimentel and Forties 1989). In many cases, these studies move from a description or content analysis to a discussion of the social impact of these images. Noting the paucity of images of fathers in picture books, Stewig argued "in an era when one child in five grows up in a home without a resident male, such books are critical" (1988, 393). In addition to studies of the mass media and picture books, research related to textbooks also suggests distorted representation of blacks (Garcia and Tanner 1985) and Australians (Birchall and Faichney 1985). The pervasiveness of this distortion, whether in picture books, mass media, or textbooks, clearly necessitates an exploration of the way these images affect public perception. If we approach this process by examining a relatively safe or neutral subject, it is highly likely that we will be able to develop a foundation of support for exploring more controversial topics.

## Appalachian Stereotypes: Hillbillies, Coal Miners, and Moonshiners

A great deal of attention in multicultural education focuses on racial representation. Much less time is given to regional representation, which offers a potentially rich and rewarding opportunity to explore the whole issue of stereotyping. In *The Celluloid South*, for example, Edward Campbell suggests that "the survival of the South in the popular imagination owes more to the cinema than any other force" (1981, 191). One region that has been very narrowly defined in literature and the mass media is Appalachia. Films like *Deliverance* (1973), *Coal Miner's Daughter* (1980), and *Winter People* (1989) have filled the public mind with images of coal miners, moonshiners, and frightening families with inbreeding and blood feuds. *L'il Abner*, Daisy Mae, Dog Patch, *The Beverly Hillbillies*, *Smokey and the Bandit,* and *The Dukes of Hazard* create a permanent portrait of Appalachia and the South where borders and separate identities blur into one indistinguishable region. Although series like *The Waltons* have recreated mountain life with great warmth and dignity, the darker images often prevail.

In children's literature, one of the most consistent creators of positive images of Appalachia has been Cynthia Rylant. *When I Was Young in the Mountains* (Rylant and Goode 1982), a Caldecott honor book, affectionately recreated family life in the West Virginia mountains, complete with an outhouse, a baptism, a swimming hole, and evenings spent on a front porch in the company of hound dogs. *Appalachia: The Voices of Sleeping Birds* (Rylant and Moser 1991) is a tour of the region conducted by an author and an illustrator who obviously love the land and the people who live there. "In a certain part of the country, called Appalachia," the book begins, "you will find dogs named Prince or King, living in little towns with names like Coal City and Sally's Backbone." Rylant's words paint tender portraits of these people and their lifestyle, while Barry Moser's illustrations evoke a stoic dignity reminiscent of *Let Us Now Praise Famous Men* (Agee and Evans 1941) and the Depression-era images captured in Farm Security Administration photographs.

Some of the most popular stories from Appalachia are the Jack Tales, which are best known in the form collected by Richard Chase in the early 1940s. Recent research, however, has begun to raise ethical questions about the validity of these tales and, more importantly, the process by which they were collected. Charles Perdue, of the University of Virginia, described Chase as "a self-serving, self-aggrandizing individual exploiting opportunities provided to him by various agencies" (1987, 94). In *Outwitting the Devil*, Perdue raises academic concerns about the impressions created in the folktales as Chase presented them. There are, he suggested, "obvious overtones of regional stereotyping, of class distinction and socioeconomic differences which affect relationships and are expressed in various ways throughout the material" (p. 94). Because Chase not only collected the stories, but interpreted them for a wider audience, which meant changing them, Perdue also raises questions about the ethics of Chase's methods. "There are the problematic ethical questions posed by the appropriation and performance of some aspect of another group or subgroup's culture. . . . Often the group from which the material is obtained finds its cultural identity compromised, stereotyped or otherwise misrepresented" (pp. 94–95). It is also likely, Perdue notes, that the group represented may find its identity and culture validated in the process.

### 158 Windows on the World: Picture Books as Social Construction and Representation

As Writer/Artist in Residence at Appalachian State University, in the mountains of her native North Carolina, Gail Haley became interested in the Jack stories because of the archetypal elements she found in them. Her location also gave her access to distinguished folklorist Cratis Williams and renowned storyteller Ray Hicks, among others. Hicks himself has said that the Jack stories reflect "how it feels to be a poor person, to be up agin it" (De Parle 1992). In two picture books, *Jack and the Bean Tree* (1986) and *Jack and the Fire Dragon* (1988), Haley created authentic images of Appalachian life sandwiched between the fantasy world of dragons and giants. The rural landscape and domestic scenes in the first seven illustrations of *Jack and the Bean Tree*, carefully construct the world of Jack and his maw, and of Poppyseed, Haley's mountain storyteller (modeled after her own grandmother). Careful examination of the pictures of cabin where Jack and his brothers live reveals many artifacts associated with Appalachia, from the familiar quilt to oaksplit baskets and earthenware jugs. Although children may have seen these objects in country stores in suburban malls, such items are part of the traditional folk arts and crafts of Appalachia; the artifacts in these illustrations provide insights into the lifestyle that cannot be found in the text alone.

The half-title page of this Appalachian story depicts the universal roots of Everyman Jack, and the hero myth evident in many cultures. (From *Jack and the Bean Tree*, retold and illustrated by Gail E. Haley.)

Fascinated with the culture, but frustrated by the limitations of the 32-page picture book, Haley created a collection of her own retellings of the Jack stories. In *Mountain Jack Tales* (1992a), she again used Poppyseed as her tale teller, but with the freedom of a larger book, she was able to flesh out the world of these stories by providing a glossary, an introduction, and notes about the stories and art. There is a bittersweet sense of the passing of an era in the introduction when she notes, "it's hard to see a cabin or house from the road that doesn't have a TV antenna or satellite dish." As technology and tourism make inroads into the mountains, Haley hopes the oral tradition will not be lost. She also argues eloquently for the preservation of these stories from another era. "The stories need retelling and translating for today's children.... I would love to bring them all back to this land before things disappear. I would like to let them feel what it was like to grow up observing the world from this place of wonder, where each day is young." In the glossary, Haley has a gentle reminder for city folk and sophisticates who have a tendency to look down on people who speak differently. Rough speech, she suggests, should not be taken as an indication of an individual's worth or intelligence. "Mountain speech is old speech. It derives not from ignorance, but from isolation." In fact, she suggests, with some good authority, much of mountain talk that exists today does so as a vestige of its roots in other lands hundreds of years ago. Though there is always a danger of idealizing Appalachia, which has for much of its existence struggled with poverty, those who romanticize and overcompensate might well be excused in light of the negative stereotypes that have gone before and that still persist in the American consciousness. Exposure to some of these recent books is one small step toward eradicating these impressions.

## *Animal Stereotypes, or Who's Afraid of the Big Bad Wolf?*

One of the most persistent and erroneous representations in myth, media, and children's literature is the depiction of members of the animal kingdom, in particular the snake, the bear, and the wolf. This includes the well-meaning and excessively cute anthropomorphism so evident in Walt Disney's approach to animals, as well as the vilification and victimization of animals in wildly exaggerated and often unsubstantiated stories that have fueled the popular imagination and helped drive some species to the brink of extinction. Exploring stereotypes of animals offers teachers, librarians, and children a relatively safe and neutral ground where they can begin to come to terms with the whole concept of misrepresentation. This, of course, builds obvious bridges to multicultural education.

A fairly simple way to begin this process is to ask children what they know about snakes. Invariably the students will create a picture of a slithering, scary, and deadly poisonous creature. The role of the serpent in the Bible clearly fostered this image in Christian cultures, where it has spread through folklore and fairy tale. In reality, however, many snakes are not poisonous, and they actually contribute much to the ecosystem. If children are given the opportunity to compare the myths with realities, and so long as they are protected by clearly understanding which snakes are safe and which ones are poisonous, they begin to be able to critically examine myth and cultural representations.

Of all the characters in children's literature, the bear and the wolf are probably the most useful to explore, to facilitate this process. In *Wolves and Men*, the author argues that "all wolves in literature are the creations of adult minds, that is, of adult fears, adult fantasies, adult allergies and adult perversions" (Lopez 1978, 250–51). Arthur (1986) and Greenleaf (1992) provide useful examples and evidence of the way wolves have been characterized in children's literature. Again, teachers who want to explore these stereotypes might start by simply asking children to describe the characteristics of wolves, or to name familiar stories in which wolves appear. Obviously, *Little Red Riding Hood* and other favorites will show up fairly consistently. The negative image of the wolf can also be found in tales from other cultures, such as the Chinese *Lon Po Po* (Young 1989). These images can be offset by reference books and encyclopedias and by children's books like *The True Story of the Three Little Pigs* (Scieszka and Smith 1989). *The Call of the Wolves* (Murphy and Weatherby 1989) is a beautifully illustrated children's book that takes young readers into the life of a wolf pack, with words and images that are moving and accurate. The book closes with a two-page discussion of the wolf—past, present, and future—and another page of reference materials for further study of these animals. Studied with excerpts from the movie *Never Cry Wolf* (1983), this book would be an excellent way of helping children compare and contrast the misrepresentation of the wolf in books and media.

Another animal traditionally maligned in the popular imagination is the bear. Goldilocks, Pooh, Paddington, Yogi, Teddy, and Smokey are just a handful of the characters through whom children are first introduced to the bear. In *The Sacred Paw: The Bear in Nature, Myth and Literature*, Shepard and Sanders provide a fascinating cross-cultural insight into the symbolic significance the bear has assumed and been assigned in various societies throughout history. "Around the world, furry creatures in both folktales, legends and myths, being both human and bear, remind us how alike are their ways and ours—and how fascinating are the difference" (1985, 1). The interest in this subject is also found in journals dedicated to the study of children's literature (Newman 1987). The presence of the bear in the mythology, religion, and literature of so many different peoples reflects one of the real but often misunderstood benefits of multicultural education, which explores commonality and continuity rather than just division and difference. Properly approached, multicultural education should not be a cause for controversy or acrimony. It is a process consistent with the critical thinking skills movement. It provides students with the skills to evaluate and analyze information, in both print and pictorial form, in terms of its content, its context, its cause, and its consequences. As such, it prepares them to be literate in the diverse information modes of the society in which they live, and to understand that information in terms of how it is both created and consumed.

## "Isms" and Attitudes That Diminish Us All: Strategies and Frameworks

To a large degree, successful multicultural education requires us to temporarily suspend learned and inherited behaviors, attitudes, and belief systems. Because our ideas, impressions, and values grow out of the way we see the world, and the way that world has been presented to us, relinquishing them requires a new way of seeing and a different perspective. Analytical frameworks provide us with new lenses for looking at our world. They draw our attention to details that we have never seen close up before, and they provide a wide view of the whole picture, which we seldom focus on.

In our own classrooms, these frameworks enable us to think about the materials we use: children's books, textbooks, trade books, and other print and audiovisual resources. In the past, published materials were not expected or required to give proper care and attention to motifs and lifestyles of groups other than those of the so-called "majority culture." Although publishers are now much more aware of and sensitive to the issues of cultural representation and minority presence, this sensitivity will be more secure and more consistent when teachers, administrators, parents, and librarians consistently evaluate educational materials from a multicultural perspective. The following list of visual biases, many of which are still found in materials present in our schools, suggests the kinds of questions that teachers and older students can ask themselves when examining these resources.

- *Ageism*: Is a distorted picture given by showing older people as silly, helpless, frail, mean, or useless?

- *Caricature*: Are the features of a person, animal, or thing ludicrously exaggerated?

- *Chauvinism*: Is a belligerent demonstration shown of someone's zealous devotion to a cause?

- *Classism*: Is subordination, lack of dignity, and loss of respect shown for someone because of social and/or economic status?

- *Cultural racism*: Is one race's culture pictured to the exclusion of cultures of other races?

- *Elitism*: Are persons portrayed as subordinate because of social position, economic class, or lifestyle?

- *Ethnocentrism*: Is the portrayal of events from one ethnic origin only?

- *Eurocentrism*: Is the portrayal of events exclusively from the perspective of those who came to the Americas from Europe?

- *Handicapsim*: Are persons shown as subordinate because of their mental or physical disabilities?

- *Patriarchy*: Is a male pictured as more important than or favored over a female, as in division of labor in the family, in educational and employment opportunities, and other spheres of life?

- *Prejudice*: Is a visual portrayal of an attitude, opinion, or feeling based on misinformation or ignorance about a person, group, gender, or object?

- *Propaganda*: Is a slanted portrayal of information shown for purpose of helping or harming a person or group?

- *Racism*: Is prejudice supported by institutional power which is used to the advantage of one race and the disadvantage of other races? (Note: The term *reverse racism* is a misnomer, because people of color are not considered as having institutional power (Home 1988, 16).

- *Religious defamation*: Is a malicious or false image shown that injures the good reputation of another's religion?

- *Scapegoatism*: Is an image of someone or something shown with blame or failure assigned to it?

- *Sexism*: Is a limitation of roles or options shown because of the character's gender?

- *Stereotype*: Is an oversimplified image shown, usually with derogatory implications for all members of a group?

- *Tokenism*: Is a very limited number of one type of person shown?

## 162 Windows on the World: Picture Books as Social Construction and Representation

Perpetuation of these kinds of overt or covert biases against groups through the print media is something that teachers have to contend with daily, and many school districts have begun to react to these biases by establishing multicultural, gender-fair, disability-aware, and age-welcoming (MCGFDAAW) guidelines for the adoption of materials. Educators in these districts have made an impact on what publishers present for use with children, because these educators are continually educating themselves concerning biases found in all children's material—not just books, but also activity cards, games, advertisements, and toys. They look more closely at any commercial materials they duplicate for children's use and are especially diligent not to unwittingly perpetuate biases in their own activities with children.

## **PWADs and PWANDs: Who Were the "Different" People?**

A most difficult challenge in American multicultural education has been for Euro-American teachers and administrators to break out of the "we" and "them" curricular attitude in the classroom, as characterized by the institutionalized setting apart of certain days, weeks, or months in which "we" celebrated "their" unique contributions, heroes, and/or traditions. In non-MCGFDAAW curriculums, "we" have been the *people who are not different* (PWANDs). Curriculum materials have historically perpetuated a composite picture of PWANDs as English-speaking, young, able-bodied, middle-class, well-adjusted males of Western European descent, of average intelligence, and from nuclear Christian families.

In the past, persons who deviated from one or more of these descriptors have been viewed as "them," *the people who are different* (PWADs): female, non-European, elderly, physically or physically challenged. If PWADs' deviations were not blatantly un-American or dramatically antisocial in nature, but resulted in some accomplishment PWANDs respected, PWADs were celebrated in the schools, their biographies read, their festivals reenacted, their accomplishments recounted on bulletin boards, often during a designated day, week, or month. Although this approach may demonstrate good intentions on the part of educators, such superficial and patronizing treatment is acutely lacking in sensitivity. This attitude implicitly places PWADs—who are often present in the classroom itself—as separate and still further from the apparently desirable mainstream and sets the stage for unwarranted and biased comparisons with PWANDs.

Discerning teachers and students are ever-watchful for continuing evidence of overt or covert biases against so-called PWADs when compared to PWANDs in print and visual materials. The following kinds of biases are subtler than the "isms" outlined earlier and are, in many cases, even more damaging in their ability to limit aspirations and produce negative self-images for those who are here, for purposes of brevity, still called PWADs.

- Are positions of importance, leadership, decision-making, and centrality shown for PWANDs; are menial, supporting, and subordinate positions shown for PWADs?

- Are PWANDs active, strong, brave, adventuresome, independent; are PWADs passive, weak, uninvolved, fearful, helpless, victimized?

- Are problems posed by PWADs in need of help; is problem-solving by the PWANDs on behalf of PWADs?

- Is solution of the PWADs' problem to become more like PWANDs? (This suits the latter's point of view and societal mores, but may not necessarily suit those of the PWADs.)

- Are PWANDs insiders, sociable, gregarious; are PWADs outsiders, loners, shy?

- Are derogatory comments or body language by PWANDs acceptable about PWADs in the beginning; do harmony and understanding between PWANDs and PWADs appear only at the end after the PWANDs have solved the problem?

- Are PWANDs unemotional, rational, linear-thinking, good strategists; are PWADs passionate, creative, flighty?

- Are PWADs pictured like PWANDs but perhaps just a different color?

- Are clothes and homes of PWADs pictured as inferior to those of PWANDs?

- Are conditions of unemployment, poverty, and/or limited resources implied or consistently cited for PWADs?

- Do PWADs have a communication problem; are PWANDs their interpreters?

- Is significance found in the uniqueness of PWADs, rather than in any basic similarities they may have with PWANDs?

- Are both PWADs' and PWANDs' group pride demonstrated rather than any sense of group humility?

- Does social history have a one-sided PWAND perspective, with a condescending tone about PWADs' "simpler" lifestyles and standards of success defined by PWANDs?

- Is little or no broad historical and/or social context given as background if PWADs have poor relationships with PWANDs?

- Are tension and conflict between PWANDs and PWADs resolved simplistically, heavy-handedly, magically, and/or tidily close-endedly rather than realistically, frankly, objectively, and open-endedly?

- Has material been created by PWANDs with no input from PWADs; are interests of PWANDs shown with no input from PWADs; are interests of PWANDs served over interests of PWADs?

- Are values of author/illustrator conveyed, with no attempt made to encourage students to think for themselves about PWADs and PWANDs?

- Is little or no motivation presented for students to examine their own attitudes, beliefs, and responsibilities about PWADs and PWANDs?

## Outsiders Looking In

One of the most delicate questions concerning representation of minority cultures in children's books is not only that of how they are represented, but also of who represents them. For the most part, many of these stories are told by cultural outsiders. Should this automatically render these books invalid or inauthentic? (Bishop 1992). Some purists argue that stories should be told only by those who "own" the story through membership in the culture. In that case, as Jane Yolen has acknowledged, "I would only be able to write books about Jewish girls growing up in New York" (Donahue 1992, 2D). In an astute article for *School Library Journal*, author Ann Cameron asked, "[W]hat entitles any writer to draw the portrait of a culture or culture? What qualifies a reader to judge that portrait?" The answer she suggested, in both cases, is the same: "knowledge, imagination and sympathy" (1992, 36). Although it is highly likely that the cultural insider will be more familiar with the nuances of the story and the role it plays in the traditions of society, it is also likely that the outsider will recognize ways of making it meaningful to a wider group—without, of course, diluting, cing the story. If the book has been thoroughly researched, and if the outsider presents the story with dignity and respect for the other culture, both mainstream and minority readers should benefit. In fact, if the story interests well-known authors or illustrators, their prominence and professional reputations are much more likely to focus attention on the story than if it were written or illustrated by a relatively unknown individual who happened to be a member of the minority culture.

Native American folktales through the eyes of a cultural outsider. Taboo, or a question of respect, accuracy and authenticity? (From *The Legend of the Indian Paintbrush*, by Tomie dePaola. Illustration copyright © 1988 by Tomie dePaola. Reprinted with permission of G. P. Putnam's Sons.)

Evaluating these books is often difficult, especially if they have won awards. In the case of the Caldecott medal, however, it is important to keep in mind that this is an award for art, not social or historical accuracy. *Ashanti to Zulu* (Musgrove, Dillon, and Dillon 1976), for example, won the medal, but its representation of African tribes and traditions has been faulted. "Many of the customs and practices identified with a particular tribe are widespread. Tribes are not generally identified with the customs and practices characteristic of their way of life. . . . They ignore the pastoral, nomadic and warrior traditions of the Massai" (Bader 1986, 282–84). In finding fault with the representation of other cultures in children's books, we must be careful not to throw the baby out with the bathwater, thereby discouraging authors and illustrators from telling such stories. Some weight must be assigned to the inaccuracy in terms of its contribution to the story as a whole and to the way the child reader would comprehend the culture. An inaccurate design on a piece of cloth or an artifact, for example, would seem to be a relatively minor flaw. On the other hand, if an attitude, an action, or an artifact plays a central role in the story, but is misplaced in the culture, this is a considerably greater infringement and infraction.

In assessing these books, it is always useful to see how the represented group responds to the story. John Akar, who served as ambassador to the United States from Sierra Leone, narrated the Weston Woods version of *A Story, A Story* (Haley 1970). In the cover notes for the program, Akar lauded the authenticity of the retelling and the contribution it made to multicultural education: "Gail Haley has retold and illustrated this ancient tale with sensitivity and with a keen awareness of African culture and oral tradition. She admirably captures the flavor of the place and the spirit of art and language. This rendition will help American and European children, black and white, become aware of the richness of the African heritage." Validation like this, provided by cultural insiders, clearly provides a meaningful context in which to assess a book.

The question of ownership is a significant one, and the dangers of exploitation and cultural imperialism should not be trivialized. Nor, however, should these concerns prevent the stories and cultures of other groups from finding wider acceptance. To argue that the stories of a group should be told only by members of the group would automatically eliminate many Caldecott titles, including *Once a Mouse* (Brown 1962), *A Story, A Story* (Haley 1970), *Arrow to the Sun* (McDermott 1973), *The Story of Jumping Mouse* (Steptoe 1984), and others. The same process applied in other media would have prevented Paul Simon from recording the hugely successful *Graceland* album and Steven Spielberg from making *The Color Purple* (1985).

The following procedures will help teachers and students evaluate representations of other cultures in children's books.

- Examine the credentials (sometimes offered in the introduction or on a book's jacket) of authors and illustrators who have created works about a group of people. If none are available, write to request such credentials from the publisher. If the authors/illustrators are not members of the group represented, is there anything in their backgrounds that specifically recommends them as creators of this material?

- Even after such scrutiny, personally apply any or all of the various study questions about biases that were previously listed in this chapter. Credentials on a book's jacket may sound very good for an author or illustrator, but some of the work still may not meet the criteria discussed here. Educators need to continue to educate themselves about what to look for by reading the professional literature and by communicating with members of groups and with publishers.

- Determine what sources were used for both text and illustrations (sometimes offered in author's or illustrator's notes). Examine these sources firsthand, if possible. If no sources are cited, request them from the publisher.

- Examine pictures for such things as the illustrator's point of view, inclusion or exclusion of background details, and ratios of certain kinds of compositions (like the number of urban settings compared to rural or male subjects compared to female).

- Scrutinize the text for words that are slanted in favor of one group, have insulting overtones, or are otherwise loaded, patronizing, ridiculing, inflammatory, insensitive, or derogatory.

- Write to publishers with a specific reason why you find a title offensive or commendable in its treatment of groups of people.

## A Rich Resource: Selected Caldecott Award Winners and Honor Books

For more than 50 years, the Caldecott medal has been awarded by the American Library Association to the illustrator(s) of the "most distinguished American picture book for children" of the previous year. Almost half of the Medal-winning illustrators created pictures for stories from parts of the world other than North America (China, Mexico, India, Africa, Great Britain, France, Eastern Europe, Japan). All but a handful of these books are folklore. Many of the Caldecott Honor Books chosen each year are also worthy of attention for multicultural education, such as Tomie dePaola's beloved *Strega Nona* (1975), the only known title about Italy in the entire collection. In fact, it is in the Honor Book list that we find two titles that make an especially excellent general introduction to multicultural studies: Natalia Belting's *Sun Is a Golden Earring* (Belting and Bryson 1962), and Byrd Baylor's *Way to Start a Day* (Baylor and Parnall 1978). Both include a variety of ethnic traditions, folk wisdom, and appropriate cultural illustrations for poetic thoughts about earth and sky.

When we look at Caldecotts with settings in the United States, the only folklore found is in half a dozen Award winners and Honor Books with Native North American stories. Eleven other Award winners and twenty more Honor Books are about twentieth century American children as main characters, in either realistic or fantasy fiction. But not all of America's children are represented. Of the Award winners, only three have characters who are non Euro-American: the now-classic *A Snowy Day* (1962), by Ezra Jack Keats and Leo Politi's *Song of the Swallows* (1949), which are important to note because they are 30 and 40 years old; and *Grandfather's Journey* (1993), by Allen Say. Of the 20 Honor Books about twentieth-century U.S. children, the overwhelming majority are about Euro-Americans; a handful are culturally specific about African-Americans; a couple portray Hispanic-Americans; a couple portray Native Americans (but are questionable as to their cultural-specificity) and none give glimpses of Asian-Americans. As a result, the Caldecott collection is perhaps as good a place as any to begin a discussion with students about what groups have historically been portrayed in American picture books, what groups have tended to be left out, and what role is played by award committees themselves in reflecting and influencing our society. The activities suggested throughout this section promote higher order thinking skills and can certainly be used with students beyond the elementary school.

*Children* are defined by the Caldecott Committee as "persons of ages up to and including fourteen." Picture books "for this entire age range are to be considered" for the award. Therefore, if students in intermediate grades or middle schools are using these books, the following activities may likewise be appropriate for them when modified to adjust for their levels of interest and sophistication. Some activities may also be adaptable for high school foreign language classes in which multicultural literacy is the goal.

This selection does not include all possible Honor Books (apologies are made for any favorites left out); many of the old ones are no longer in print and are nearly impossible to find. The dates listed here are publication years, not the years that the books won their Medals. All cited books are also included in this chapter's reference list, to facilitate bibliographic searches.

## *Caldecott "Who, What, Why, and How" Stories from Africa*

- Leo Dillon and Diane Dillon's illustrations for Verna Aardema's *Why Mosquitoes Buzz in People's Ears* (1975) show how exaggerated misunderstandings lead jungle animals into tragedy and trouble through a chain reaction of unfortunate events.

- The same artists' portraits for Margaret Musgrove's ABC text in *Ashanti to Zulu: African Traditions* (1976) depict lifestyles of 26 tribes, including a man, a woman, a child, their living quarters, an artifact, and a local animal.

- Gail E. Haley's *A Story, A Story* (1970) shows how Ananse the spider man captures a leopard, hornets, and a fairy as payment to the Sky God in order to bring his box of stories to the people of the world.

- Marcia Brown's *Shadow* (1982) illustrates a mystical shadow from African traditions as mute, blind, and magical, to accompany a poem by Blaise Cendrars.

### Cultural Strategies and Activities

- Study other "how and why" stories, like Award winner *Arrow to the Sun* (McDermott 1974) and Honor Books *Feather Mountain* (Olds 1951) and *Why the Sun and the Moon Live in the Sky* (Dayrell and Lent 1968). Write and illustrate original ones.

- As Brown stated in her Caldecott acceptance speech, no one book can give the whole picture of the continent that is Africa. Compare what is learned from these books to what can be learned about African countries in reference books, other books of folklore, and poetry. Discuss what has been included in the Award winners and what has been omitted.

- Contrast African cities, villages, and countryside as shown.

- Discuss who the heroes are in these stories and who or what is revered or feared.

- Study African batik as background for *Mosquitoes* (Aardema 1975) and floral designs for *A Story, A Story* (Haley 1970).

- Compare Ananse in *A Story, A Story* (Haley 1970) to Honor Book *Anansi the Spider* (McDermott 1972).

- Research the professional literature for criticisms of racial stereotyping (Africans as only a primitive people) in *Shadow* (Brown 1982).

- Notable Honor Books about Africa: *Why the Sun and the Moon Live in the Sky* (Dayrell and Lent 1968), *Mufaro's Beautiful Daughters: An African Tale* (Steptoe 1987), *Village of Round and Square Houses* (Grifalconi 1986), *Moja Means One* (Feelings and Feelings 1971), *Jambo Means Hello* (Feelings and Feelings 1974), and *Anansi the Spider* (McDermott 1972).

## Caldecotts About Long-Ago China

- Ed Young's *Lon Po Po: A Red-Riding Hood Story from China* (1989), is about three sisters home alone who are threatened by a hungry wolf disguised as their grandmother.

- Thomas Handforth's *Mei Li* (1938) is the story of a young country girl's adventures during the New Year's Fair inside a walled city in Northern China.

### Cultural Strategies and Activities

- Contrast Young's illustrative style in *Lon Po Po* (Young 1989) in which he combined Chinese panel art with a contemporary palette of watercolors and pastels, to the different style, using an authentic Chinese papercut technique, he demonstrated in his illustrations for Honor Book *Emperor and the Kite* (Yolen and Young 1967).

- *Lon Po Po* (Young 1989) is translated from a collection of Chinese folktales. Discuss how this "Granny Wolf" is similar to and different from the European tale told in Honor Book *Little Red Riding Hood* (Hyman 1983).

- Study stereotypes of wolves as villains in literature; write stories in which a "Granny Wolf" could be the hero instead.

- Contrast rural versus urban settings in these two books.

- Both author/illustrators Young and Handforth lived for a time in China. Gather books about China and guide students in looking for influences on both books.

- Bring in chopsticks for students to experiment with; have them eat popcorn, which is easier to eat than rice.

- Discuss ancient Chinese attitudes about females that result in sexism in *Mei Li* (Handforth 1938).

- Notable Honor Books about China: *You Can Write Chinese* (Wiese 1945), *Good Luck Horse* (Wiese 1943), *Fish in the Air* (Wiese 1948), and *Emperor and the Kite* (Yolen and Young 1967).

## Caldecott Folklore from Eastern Europe

- Nicholas Sidjakov's illustrations for Ruth Robbins's *Baboushka and the Three Kings* (1960) portray a Russian legend of the peasant woman Baboushka, who visits children each year at Christmas time as she searches for the Christ child.

- Uri Shulevitz's illustrations for Arthur Ransome's retelling of *The Fool of the World and the Flying Ship* (1968) show impossible tasks set by a Russian feudal czar for a boy who succeeds only through the help of magical friends.

- Nonny Hogrogian's *One Fine Day* (1971) is an Armenian folktale about an old woman who cuts off a thieving fox's tail, and the events that occur as the fox obtains milk to replace what he has taken.

# A Rich Resource: Selected Caldecott Award Winners and Honor Books

## Cultural Strategies and Activities

- Study recurring literary themes around the world of generous holiday gift-givers, magical friends, and flying ships.

- Study eastern European peasant life long ago as pictured in these folktales; discuss the old use of the word *fool* here as describing a simple, gentle person who does no one any harm.

- Discuss portrayals of ancient classist societies; gather reference books about eastern Europe and study changes since 1919 (particularly in 1991 for the political boundaries of the Commonwealth of Independent States).

- Research Russian folk art and pictures from the Middle Ages as inspiration for Shulevitz's illustrations in *Fool of the World* (Ransome 1968).

- Notable Honor Books about Eastern Europe: *Contest* (Hogrogian 1976), *Golem* (McDermott 1976), *Hershel and the Hanukkah Goblins* (Kimmel and Hyman 1989), *Treasure* (Shulevitz 1979), *My Mother Is the Most Beautiful Woman in the World* (Reyher 1945), and *Stone Soup* (Brown 1947).

## Heroes and Heroines in Caldecotts About France

- Marcia Brown illustrated and translated Charles Perrault's *Cinderella* (1954), the classic fairy tale of a mistreated girl whose fairy godmother helps her go to the royal ball.

- Ludwig Bemelmans's *Madeline's Rescue* (1953) is about Genevieve the dog, who rescues Madeline from the Seine and is taken to live at Madame Clavel's boarding school.

- Alice Provensen and Martin Provensen's *The Glorious Flight: Across the Channel with Louis Bleriot* (1983) is a biography of the Frenchman who built a series of flying machines until he perfected an airplane he could fly across the English Channel.

- Emily Arnold McCully's *Mirette on the High Wire* (1992) is about a girl in nineteenth-century Paris who learns tightrope walking from a celebrated performer who has quit because he is afraid.

## Cultural Strategies and Activities

- Find ways in which western European fairy tales like *Cinderella* (Perrault 1954) are often different from other cultures' folktales, legends, and fables.

- Read other titles about Madeline in different places around the world, including Honor Book *Madeline* (Bemelmans 1939).

- Compare Perrault's *Cinderella* (1954) to variants around the world, including an African version in Honor Book *Mufaro's Beautiful Daughters: An African Tale* (Steptoe 1987).

- Make a timeline of historic events in aviation, noting that Bleriot's flight was of equal importance to those of the American Wright brothers and Lindbergh.

- Using a map and photographs of Paris, trace the plot in *Madeline's Rescue* (Bemelmans 1953) to find real buildings and places shown.

- Research the great French tightrope walker Blondin, whose stunts high over Niagara Falls in 1859 and 1860 provided the inspiration for *Mirette on the High Wire* (McCully 1992).

- Notable Caldecott Honor Books about France: *Madeline, Anatole* (Titus 1956), *Anatole and the Cat* (Titus 1957), *Pierre Pigeon* (Kingman 1943), and *The House That Jack Built* (Frasconi 1958) (the latter's text is in both French and English).

## *Caldecott Classics About Great Britain*

- In Trina Schart Hyman's illustrations for Margaret Hodges' retelling of Edmund Spenser's *Saint George and the Dragon* (1984), the Red Cross Knight battles a dragon, wins the hand of Princess Una, and becomes known as Saint George.

- In Barbara Cooney's art and adaptation of Geoffrey Chaucer's *Chanticleer and the Fox* (1958), a rooster learns not to trust a fox's flattery.

- In Margot Zemach's pictures for husband Harve's retelling of the folktale *Duffy and the Devil* (1973), the devil spins for Duffy until she guesses his name is Taraway and is freed of her promise to marry him.

- In Nonny Hogrogian's illustrations for Sorche Nic Leodhas' *Always Room for One More* (1965), a generous man builds onto his house to make room for all the passers-by who take advantage of his hospitality.

- In Feodor Rojankovsky's art for John Langstaff's retelling of the old Scottish ballad *Frog Went A-Courtin'* (1955), many animal guests attend the wedding of Frog and Miss Mousie.

### Cultural Strategies and Activities

- Research medieval England for authentic examples of architecture, clothing, animals and plants shown in *Saint George* (Hodges 1984) and *Chanticleer* (Chaucer 1958).

- Study Welsh Folklore tradition to enrich appreciation of *Duffy* (Harve 1973); study Scotland for increased enjoyment of *Always Room* (Nic Leodhas 1965), and *Frog* (Langstaff 1955).

- Contrast Hyman's portrayal of Saint George and the dragon to those in famous works of art; study illuminated manuscripts and decorative borders to compare to *Saint George* (Hodges 1984) and *Chanticleer* (Chaucer 1958).

- Compare *Duffy* (Harve 1973) to stories in Honor Books *Rumpelstiltskin* (Zelinsky 1986), and *Tom Tit Tot* (Ness 1965).

- Study Chaucer's Canterbury Tales and Aesop's Fables as background for Cooney's illustrations in *Chanticleer* (Chaucer 1958); read Spenser's Faery Queen as background for Hodges's retelling of *Saint George* (1984).

- Study dragons, foxes, and cats as villains; write stories in which they are the heroes instead.

- Define new words in *Always Room* (Nic Leodhas 1965) and *Chanticleer* (Chaucer 1958).

- Discuss stereotyping of fat people as all looking alike and all acting foolishly, as has been criticized of Zemach's drawings in *Duffy* (Harve 1973).

- Notable Honor Books about Great Britain: *A Visit to William Blake's Inn* (Willard and Provensen 1981), *Three Jovial Huntsmen* (Jeffers 1973), *All in the Morning Early* (Nic Leodhas and Ness 1963), *Song of Robin Hood* (Malcolmson and Burton 1947), and *Wee Gillis* (Leaf and Lawson 1938).

## *Ancient Wisdom in a Caldecott Tale from India*

- Marcia Brown's *Once a Mouse* (1961) is a fable from India, in which a hermit rescues a mouse from its attackers by changing it into a variety of other animals until its arrogance results in the hermit changing it back again.

### Cultural Strategies and Activities

- Research India, where scholars say fables originated; study Buddhism and Hinduism as background for fables and parables.

- Study the class society of ancient India, with its rajahs, princes, ministers, sages, philosopher hermits.

- Research the ancient Hitopadesa, or "Book of Good Counsel" originally written to instruct a rajah's sons in moral principles, which is the Sanskrit literature from which *Mouse* was taken and from which "beast-fables" have passed into almost all the civilized literatures of the world, including Aesop's fables and the Arabian Nights.

## *Homecomings in Caldecotts About Japan*

- Blair Lent's illustrations for Arlene Mosel's *Funny Little Woman* (1972) show a Japanese woman who follows a rolling dumpling down a hole, where she is captured and held underground by wicked monsters until she escapes with their magic paddle that turns one grain of rice into a potful.

- Allen Say in *Grandfather's Journey* (1993) relates his family's history in America and Japan and the love he and his grandfather have felt for both countries.

### Cultural Strategies and Activities

- Research Lent's authentic Japanese garden, stone lanterns, masks, kimonos, architecture, and jizo samas—the guardian gods of farmers and protectors of children, statues of whom are often placed along roads in Japan.

- Research the collections of folktales by Lafcadio Hearn.

- Contrast differences among Japanese and American landscapes, interior scenes and clothing in *Grandfather's Journey* (Say 1993).

- Study reproductions of portrait photography by Say and Robert Lawson in his award winner *They Were Strong and Good* (1940) and practice drawing pictures from family photographs.

**172** Windows on the World: Picture Books as Social Construction and Representation

- Discuss the feelings of being torn by love for two places described in *Grandfather's Journey* (Say 1993) and in Paul Goble's *The Girl Who Loved Wild Horses* (1978).

- Compare Say's loving relationship with his grandfather to that in other award winners with cross-generational themes, like *Song of the Swallows* (Politi 1949), *Song and Dance Man* (Ackerman and Gammell 1988), and *Owl Moon* (Yolen and Schoenherr 1987).

- Notable Caldecott Honor Books about Japan: *The Wave* (Hodges and Lent 1964), *The Boy of the Three-Year Nap* (Snyder and Say 1988), *The Tale of the Mandarin Ducks* (Patterson, Dillon, and Dillon 1990), *Crow Boy* (Yashima 1955), *Umbrella* (Yashima 1958), and *Seashore Story* (Yashima 1967).

## *Breaking Down Hispanic Stereotypes in a Caldecott About Mexico*

- Marie Hall Ets's collaboration with Aurora Labistida for *Nine Days to Christmas* (1959) is about a little girl who chooses her first piñata and attends her first *posada*, or special Christmas party.

### Cultural Strategies and Activities

- Study winter holiday celebrations around the world.

- Compare *Nine Days* (Labistida 1959) to other Award winners about Christmas: *The Polar Express* (Van Allsburg 1985) and *Baboushka and the Three Kings* (Robbins and Sidjakov 1960).

- Research the holiday tradition of the *posada*; compare the party in *Nine Days* (Labistida 1959) to the one in Honor Book *Pedro, the Angel of Olvera Street* (Politi 1946).

- Compare Ets's art to that of Mexican artists, especially to Diego Rivera's 1953 painting, *La Piñata*.

- Ets lived in Mexico City. She and her friend, children's librarian Labistida, hoped in *Nine Days* (Labistida 1959) to dispel stereotypic notions children in the United States have about the Mexican people. Discuss these stereotypes and look for examples of real people and places and old versus modern Mexico in Ets's 1959 pictures of Mexico City.

## *Synthesized Legends in Caldecotts About Native North America*

- In Gerald McDermott's *Arrow to the Sun* (1974), an arrowmaker makes a Pueblo Indian boy into an arrow that flies to the sun, where the boy passes three tests and returns home with the power of the sun, his father.

- In Paul Goble's *The Girl Who Loved Wild Horses* (1978), a Plains Indian girl runs away from her people to live with wild horses and finally becomes one of them.

# A Rich Resource: Selected Caldecott Award Winners and Honor Books

## Cultural Strategies and Activities

- Discuss quests by young heroes, what the heroes contribute to their people, how they change, what might happen next; compare to the quest in Award winner *Saint George and the Dragon* (Hodges and Hyman 1984).

- Both McDermott and Goble have stated that these stories are their own original synthesizing of stories from southwestern and western tribal people. Study traditions of the Pueblo and Plains tribal people to determine whether the stories have foundations in native beliefs.

- Compare McDermott's artistic style in *Arrow to the Sun* (1974) to geometric designs in southwestern tribal art.

- Compare Goble's artistic style in *Wild Horses* (1978) to nineteenth-century Native American pictures drawn on animal hides and ledger-book paper.

- Contrast the representation of Native Americans in *Arrow* or *Wild Horses* with past stereotypic portrayals, as in the Honor Book *Mighty Hunter* (Hader and Hader 1943).

- Research authenticity in both *Arrow* (McDermott 1974) and *Wild Horses* (Goble 1978), not only for an overall look, but also for specific nonstereotypical details in clothing, dwellings, and natural environments.

- Notable Honor Books about Native North America: *Angry Moon* (Sleator and Lent 1970), *Feather Mountain* (Olds 1951), *Paddle-to-the-Sea* (Holling 1941), *In My Mother's House* (Clark and Herrera 1941), *The Story of Jumping Mouse* (Steptoe 1984), *Hawk, I'm Your Brother* (Baylor and Parnall 1976), *Desert Is Theirs* (Baylor and Parnall 1975), *When Clay Sings* (Baylor and Bahti 1972), and *Where the Buffaloes Begin* (Baker and Gammell 1981).

## *Contemporary American Children in the Caldecotts*

- In Maurice Sendak's *Where the Wild Things Are* (1963) and Chris Van Allsburg's *The Polar Express* (1985), boys escape from their rooms on flights of fantasy and assume positions of importance in magical lands.

- In Karen Ackerman and Stephen Gammell's *Song and Dance Man* (1988), Chris Van Allsburg's *Jumanji* (1981), and David Macaulay's *Black and White* (1990), boy-and-girl siblings amuse themselves and are amused by their elders.

- In Jane Yolen and John Schoenherr's *Owl Moon* (1987) and Evaline Ness's *Sam, Bangs & Moonshine* (1966), girls receive sound advice from their fathers.

- In Lynd Ward's *Biggest Bear* (1952) and Robert McCloskey's *Time of Wonder* (1957), children find much to learn about the love of natural environments far from the city.

- In Ezra Jack Keats's *A Snowy Day* (1962) and Leo Politi's *Song of the Swallows* (1949), boys respond to acts of nature that intrigue them.

## Cultural Strategies and Activities

- Rewrite some of theses stories and change the characterization and/or plot to fit children of another cultural background, region of the country, opposite sex, physical ability, or family structure.

- Make a list of the things someone from another country could possibly learn about many contemporary Euro-American children from the first nine titles. Discuss whether any or all of these things are true of all Euro-American children.

- Discuss adult controversies over monsters and Max's antisocial behavior in *Wild Things* (Sendak 1963) and "Communist overtones" in Honor Book *Two Reds* (Lipkind and Mordvinoff 1950).

- Compare the boys' fantasy adventures in *Wild Things* (Sendak 1963) and *Polar Express* (Van Allsburg 1985) to Honor Book *Free Fall* (Wiesner 1988).

- Discuss ways in which *A Snowy Day* (1962), conceived by Keats as a universal story, was or was not culturally specific to the African-American inner-city experience in the 1960s.

- Find examples in *Swallows* (Politi 1949) of regional history, the Mexican culture, and use of the Spanish language as Politi's intentional culturally specific reflections of the Hispanic-American experience in southern California.

- Discuss which of these stories exhibit a "generation gap" between children and their elders; which imply the existence of other family members; which have exciting events when elders are absent and which when elders are present.

- Three of these illustrators also created pictures in Honor Books with family themes. Gather the titles and discuss the continuities/divergences between Ackerman and Gammell's *Song and Dance Man* (1988) and Honor Book *The Relatives Came* (Rylant and Gammell 1985); McCloskey's *Time of Wonder* and Honor Book's *One Morning in Maine* (1952), and *Blueberries for Sal* (1948); Sendak's *Wild Things* (1963) and Honor Book *Mr. Rabbit and the Lovely Present* (Zolotow and Sendak 1962).

- Gather other Caldecotts about American children not too long ago in our nation's past: Katherine Milhous's Award winner *Egg Tree* (1950) to discuss the Pennsylvania Dutch tradition of decorating eggs at Easter; Jerry Pinkney's illustrations for Patricia C. McKissack's Honor Book *Mirandy and Brother Wind* (1988) to discuss the African-American tradition of a cakewalk in the rural South; and Robert McCloskey's illustrations for Ruth Sawyer's Honor Book *Journey Cake, Ho!* (1953) to discuss an Appalachian mountain version of the "Gingerbread Man."

- Study stereotypic visuals about African-Americans in past Award winners *They Were Strong and Good* (Lawson 1940), *Abraham Lincoln* (d' Aulaire 1939), and *Rooster Crows* (Petersham 1945).

- Discuss possible reasons for the disproportionate numbers of books about ethnic groups other than Euro-American in the Caldecott collection (including the Honor Books listed by groups later in this section) and in other collections of children's books (the school media center, lists for winners of other awards, etc.). Compare these numbers to U.S. population statistics.

- Notable Honor Books with contemporary Euro-American children: *The Relatives Came* (Rylant and Gammell 1989), *Chair for My Mother* (Williams 1982), *The Garden of Abdul Gasazi* (Van Allsburg 1979), *In the Night Kitchen* (Sendak 1970), *Just Me* (Ets 1965), *Pocketful of Cricket* (Caudill and Ness 1964), *Moon Jumpers* (Udry and Sendak 1959), *What Do You Say, Dear?* (Joslin and Sendak 1958), *Very Special House* (Krauss and Sendak 1953), *Play with Me* (Ets 1955), *One Morning in Maine* (McCloskey 1952), *Blueberries for Sal* (McCloskey 1948), *Two Reds* (Lipkind and Mordvinoff 1950), and *Free Fall* (Wiesner 1988).

- Notable Honor Books with contemporary African-American children: *Tar Beach* (Ringgold 1991); *"More More More," Said the Baby* (Williams 1990), *Ben's Trumpet* (Isadora 1979), *Goggles* (Keats 1969), and *Ten, Nine, Eight* (Bang 1983).

- Notable Honor Books with contemporary Native American children: *Desert Is Theirs* (Baylor and Parnall 1975), *Hawk, I'm Your Brother* (Baylor and Parnall 1976), and *When Clay Sings* (Baylor and Bahti 1972).

- Notable Honor Books with contemporary Hispanic-American children: *Juanita* (Politi 1948), and *Pedro, the Angel of Olvera Street* (Politi 1946).

- Notable Honor Books with contemporary Asian-American children: None to date.

## Case Studies in Social Construction

A single, insensitive image does not make a stereotype. It takes many, over time—the same image seen again and again, from generation to generation. No other group of people in America continues to be as stereotyped as the Native American. Visual clichés of war-painted Indians from old Hollywood Westerns are recognized anywhere by anyone around the world. The creators of those movies—and most non-Native Americans in general—apparently never considered that Native peoples might be offended by such caricatures of their ancestors. But media literacy requires that we distinguish between intent and impact.

Rennard Strickland explained in *Native Peoples* magazine, "Film gave light and motion to longstanding images of deeply entrenched stereotypes . . . rooted in almost five hundred years of white portrayals of Native Americans . . . of good Indians and bad Indians . . . few, if any, 'real Indians'" (Strickland 1989, 48–50). The result, according to the Council on Interracial Books for Children publication, *Unlearning "Indian" Stereotypes*, is that the "unreal image distributed by Hollywood . . . has degraded Native American people and distorted non-Native people's perceptions of Native Americans" (Moore and Hirschfelder 1977, 8). We are left with homogenized movie stereotypes that are hard to erase. The box-office success *Dances with Wolves* (1990) attempted to remedy this public perception by showing Indian characters as real human beings with emotional and motivational dimensions and by casting Native Americans themselves in the roles. A criticism of the film remains, however, that it perpetuated one of Hollywood's oldest and most Eurocentric of formulas: an outsider coming into an Indian community is, as always, still the hero. The process of changing the image of the Native American in the mass media and in children's books is a slow and subtle one that requires sophisticated objective analysis. The publishing industry is well aware of the changes and of course of the potential profit to be derived from tapping into the growing interest in this cultural heritage. The editors of *Publishers Weekly*, for example, described the "reawakening of pride in, and respect for, Native American heritage, that has been sweeping the country" (Ruback and Maughan 1992, 23). But these changing attitudes cannot be locked inside our classroom or curricula, and they are often controversial. In 1991, for example, the National Museum of American Arts featured an exhibit called "The West as America." The revisionist view of manifest destiny and the cultural clash between whites and Native Americans outraged many, including the Librarian of Congress, Daniel Boorstin. If the art world can generate anger about Native American images, the wider world of sport can generate fury.

## *Sports Mascots and Picture Books*

The head-dressed and whooping stereotype of old invades our living rooms yet today through televised sports events that show contemporary non-Native Americans dressed up like Hollywood Indians as mascots for teams with names like Braves, Chiefs, Indians, and Redskins. The fans in the stadium mirror the mascots' antics with war paint and turkey-feather headdresses or make up new antics of their own, like Atlanta's baseball fans who wave foam-rubber hatchets in the "Tomahawk Chop" while chanting a pseudo-Indian "war song." When the Braves played the Minnesota Twins in Minneapolis during the 1991 World Series, Atlanta fans were bemused, surprised, defensive, and downright angry to find protesters of all races, ages, and walks of life rallied outside the Metrodome, demanding "Stop the Chop! The Chop stops here!"

Minnesota's large, active Native population had been protesting Indian stereotyping for decades through such organizations as Concerned Indian Parents and the American Indian Movement (AIM). The 1991 protest, planned as an educational platform, included a drum group to demonstrate real Native American music, as well as many speakers, one of whom called out repeatedly over a bullhorn, "Atlanta fans, we're not here to keep you from having a good time! We WANT you to have a good time! Just don't do it at OUR expense!" By the time the Washington Redskins arrived at the Super Bowl the next January, once again in the Minneapolis Metrodome, a summit conference had been organized by the newly formed National Coalition on Racism in Sports and the Media, supported by three dozen organizations. Protesters continued to call for an end to Indian team names and their mascots across the nation.

The mascot issue is a classic example of culture clash. A brief review of the debate in the press over sports teams with Indian names presents invaluable insight into adult attitudes. Even though each of the following 10 conflicting attitudes appeared in the press as either pro-mascot or anti-mascot, they are generically transferable as either pro-stereotype ("Indian people are hypersensitive and are overreacting") or anti-stereotype, in terms of the portrayal of Native American peoples in children's books:

1. Pro-stereotype attitude is that telling other people what they can and cannot do, within the law, is not the American way. It's censorship and it's wrong. Anti-stereotype attitude is that the American way is that all people have the right to equal and fair treatment and to historically accurate access to their own culture. Although none of us today is responsible for the acts of our ancestors, we are collectively responsible as Americans to correct them.

2. Pro-stereotype is that this is all in good fun and nobody means any harm. Anti-stereotype is that "having fun" becomes "making fun" when someone dresses up as someone else and acts foolishly. Indians also want to have fun, but are not amused by demeaning images such as "Injun Joe" logos that are derogatory about Native Americans, just as Stepin Fetchit and black-faced minstrels were about African-Americans. Because someone is not acting maliciously does not mean that harm is not still done. Native American children are suffering from the outside imposition of these negative self-images.

3. Pro-stereotype is that this is intended to honor the bravery and colorful heritage of Indian people. Anti-stereotype is that Native Americans are not flattered by savage and warlike portrayals. Their traditional beliefs and spirituality are insulted by parodies of ceremonial symbols such as the headdress, sacred music, and peace pipe. No one would consider names like New York Negroes or Chicago Jews as honoring those groups and, according to the dictionary, *redskins* is an ethnic slur as bad as *wop*, *kike*, or *nigger*.

4. Pro-stereotype is that Indian people are squandering their energies over trivial issues when much more important ones exist. Anti-stereotype is that falsely portraying another's way of life is a basic denial of human dignity. It transcends entertainment, because it condones an idea that Native Americans are somehow less than other humans, and it directly affects contemporary social policies concerning other issues. Nothing is going to change—neither behavior, attitudes, nor policies—until the stereotype is erased.

5. Pro-stereotype is that other groups are still stereotyped and they don't complain. Anti-stereotype is that each group speaks for itself and has a right to be treated as it desires. Some stereotyped groups often mentioned are mythical beings or vanished warriors as sports mascots, like the Giants and the Vikings, but Indians are real and live in the present. Other groups are occupational, like the Steelers, but being a Native American is not a role a person can play. Still other mascots are animals and have no voice in the matter, like the Bears—which is disrespectful to the dignity of another living creature for Native American people.

6. Pro-stereotype is that not all Indians complain and some even participate. Anti-stereotype is that, as in all other cultures, Native people also are not all the same, but vary in their knowledge of traditions and in their beliefs, opinions, and commitments. Inconsistent reactions often also occur because of national (tribal) differences. Particularly true is that Native Americans most often do not presume to speak for others, and many will not speak out at all because to be in the public eye is not in their culture.

7. Pro-stereotype is that Indians didn't complain until they got in the national spotlight and this idea became politically correct. Anti-stereotype is that, along with other people of color, Native Americans have protested for decades against institutionalized stereotypes. Now the protest is more visible in the media because the protesters' numbers are growing, organizations have broader bases, and various groups are banding together, including many non-Indians.

8. Pro-stereotype is that this has been around for years and we resist the idea of giving up what we have. Anti-stereotype is that if multiculturalism is to become a reality in this country, Native Americans must assert their right to define themselves and to expect others to abide by their definition. Indians and non-Indians must communicate with each other and understand what the other is upset about. S. I. Hayakawa once called stereotypes substitutes for observation. All of us must learn to really observe and really listen to each other.

9. Pro-stereotype is that American culture is a rich mixture of many people's traditions. Everyone has the right to use cultural symbols even though they have no ancestral connection to them. Anti-stereotype is that many traditions are spiritual in nature to Native American people, and parodying them for one's own amusement is trivializing and abusive. When one knows what symbols mean and how to use them properly, one does not use them frivolously and looks with disdain on those who do.

10. Pro-stereotype is that we're all Americans after all and should look at things the same way. Anti-stereotype is that, historically, many Indians have never desired assimilation to the degree of other groups. Today they attempt to mesh traditional values with contemporary settings, living in two worlds. By race they are American Indian, by citizenship American, and by nationality they may be not only enrolled members of a tribal nation, but also hereditary members of other nations. They identify themselves in all these ways, with no single label, no single way of looking at things, no one "American Indian"— no stereotype.

## *Unlearning Stereotypes: Case Study on Images of Native Americans*

The fact that attitudes about sports-mascot Indian stereotypes reflect attitudes about children's book stereotypes is not the only indication that we have far to go before we have real multicultural education for all our children. More alarming is proof of institutionalized acceptance of these stereotypes within the educational system itself. An example is novels like those by Lynne Reid Banks, such as *Indian in the Cupboard* (1980), with their racist slurs, lockjawed "Indian" dialogue, and acts of snarling violence full of hatred and rage, which are recommended, even required, on elementary reading lists in language arts curriculums across the nation. As a reviewer said in *Books Without Bias*, "My heart aches for the Native child unfortunate enough to stumble across, and read, these books . . . . [H]ow could a white child fail to believe that he is far superior to the bloodthirsty, sub-human monsters portrayed here?" (Slapin and Seale 1988, 161).

Lenore Weitzman states in *The American Journal of Sociology* that "children's books reflect cultural values and are an instrument for persuading children to accept those values" (Weitzman 1972, 1126). If picture books are indeed one way in which we educate, persuade, and pass down values to our children, then books that repeat the Hollywood, sports-mascot, and *Indian in the Cupboard* stereotypes set them firmly in minds of each new generation. These images can stay in a child's mind—sometimes forever—and the damage can be hard to undo. As educators, we can help reverse that tide when we accept our role as transmitters of equally rich and diverse cultures, about "how it was, how it is and—with hope and a little luck—maybe how it will come to be, for all of us" (Slapin and Seale 1988, 316).

Several things have been happening in the field of children's literature that help all educators in their struggle to know what, why, and how to teach about Native Americans. First is the publication of excellent annotated bibliographies and reference tools written from an Indian perspective, such as the following:

- Beverly Slapin and Doris Seale's *Books Without Bias: Through Indian Eyes* (1988), revised in 1992 by New Society Press as *Through Indian Eyes: The Native Experience in Books for Children.*

- Barbara J. Kuipers's *American Indian Reference Resource Books for Children and Young Adults* (1995).

- Arlene Hirschfelder's edited essays in *American Indian Stereotypes in the World of Children* (1982).

There has been increased exposure for Native American periodicals and small-press publishers whose goals are to combat stereotypes that "offend Native peoples and cheat non-Native people of information that may enrich their lives" (Slapin and Seale 1988, 389). Addresses can be found in the bibliographies mentioned here.

A third trend is increased sensitivity on the part of some of the major publishers. For instance, blatant stereotypes by Richard Scarry in the first edition of his *Best Word Book Ever* (1974) were omitted in the 1980 edition. Paul Goble considered nuances in text important enough that he rewrote his *Friendly Wolf* (1974) to create a subtly new version of the story in *Dream Wolf* (1988a) (he also revised the art for the book jacket). Would that all creators of children's books should act as conscientiously.

Publishers of many books with stereotypic images have dealt with them by simply allowing the books to go out of print. However, unless the publishing community is pressured to change dramatically, books such as Caldecott Award winners (which remain in print) will continue to perpetuate the stereotypes. For example, Robert Lawson's *They Were Strong and Good* (1940) and Ingri and Edgar Parin d'Aulaire's *Abraham Lincoln* (1939) both have stereotypes of Native Americans and African-Americans as inferior to Euro-Americans. Revised editions of either title seem highly unlikely. Neither can a revision be anticipated for so recent an Honor Book as *Bill Peet: An Autobiography* (1989), with its illustration of a non-Indian child wearing a feathered headdress, similar to an image half a century before in Berta and Elmer Hader's Award winner *Rooster Crows* (1945). This latter title also had stereotypes of African-Americans, which were eliminated by the publisher as early as 1966, but as Raymond William Stedman pointed out in *Shadows of the Indian*, "while the offensiveness of demeaning [images] was realized long ago in regard to most minorities, with the Indian it has gone largely unrecognized—even by those who think of themselves as sensitive in such matters" (Stedman 1982, 228).

In *Unlearning "Indian" Stereotypes* (1977), authors Robert Moore and Arlene Hirschfelder cited 75 picture books from 1950 to 1976 with hundreds of stereotypes. Their expectations were that most of the books would be older titles from the 1940s, but the alarming fact was that all but 6 of the 75 were published in the 1960s and 1970s. Also, although more than 60 percent of the titles are now out of print, many are still found on library shelves today. Many illustrators were involved, and two dozen of them are still top names in children's literature today: Maurice Sendak, Richard Scarry, Paul Galdone, Tomi Ungerer, H. A. Rey, Arnold Lobel, Norman Bridwell, Dick Bruna, Marcia Brown, Lillian Hoban, Mercer Mayer, Robert Kraus, Beni Monstresor, Bruno Munari, Ellen Raskin, William Steig, Gyo Fujikawa. Editorial irresponsibility was demonstrated by 33 publishing houses. Harper and Row was the worst offender, with 8 titles cited over 10 years, but Golden Press and Random House combined had 11 because of repeated association with illustrator Richard Scarry, who was the individual offender most frequently found in the sampling.

Moore and Hirschfelder established several categories of stereotyping, which have been augmented in a study (cited below) by others mentioned in *Books Without Bias* (Slapin and Seale 1988) and other resources and talks with Native educators. The study here is certainly not exhaustive, but does allow the drawing of certain general conclusions. The good news is that this study did not reveal as many blatantly stereotypic newer books as in the past. The bad news is that problems associated with visual bias have now become subtler and trickier, perhaps reflecting good intentions by authors and illustrators, but also revealing sloppy research and publishers' misguided notions that any material at all about Native peoples will be welcomed and acceptable. This study concludes with positive publishing trends to be encouraged and a few examples of research ideas for students using specific titles.

A list for adults and students begins with Native American stereotypes found not only in older picture books still on library shelves, but also in some later books; the study ends with newer, subtler types of inaccuracies. This overview is not an indepth study but is intended simply to raise awareness of specific stereotypic patterns. An ability to further analyze materials meaningfully requires that readers review the professional literature dealing with Indians in children's literature and acquaint themselves with Native American cultures and traditions. Only a few of many picture-book titles are suggested here as examples.

- Native people are sometimes shown colored red, perpetuating a nineteenth-century stereotype of Indians as "redmen." Look at the cigar-store Indian in *Hailstones and Halibut Bones: Adventures in Color* (O'Neill and Weisgard 1961).

- Dictionary and alphabet books often have "I is for Indian" or "E is for Eskimo," implying that Native people are *things* to be alphabetized or categorized (as in counting books), which is as ludicrous as having "C is for Caucasian" or "T is for Texan." Look at Maurice Sendak's *Alligators All Around: An Alphabet* (1962) or Richard Scarry's *Find Your ABCs* (1973).

- Cartoon-like drawings show Indian people as comical caricatures, implying that all Native Americans look alike and dress the same way. Look at Walt Disney American Classics book versions of films like *Peter Pan* (1990b) and *Little Hiawatha* (1990a). It goes without saying that the Disney movies themselves are just as offensive.

- Indians are shown as fierce and warlike, stealthy or stoic, and making unreasonable demands on non-Indians. Look at *Good Giants and the Bad Puckwudgies* (Fritz and dePaola 1982), Caldecott Award winner *They Were Strong and Good* (Lawson 1940), and *Josephina Story Quilt* (Coerr and Degen 1986).

- Non-Indian children are shown "playing Indian," almost always whooping or lurking, and are sometimes called "Indian" in the text as if being a Native American were a role to be played like being a firefighter or nurse. Look at Charlotte Zolotow's *If It Weren't for You* (Zolotow and Shecter 1966), Leo Politi's *Little Leo* (1951), and Sesyle Joslin's *What Do You Say, Dear?* (Joslin and Sendak 1961).

- Indians are portrayed as cute, fantasy creatures like elves. Look at Nathaniel Benchley's *Running Owl the Hunter* (Benchley and Funai 1979) and *Red Fox and His Canoe* (Benchley and Lobel 1964).

- Animals are dressed up like Indians, implying that Native people are not fully human. Other ethnic groups may not object to being portrayed as animals, but for Native people this is the most dehumanizing of all stereotypes, and is doubly offensive because it also degrades animals, regarded as co-inhabitants of a fragile ecological system. Look at *Arthur's Thanksgiving* (Brown 1983), *Best Times Ever* (Scarry 1988), *Great Big Schoolhouse* (Scarry 1979), *Spot Goes to School* (Hill 1984), *Stupids Step Out* (Allard and Marshall 1974), *George and Martha Encore* (Marshall 1983), *Doctor Coyote* (Bierhorst and Watson 1987), *Crow and Weasel* (Lopez and Pohrt 1990), and *Ten Little Rabbits* (Grossman and Long 1991).

- Traditional clothes and motifs with religious and cultural significance are shown in everyday use by Indian people. Look at Caldecott Award winner *Arrow to the Sun* (McDermott 1974), *Little Runner of the Longhouse* (Baker and Lobel 1962), and *They Put on Masks* (Baylor and Ingram 1974). The feathered headdress, often disrespectfully called a "hat," is a popular cliché. Look at the Caldecott Honor Books *Mighty Hunter* (Hader and Hader 1943) and, 50 years later, *Bill Peet: An Autobiography* (Peet 1989).

- All Native people are generically portrayed as Plains Indians, and stories from different nations are mixed up as if all tribal histories were the same. Look at children's book versions of Longfellow's "Song of Hiawatha" by Susan Jeffers (1983), Keith Mosely (1988), and Chris Molan (1985).

- Artwork that appears authentic on the surface often has inaccuracies regarding a specific Native nation, period of history, or general Native frame of reference. Further research must necessarily be encouraged for the reader to recognize many of these inaccuracies. For instance, regarding Gerald McDermott's illustrations in *Arrow to the Sun* (1974), research indicates that a Pueblo elder would not have a long beard down to his knees, as Native people long ago did not have facial hair. Another example is *Dreamcatcher* (Osofsky and Young 1992), in which Ojibway educators point to pictures with the wrong kind of dress for an Ojibway female, containers that should have been birch bark, and a dreamcatcher itself that should be irregular in its spacing, as they were made long ago, rather than symmetrical, as they are often made today. When exploring the aesthetic elements of these books, teachers and librarians need to ask whether "the artwork is predominated by generic Indian designs" or whether the artist has "taken care to reflect the traditions and symbols of the particular people in the book" (MacCann 1992, 161).

- Indians are depicted acting in a manner generally considered inappropriate in Native cultures. Study of Native American customs will be required to recognize such inaccuracies. For instance, look at *Knots on a Counting Rope* (Martin, Archambault, and Rand 1987), in which a youngster repeatedly interrupts an elder; *Hawk, I'm Your Brother* (Baylor and Parnall 1976), in which a boy steals a hawk and is allowed to put it in a cage; and *Iktomi and the Buffalo Skull* (Goble 1991), in which disrespect for the sacred buffalo skull is an unpleasant point of the story.

- Artwork reflects illustrators' training in western European art traditions and makes no attempt to replicate Native artistic traditions themselves. Fundamentally, pictures lack substance as representing an Indian story in an Indian way. Look at *Brother Eagle, Sister Sky* (Jeffers and Seattle 1991), *Star Maiden* (Esbensen and Davie 1988), and *Ladder to the Sky* (Esbensen and Davie 1989).

## **Positive Trends and Titles**

Consultations with Native people and a review of the professional literature suggest the following positive trends to be encouraged in children's literature dealing with American Indians. Titles representative of these trends are recommended for study by students and educators.

- Materials have begun to portray Native American values generally held in common today, such as harmony between nature and human beings and respect for family and traditions. Look at *Trees Stand Shining* (Jones and Parker 1971), *Alice Yazzie's Year* (Maher and Gammell 1977), *The Girl Who Loved Wild Horses* (Goble 1978), and *Buffalo Woman* (Goble 1984).

- Portrayals are more prevalent of Native people in the past as multidimensional human beings. Look at *Bright Fawn and Me* (Leech, Spencer, and Coalson 1979), *The Legend of the Bluebonnet* (dePaola 1983), and *Encounter* (Yolen and Shannon 1992).

- Author, illustrator, and/or consultant notes refer to sources respected by today's Native people themselves. It is important that text and pictures reflect not only the source material's original intent, but also an understanding for all other varied aspects of Native

American history and culture. Look at Paul Goble's notes in *Her Seven Brothers* (1988b) and *The Great Race* (1985).

- Accurate representation of tribal histories is being published. Look at *People Shall Continue* (Ortiz and Graves 1988) and *Death of the Iron Horse* (Goble 1987).

- Major publishing houses have begun to publish materials compiled, written, and/or illustrated by Native Americans themselves. Look at *Mud Pony* (Cohen and Begay 1988), *Dancing Teepees* (Sneve and Gammell 1989), and *Rising Voices: Writings of Young Native Americans* (Hirschfelder and Singer 1992).

- Accurate and sensitive understanding of the original spirit of a text can be found in retellings and/or illustrations by non-Native persons. Look at *The Story of Jumping Mouse* (Steptoe 1984), *Where the Buffaloes Begin* (Baker and Gammell 1981), *Star Boy* (Goble 1983), *Angry Moon* (Sleator and Lent 1970), *Quail Song* (Carey and Barnett 1990), and *Who-Paddled-Backward-With-Trout* (Norman and Young 1987).

- Publication of more materials portrays contemporary Native Americans or a Native frame of reference, as opposed to books that depict Indians solely as people of the past. Look at *Very Last First Time* (Andrews and Wallace 1986), *A Promise Is a Promise* (Munsch and Kusugak 1988), *On Mother's Lap* (Scott and Coalson 1972), *Candle for Christmas* (Speare and Blades 1986), and *Goat in the Rug* (Blood, Link, and Parker 1976).

The text by Acoma Poet Simon Ortiz was praised by Native people for presenting history from their perspective. (Used by permission of BookStop Literary Agency, Agent for Children's Book Press, from the book *The People Shall Continue* by Simon Ortiz, illustrated by Sharol Graves. © 1988, original edition, © 1977 by Children's Book Press.)

# Strategies and Learning

The following study ideas suggest specific titles for comparison.

- Contrast examples of animal how-and-why stories, such as *Story of Light* (Roth 1990), with *How Rabbit Stole the Fire* (Troughton 1986) and Caldecott Honor Book *Feather Mountain* (Olds 1951) with *How the Birds Got Their Colours* (Johnston and Ashkewe 1978).

- Find examples of Plains tribal hide-paintings in reference material to contrast to the illustrations in *Legend of the Indian Paintbrush* (dePaola 1988). Also find examples from past Indian art for an illustrative convention of drawing faces without distinct individual features, which leaves the reader to supply personalities rather than having them dictated by the visual maker. Study illustrations for many books by both dePaola and Paul Goble that reflect this artistic convention.

- Compare dramatic differences in text by Paul Goble for *Friendly Wolf* (1974) and the revised version of the same story in *Dream Wolf* (1988a). Note that the only changes in artwork appear subtly on the newer book's jacket. Discuss why these changes in text and art might have been made by the author/illustrator.

- Contrast the main character in Longfellow's "Hiawatha" to the Plains story of "Falling Star" in *Crow Chief* (Goble 1992a).

- Compare two versions of the same story in Robert San Souci's *Legend of Scarface* (1978) and Paul Goble's *Star Boy* (1983). Research the Blackfeet nation in reference books and decide which picture book depicts the most authentic traditional clothes and environment. Also compare the story to a similar hero-quest in Gerald McDermott's *Arrow to the Sun* (1974).

- Specific analyses of numerous and very subtle inaccuracies in some books cannot be made in a brief case study such as this, and many of these criticisms have already been thoroughly reviewed in works like *Books Without Bias* (Slapin and Seale 1988). Readers are encouraged to study non-Indian educators alongside Indian educators, and to take the time to communicate with each other so awareness will spread about images that are appropriate to a tribal nation and best represent a specific group of Native American people.

# References

Aardema, Verna, Leo Dillon, and Diane Dillon (1975). *Why Mosquitoes Buzz in People's Ears*. New York: Dial.

Ackerman, Karen, and Stephen Gammell (1988). *Song and Dance Man*. New York: Alfred A. Knopf.

Agee, James, and Walker Evans (1941). *Let Us Now Praise Famous Men*. New York: Ballantine.

Akar, John (1971). Cover notes for *A Story, A Story*. Weston, CT: Weston Woods Studios. Audiocassette.

Alexander, Lloyd, and Trina Schart Hyman (1992). *The Fortune-Tellers*. New York: Dutton.

Allard, Harry, and James Marshall (1974). *Stupids Step Out*. Boston: Houghton Mifflin.

American Association of University Women (1992). *How Schools Shortchange Girls*. Washington, DC.

Andrews, Jan, and Ian Wallace (1986). *Very Last First Time*. New York: Atheneum.

Arthur, Arnold (1986). Big Bad Wolf. *Children's Literature in Education* 17 (2): pages not available.

Bader, Barbara (1986). The Caldecott Spectrum. In *Newbery and Caldecott Medal Books, 1976–1985*. Boston: Horn Book.

Baker, Betty, and Arnold Lobel (1962). *Little Runner of the Longhouse*. New York: Harper & Row.

Baker, Olaf, and Stephen Gammell (1981). *Where the Buffaloes Begin*. New York: Warne.

Bang, Molly (1983). *Ten, Nine, Eight*. New York: William Morrow.

Banks, Lynne Reid (1980). *Indian in the Cupboard*. Garden City, NY: Doubleday.

Baylor, Byrd, and Tom Bahti (1972). *When Clay Sings*. New York: Scribners.

Baylor, Byrd, and Jerry Ingram (1974). *They Put on Masks*. New York: Scribners.

Baylor, Byrd, and Peter Parnall (1975). *Desert Is Theirs*. New York: Scribners.

——— (1976). *Hawk, I'm Your Brother*. New York: Scribners.

——— (1978). *Way to Start a Day*. New York: Scribners.

Belting, Natalia M., and Bernarda Bryson (1962). *Sun Is a Golden Earring*. New York: Henry Holt.

Bemelmans, Ludwig (1939). *Madeline*. New York: Viking.

——— (1953). *Madeline's Rescue*. New York: Viking.

Benchley, Nathaniel, and Mamoru Funai (1979). *Running Owl the Hunter*. New York: Harper & Row.

Benchley, Nathaniel, and Arnold Lobel (1964). *Red Fox and His Canoe*. New York: Harper & Row.

Berger, John (1972). *Ways of Seeing*. Middelsex, England: Penguin.

Bernhard, Emery, and Durga Bernhard (1993). *Spotted Eagle and Black Crow*. New York: Holiday House.

Bierhorst, John, and Wendy Watson (1987). *Doctor Coyote: A Native American Aesop's Fables*. New York: Macmillan.

Binklen, Douglas, and Robert Bodgen (1977). Media Portrayals of Disabled People: A Study in Stereotypes. *Interracial Books for Children* 8 (6/7).

Birchall, Gregory, and Gavin Faichney (1985). Images of Australia in Elementary Social Studies Texts. *Social Studies* 76 (3): 120–24.

Bishop, Rudine Sims (1992). Multicultural Literature for Children: Making Informed Choices. In *Teaching Multicultural Literature in Grades K8*, edited by Violet J. Harris. Norwood, MA: Christopher Gordon.

Blood, Charles L., Martin Link, and Nancy Winslow Parker (1976). *Goat in the Rug*. New York: Four Winds.

Bogen, D. (1974). *Toms, Coons, Mulattoes, Mammies and Bucks*. New York: Bantam Books.

Brown, Marc (1983). *Arthur's Thanksgiving*. Boston: Little, Brown.

Brown, Marcia (1947). *Stone Soup*. New York: Scribners.

——— (1961). *Once a Mouse*. New York: Scribners.

Brown, Morgan (1975). Sexism in Western Art. In *Women: A Feminist Perspective*, edited by Jo Freeman. Palo Alto, CA: Mayfield.

Bruchac, Joseph, Jonathan London, and Thomas Locker (1992). *Thirteen Moons on Turtle's Back*. New York: Philomel.

Butler, Francelia (1987). Portraits of Old People in Children's Literature. *The Lion and the Unicorn* 11 (1): 26–37.

Caduto, Michael J., and Joseph Bruchac (1988). *Keepers of the Earth*. Golden, CO: Fulcrum.

Cameron, Ann (1992). The Many Faces of Children's Literature. *School Library Journal*, January: 28–30.

Campbell, Edward (1981). *The Celluloid South: Hollywood and the Southern Myth*. Knoxville: University of Tennessee Press.

Carey, Valerie Scho, and Ivan Barnett (1990). *Quail Song*. New York: Putnam.

Carlsdon, Margaret (1992). All Eyes on Hillary. *Time*, September 14: 30.

Caudill, Rebecca, and Evaline Ness (1964). *Pocketful of Cricket*. New York: Henry Holt.

Cendrars, Blaise, and Marcia Brown (1982). *Shadow*. New York: Scribners.

Chaucer, Geoffrey, and Barbara Cooney (1958). *Chanticleer and the Fox*. New York: Crowell.

Clark, Ann Nolan, and Velino Herrera (1941). *In My Mother's House*. New York: Viking.

Coerr, Eleanor, and Bruce Degen (1986). *Josephina Story Quilt*. New York: Harper & Row.

Cohen, Caron Lee, and Shonto Begay (1988). *Mud Pony*. New York: Scholastic.

Considine, David M. (1985a). *The Cinema of Adolescence*. Jefferson, NC: McFarland.

——— (1985b). The Decline and Possible Rise of the Movie Mother. *Journal of Popular Film and Television* 113 (1): 4–15.

Council on Interracial Books for Children (1976). *Human and Anti-Human Values in Children's Books*. New York.

Czaplinski, Suzanne (1976). Sexism in Award-Winning Picture Books. In *Sexism in Children's Books: Facts, Figures, and Guidelines*. London: Writers and Readers.

d'Aulaire, Ingri, and Edgar d'Aulaire (1939). *Abraham Lincoln*. Garden City, NY: Doubleday.

Dayrell, Elphinstone, and Blair Lent (1968). *Why the Sun and the Moon Live in the Sky*. Boston: Houghton Mifflin.

dePaola, Tomie (1975). *Strega Nona*. Englewood Cliffs, NJ: Prentice-Hall.

——— (1983). *The Legend of the Bluebonnet*. New York: Putnam.

——— (1988). *The Legend of the Indian Paintbrush*. New York: Putnam.

De Parle, Jason (1992). Mountain Voice Shares Ageless Magic Tales. *New York Times*, June 2, 22C.

De Sauza, James, Harriet Rohmer, and Stephen Von Mason (1989). *Brother Anansi and the Cattle Ranch*. San Francisco: Children's Books Press.

Donahue, Deidre (1992). *USA Today*, March 18, 1D.

Donovan, Ann (1983). New Mothers in Current Children's Fiction. *Children's Literature in Education* 14 (3): 131–41.

Dorros, Arthur, and Elisa Kleven (1991). *Abuela*. New York: Dutton.

Dougherty, Wilma Holden, and Rosalind Engel (1987). An 80s Look for Sex Equality in Caldecott Winners and Honor Books. *The Reading Teacher*, January: 394–98.

Esbensen, Barbara Juster, and Helen K. Davie (1988). *Star Maiden*. Boston: Little, Brown.

——— (1989). *Ladder to the Sky*. Boston, MA: Little, Brown.

Ets, Marie Hall (1955). *Play with Me*. New York: Viking.

——— (1965). *Just Me*. New York: Viking.

Feelings, Muriel, and Tom Feelings (1971). *Moja Means One: A Swahili Counting Book*. New York: Dial.

——— (1974). *Jambo Means Hello: A Swahili Alphabet Book*. New York: Dial.

Frasconi, Antonio (1958). *The House That Jack Built: A Picture Book in Two Languages*. New York: Harcourt Brace Jovanovich.

Fritz, Jean, and Tomie dePaola (1982). *Good Giants and the Bad Puckwudgies*. New York: Putnam.

Garcia, Jesus, and David Tanner (1985). The Portrayal of Blacks in US History Textbooks. *Social Studies,* September/October: 200–204.

Goble, Paul (1974). *Friendly Wolf*. New York: Bradbury.

——— (1978). *The Girl Who Loved Wild Horses*. New York: Bradbury.

——— (1983). *Star Boy*. New York: Bradbury.

——— (1984). *Buffalo Woman*. New York: Bradbury.

——— (1985). *The Great Race*. New York: Bradbury.

——— (1987). *Death of the Iron Horse*. New York: Bradbury.

——— (1988a). *Dream Wolf*. New York: Bradbury.

——— (1988b). *Her Seven Brothers*. New York: Bradbury.

——— (1991). *Iktomi and the Buffalo Skull*. New York: Orchard.

——— (1992a). *Crow Chief*. New York: Orchard.

——— (1992b). *Love Flute*. New York: Bradbury.

Greenleaf, Sarah (1992). The Beast Within. *Children's Literature in Education* 23 (1): 49–55.

Grifalconi, Ann (1986). *Village of Round and Square Houses*. Boston: Little, Brown.

Grossman, Virginia, and Sylvia Long (1991). *Ten Little Rabbits*. San Francisco: Chronicle Books.

Hader, Berta (1945). *Rooster Crows*. New York: Macmillan.

Hader, Berta, and Elmer Hader (1943). *Mighty Hunter*. New York: Macmillan.

Haley, Gail E. (1970). *A Story, A Story*. New York: Atheneum.

——— (1977). *Go Away, Stay Away*. New York: Scribners.

——— (1986). *Jack and the Bean Tree*. New York: Crown.

——— (1988). *Jack and the Fire Dragon*. New York: Crown.

——— (1992a). *Mountain Jack Tales*. New York: Dutton.

——— (1992b). Puppetry as Illustration, Part I. *The Puppetry Journal* 43 (3): 89–104.

Haley, Gail E., and David Considine (1987). *Tradition and Technique: Creating Jack and the Bean Tree*. Weston, CT: Weston Woods Studio. Audiocassette and filmstrip.

Hamilton, Virginia (1986). On Being a Black Writer in America. *The Lion and the Unicorn* 10: 15–17.

Handforth, Thomas (1938). *Mei Li*. Garden City, NY: Doubleday.

Harris, Violet J. (1992). Contemporary Griots: African American Writers of Children's Literature. In *Teaching Multicultural Literature in Grades K-8*, edited by Violet Harris. Norwood, MA: Christopher Gordon.

Haskell, Molly (1973). *From Reverence to Rape: The Treatment of Women in the Movies*. New York: Holt, Rinehart & Winston.

Henry, William (1990). Beyond the Melting Pot. *Time,* April 9: 28–31.

Heyer, Marilee (1986). *The Weaving of a Dream*. New York: Viking.

Hill, Eric (1984). *Spot Goes to School*. New York: Putnam's.

Hirschfelder, Arlene B., ed. (1982). *American Indian Stereotypes in the World of Children*. Metuchen, NJ: Scarecrow Press.

Hirschfelder, Arlene B., and Beverly R. Singer, eds. (1992). *Rising Voices: Writings of Young Native Americans*. New York: Scribners.

Hodges, Margaret, and Trina Schart Hyman (1984). *Saint George and the Dragon*. Boston: Little, Brown.

Hodges, Margaret, and Blair Lent (1964). *The Wave*. Boston: Houghton Mifflin.

Hoffman, Mary, and Caroline Binch (1991). *Amazing Grace*. New York: Dial.

Hogrogian, Nonny (1971). *One Fine Day*. New York: Macmillan.

——— (1976). *Contest*. New York: William Morrow.

Holling, Holling C. (1941). *Paddle-to-the-Sea*. Boston: Houghton Mifflin.

Home, Gerald, ed. (1988). *Thinking and Rethinking U.S. History*. New York: Council on Interracial Books for Children, No. 16.

Howard, Elizabeth (1983). Shadow and Marcia Brown's *Shadow*. *Horn Book*, October: 621–23.

Hyman, Trina Schart (1983). *Little Red Riding Hood*. New York: Holiday House.

Isadora, Rachel (1979). *Ben's Trumpet*. New York: William Morrow.

Jeffers, Susan (1973). *Three Jovial Huntsmen*. New York: Bradbury.

——— (1983). *Hiawatha*. New York: Dial.

Jeffers, Susan, and Chief Seattle (1991). *Brother Eagle, Sister Sky*. New York: Dial.

Johnston, Basil H., and Del Ashkewe (1978). *How the Birds Got Their Colours*. Toronto: Kids Can Press.

Jones, Hettie, compiler, and Robert Andrew Parker (1971). *Trees Stand Shining*. New York: Dial.

Jones, Malcolm (1991). It's a Not So Small World. *Newsweek*, September 9: 64–65.

Joslin, Sesyle, and Maurice Sendak (1961). *What Do You Say, Dear?* New York: Scott.

Keats, Ezra Jack (1962). *A Snowy Day*. New York: Viking.

——— (1969). *Goggles*. New York: Macmillan.

Kimmel, Eric, and Trina Schart Hyman (1989). *Hershel and the Hannukah Goblins*. New York: Holiday House.

Kingman, Lee (1943). *Pierre Pigeon*. Boston: Houghton Mifflin.

Krauss, Ruth, and Maurice Sendak (1953). *Very Special House*. New York: Harper & Row.

Kuipers, Barbara J. (1991). *American Indian Reference Books for Children and Young Adults*. Englewood, CO: Libraries Unlimited.

Labistida, Aurora, and Marie Hall Ets (1959). *Nine Days to Christmas*. New York: Viking.

Lacy, Lyn Ellen (1986). *Art and Design in Children's Picture Books: An Analysis of Caldecott Award-Winning Illustrations*. Chicago: American Library Association.

Langstaff, Joun, and Feodor Rojankovsky (1955). *Frog Went A-Courtin'*. New York: Harcourt Brace Jovanovich.

Larrick, Nancy (1965). The All White World of Children's Books, *Saturday Review* September: 64.

Lawson, Robert (1940). *They Were Strong and Good*. New York: Viking.

Leab, Daniel (1975). *From Sambo to Superspade: The Black Experience in Motion Pictures*. Boston: Houghton Mifflin.

Leaf, Munro, and Robert Lawson (1938). *Wee Gillis*. New York: Viking.

Lee, Jeanne (1991). *Silent Lotus*. New York: Farrar, Straus & Giroux.

Leech, Jay, Zane Spencer, and Glo Coalson (1979). *Bright Fawn and Me*. New York: Crowell.

Lipkind, Will, and Nicolas Mordvinoff (1950). *Two Reds*. New York: Harcourt Brace Jovanovich.

Lobel, Arnold (1980). *Fables*. New York: Harper and Row.

Lopez, Barry (1978). *Of Wolves and Men*. New York: Charles Scribner's Sons.

Lopez, Barry, and Tom Pohrt (1990). *Crow and Weasel*. New York: Harper-Perennial.

Macaulay, David (1990). *Black and White*. Boston: Houghton Mifflin.

MacCann, Donnarae (1992). Native Americans in Books for the Young. In *Teaching Multicultural Literature in Grades K-8,* edited by Violet Harris. Norwood, MA: Christopher Gordon.

Maher, Ramona, and Stephen Gammell (1977). *Alice Yazzie's Year*. New York: Coward.

Malcolmson, Anne, ed., and Virginia Lee Burton (1947). *Song of Robin Hood*. Boston: Houghton Mifflin.

Marshall, James (1983). *George and Martha Encore*. Boston: Houghton Mifflin.

Martin, Jr., Bill, John Archambault, and Ted Rand (1987). *Knots on a Counting Rope*. New York: Henry Holt.

McCloskey, Robert (1948). *Blueberries for Sal*. New York: Viking.

——— (1952). *One Morning in Maine*. New York: Viking.

——— (1957). *Time of Wonder*. New York: Viking.

McCully, Emily Arnold (1992). *Mirette on the High Wire*. New York: Putnam.

McDermott, Beverly Brodsky (1976). *Golem*. Philadelphia: Lippincott.

McDermott, Gerald (1972). *Anansi the Spider*. New York: Henry Holt.

——— (1974). *Arrow to the Sun*. New York: Viking.

——— (1993). *Raven: A Trickster Tale of the Pacific Northwest*. San Diego, CA: Harcourt Brace Jovanovich.

McKissack, Patricia, and Jerry Pinkney (1988). *Mirandy and Brother Wind*. New York: Alfred A. Knopf.

Mikkelsen, Nina (1982). Censorship and the Black Child: Can the Real Story Ever Be Told? *Proceedings of the 9th Annual Conference of the Children's Literature Association*. Boston: Children's Literature Association.

Milhous, Katherine (1950). *Egg Tree*. New York: Scribners.

Molan, Chris (1985). *Hiawatha*. Chicago: Rand McNally.

Moore, Robert, and Arlene Hirschfelder (1977). *Unlearning "Indian" Stereotypes*. New York: Council on Interracial Books for Children.

Mosel, Arlene, and Blair Lent (1972). *Funny Little Woman*. New York: Dutton.

Moseley, Keith (1988). *Hiawatha*. New York: Philomel.

Munsch, Robert, and Michael Kusugak (1988). *A Promise Is a Promise*. Toronto: Annick.

Murphy, Jim, and Mark Alan Weatherby (1989). *The Call of the Wolves*. New York: Scholastic.

Musgrove, Margaret, Leo Dillon, and Diane Dillon (1976). *Ashanti to Zulu: African Traditions*. New York: Dial.

National Committee on Excellence in Education (1983). *A Nation At Risk: The Imperative for Educational Reform*. Washington, DC.: U.S. National Commission on Excellence in Education.

Ness, Evaline (1965). *Tom Tit Tot*. New York: Scribner's.

——— (1966). *Sam, Bangs & Moonshine*. New York: Henry Holt.

Newman, Anne Royall (1987). Images of the Bear in Children's Literature. *Children's Literature in Education* 18 (3): 131–38.

Nic Leodhas, Sorche, and Nonny Hogrogian (1965). *Always Room for One More*. New York: Henry Holt.

Nic Leodhas, Sorche, and Evaline Ness (1963). *All in the Morning Early*. New York: Henry Holt.

Nilsen, Aileen Pace (1978). Five Factors Contributing to the Unequal Treatment of Females in Children's Picture Books. *Top of the News* 34: 255–59.

Norman, Howard, and Ed Young (1987). *Who-Paddled-Backward-With-Trout*. Boston: Little, Brown.

Olds, Elizabeth (1951). *Feather Mountain*. Boston: Houghton Mifflin.

O'Neill, Mary, and Leonard Weisgard (1961). *Hailstones and Halibut Bones*. Garden City, NY: Doubleday.

Orodovensky, Pat (1992). *USA Today,* July 7, 1.

Ortiz, Simon and Sharol Graves (1988). *The People Shall Continue*. San Francisco: Children's Book Press.

Osofsky, Audrey, and Ed Young (1992). *Dreamcatcher*. New York: Orchard.

Paterson, Katherine, Leo Dillon, and Diane Dillon (1990). *The Tale of the Mandarin Ducks*. New York: Dutton.

Patrick, Denise Lewis, and James Ransome (1993). *Red Dancing Shoes*. New York: Tambourine.

Peet, Bill (1989). *Bill Peet: An Autobiography*. Boston: Houghton Mifflin.

Perdue, Charles L. (1987). *Outwitting the Devil: Jack Tales from Wise County, Virginia*. Santa Fe, NM: Ancient City Press.

Perrault, Charles, and Marcia Brown (1954). *Cinderella*. New York: Scribners.

*Perspectives* (1986). Review of *Jack and the Bean Tree*. 3 (1): 4.

Petersham, Maud, and Miska Petersham (1945). *Rooster Crows*. New York: Macmillan.

Pimentel, Graziella, and Mark Forties (1989). Representations of the Family in Four Recent Films for Children. *Journal of Youth Services* 2 (4): 341–47.

Politi, Leo (1946). *Pedro, the Angel of Olvera Street*. New York: Scribners.

——— (1948). *Juanita*. New York: Scribners.

——— (1949). *Song of the Swallows*. New York: Scribners.

——— (1951). *Little Leo*. New York: Scribners.

Provensen, Alice, and Martin Provensen (1983). *The Glorious Flight: Across the Channel with Louis Bleriot*. New York: Viking.

*Publishers Weekly* (1993). Review of *Joshua's Massai Mask*. May 10: 71.

Ransome, Arthur, and Uri Shulevitz (1968). *The Fool of the World and the Flying Ship*. New York: Farrar, Straus & Giroux.

Reinartz, Kay (1975). The Paper Doll: Images of Women in Popular Songs. In *Women: A Feminist Perspective,* edited by Jo Freeman. Palo Alto, CA: Mayfield.

Reyher, Becky (1945). *My Mother Is the Most Beautiful Woman in the World*. New York: Lothrop.

Ringgold, Faith (1991). *Tar Beach*. New York: Scholastic.

Robbins, Ruth, and Nicholas Sidjakov (1960). *Baboushka and the Three Kings*. Berkeley, CA: Parnassus.

Rosen, Marjorie (1974). *Popcorn Venus: Women, Movies and the American Dream*. New York: Avon.

Roth, Susan (1990). *Story of Light*. New York: William Morrow.

Ruback, Diane, and Shannon Maughan (1992). Keeping Traditions Alive. *Publishers Weekly,* December 14: 23.

Rubin, Ellen, and Emily Strauss Watson (1987). Disability Bias in Children's Literature, *The Lion and the Unicorn* 11 (1): 60–67.

Rylant, Cynthia, and Stephen Gammell (1985). *The Relatives Came*. New York: Bradbury.

Rylant, Cynthia, and Diane Goode (1982). *When I Was Young in the Mountains*. New York: Dutton.

Rylant, Cynthia, and Barry Moser (1991). *Appalachia: The Voices of Sleeping Birds*. San Diego, CA: Harcourt Brace Jovanovich.

San Souci, Robert (1978). *Legend of Scarface*. New York: Doubleday.

Sapon-Shevin, Mara (1982). Mentally Retarded Characters in Children's Literature. *Children's Literature in Education* 13 (1): 19–31.

Sawyer, Ruth, and Robert McCloskey (1953). *Journey Cake, Ho!* New York: Viking.

Say, Allen (1991). *Tree of Cranes*. Boston: Houghton Mifflin.

——— (1993). *Grandfather's Journey*. Boston: Houghton Mifflin.

Scarry, Richard (1973). *Find Your ABCs*. New York: Random House.

——— (1974). *Best Word Book Ever*. New York: Golden Press.

——— (1979). *Great Big Schoolhouse*. New York: Random House.

——— (1988). *Best Times Ever*. New York: Golden Press.

*School Library Journal* (1991). Review of *Amazing Grace*. October: 97.

——— (1993a). Review of *The Fortune Tellers*. January: S4.

——— (1993b). Review of *Raven*. May: 100.

Schwartz, Amy (1987). Mrs. Moskowitz and Yossel Zissel. *The Lion and the Unicorn* 11 (1): 88–97.

Scieszka, Jon, and Lane Smith (1989). *The True Story of the Three Little Pigs*. New York: Viking.

Scott, Ann Herbert, and Glo Coalson (1972). *On Mother's Lap*. New York: McGraw-Hill.

Sendak, Maurice (1962). *Alligators All Around: An Alphabet*. New York: Harper & Row.

——— (1963). *Where the Wild Things Are*. New York: Harper & Row.

——— (1970). *In the Night Kitchen*. New York: Harper & Row.

Shepard, Paul, and Barry Sanders (1985). *The Sacred Paw: The Bear in Nature, Myth and Literature*. New York: Viking.

Shepard, Ray Anthony (1971). Adventures in Blackland with Keats and Steptoe. *Interracial Books for Children*, no. 2: 2–3.

Shulevitz, Uri (1979). *Treasure*. New York: Farrar, Straus & Giroux.

Slapin, Beverly, and Doris Seale, eds. (1988). *Books Without Bias: Through Indian Eyes*. Berkeley, CA: Oyate.

Sleator, William, and Blair Lent (1970). *Angry Moon*. Boston: Little, Brown.

Sleeter, Christian (1992). Restructuring Schools for Multicultural Education. *Journal of Teacher Education* 43 (2): 141–48.

Sneve, Virginia Driving Hawk, and Stephen Gammell (1989). *Dancing Teepees*. New York: Holiday House.

Snyder, Dianne, and Allen Say (1988). *The Boy of the Three-Year Nap*. Boston: Houghton Mifflin.

Speare, Jean, and Ann Blades (1986). *Candle for Christmas*. New York: Macmillan.

Stanley, Diane (1990). *Fortune*. New York: Morrow Junior Books.

Stedman, Raymond William (1982). *Shadows of the Indian: Stereotypes in American Culture*. Norman and London: University of Oklahoma Press.

Steenland, Sally, ed. (1988). *Growing Up in Prime Time: An Analysis of Adolescent Girls on Television*. Washington, DC.: National Commission on Working Women of Wider Opportunities for Women.

Steptoe, John (1984). *The Story of Jumping Mouse*. New York: Mulberry.

——— (1987). *Mufaro's Beautiful Daughters: An African Tale*. New York: Lothrop, Lee & Shepard.

Stewig, John Warren (1988). Fathers: A Presence in Picture Books? *Journal of Youth Services* 1 (4): 391–95.

Strickland, Rennard (1989). Coyote Goes Hollywood. *Native Peoples* 2 (3): 48–50.

Tan, Amy, and Gretchen Schields (1992). *Moon Lady*. New York: Macmillan.

Tatar, Maria (1992). *Off with Their Heads: Fairy Tales and the Culture of Childhood*. Princeton, NJ: Princeton University Press.

Taxel, Joel (1992). The Politics of Children's Literature: Reflections on Multiculturalism, Political Correctness and Christopher Columbus. In *Teaching Multicultural Literature in Grades K-8*, edited by Violet J. Harris. Norwood, MA: Christopher Gordon.

Titus, Eve (1956). *Anatole*. New York: McGraw-Hill.

——— (1957). *Anatole and the Cat*. New York: McGraw-Hill.

Troughton, Joanna (1986). *How Rabbit Stole the Fire*. New York: Peter Bedrick.

Troy, Lily (1991). *How the Ox Star Fell from Heaven*. St. Niles, IL: Albert Whitman.

Udry, Janice, and Maurice Sendak (1959). *Moon Jumpers*. New York: Harper & Row.

U.S. Commission on Civil Rights (1989). *Window Dressing on the Set*. Washington, DC.: Government Printing Office.

Van Allsburg, Chris (1979). *The Garden of Abdul Gasazi*. Boston, MA: Houghton Mifflin.

——— (1981). *Jumanji*. Boston: Houghton Mifflin.

——— (1985). *The Polar Express*. Boston: Houghton Mifflin.

Walt Disney American Classics (1990a). *Little Hiawatha*. Greenwich, CT: Marboro Books.

Walt Disney American Classics (1990b). *Peter Pan*. Greenwich, CT: Marboro Books.

Ward, Lynd (1952). *Biggest Bear*. Boston: Houghton Mifflin.

Weitzman, J. (1972). Sex-Role Socialization in Picture Books for Pre-School Children. *American Journal of Sociology* 77: 1125–30.

Weitzman, Lenore, et al. (1976). Sex-Role Socialization in Picture Books for Pre-School Children. In *Sexism in Children's Books: Facts, Figures and Guidelines*. London: Writers and Readers.

Wiese, Kurt (1943). *Good Luck Horse*. New York: Viking.

——— (1945). *You Can Write Chinese*. New York: Viking.

——— (1948). *Fish in the Air*. New York: Viking.

Wiesner, David (1988). *Free Fall*. New York: Clarion.

Willard, Nancy, Alice Provensen, and Martin Provensen (1981). *Visit to William Blake's Inn*. New York: Harcourt Brace Jovanovich.

Williams, Sherely Anne, and Carol Byard (1992). *Working Cotton*. San Diego, CA: Harcourt Brace Jovanovich.

Williams, Vera (1982). *A Chair for My Mother*. New York: William Morrow.

——— (1990). *"More More More," Said the Baby*. New York: William Morrow.

Wolf, Naomi (1990). *The Beauty Myth*. London, England: Chatto and Windus.

Xiong, Blia, Cathy Spagnoli, and Nancy Hom (1989). *Nine-in-One Grr! Grr!* San Francisco: Children's Book Press.

Yashima, Taro (1955). *Crow Boy*. New York: Viking.

——— (1958). *Umbrella*. New York: Viking.

——— (1967). *Seashore Story*. New York: Viking.

Yeh, Phoebe (1993). Multicultural Publishing: The Best and Worst of Times. *Journal of Youth Services in Libraries* 6 (6): 157–160.

**196** Windows on the World: Picture Books as Social Construction and Representation

Yolen, Jane, and John Schoenherr (1987). *Owl Moon*. New York: Philomel.

Yolen, Jane, and David Shannon (1992). *Encounter*. San Diego, CA: Harcourt Brace Jovanovich.

Yolen, Jane, and Ed Young (1967). *Emperor and the Kite*. New York: Putnam.

Young, Ed (1989). *Lon Po Po*. New York: Philomel.

Zelinsky, Paul O. (1986). *Rumpelstiltskin*. New York: Dutton.

Zemach, Harve, and Margot Zemach (1973). *Duffy and the Devil*. New York: Farrar, Straus & Giroux.

Zolotow, Charlotte, and Maurice Sendak (1962). *Mr. Rabbit and the Lovely Present*. New York: Harper & Row.

Zolotow, Charlotte, and Ben Shecter (1966). *If It Weren't for You*. New York: Harper & Row.

Controversy and conflict have often greeted multicultural education and the effort to recognize cultural diversity. (Signe, Philadelphia Daily News. Courtesy of Cartoonists and Writers Syndicate.)

# Index

Aardema, Verna, 46, 51, 77, 90
*Abominable Swampman, The*, 91
*Abraham Lincoln*, 179
*Abuela*, 150
Ackerman, Karen, 51, 62, 126, 173
*Adoration of the Magi*, 87
Africa—stories from, 167
African-Americans, 151
African Ananse (character), 11
Agee, James, 157
Ageism, 161
*Aida*, 4, 14, 46, 77
AIME (Amount of Invested Mental Energy), 27, 29
Aims (of the book), xvi-xix
Akar, John, 165
Alexander, Lloyd, 75, 127, 152
*Alice in Wonderland*, 43
*Alice Yazzie's Year*, 181
Allard, Harry, 180
Alles, Hamesh, 8
*Alligators All Around*, 180
*Always Room for One More*, 170
*Amazing Grace*, 46, 150
Amelia-Frances Howard-Gibbon Medal, 98
American children—stories of, 173-75
*American Indian Reference Books for Children and Young Adults*, 178
*American Indian Stereotypes in the World of Children*, 178
*American Journal of Sociology, The*, 148
Amount of Invested Mental Energy (AIME), 27, 29
*Anancy and Mr. Dry-Bone*, 46, 79
Anansi, 149
*Anansi the Spider*, 155
Andres, Jan, 182
Andrew, Robert, 113
*Angry Moon*, 182
Animal stereotypes, 159-60
*Animals in Danger*, 113
*Annabel's House*, 114
Anno, Mitsumasa, 113
*Anno's Journey*, 87
*Anno's Sundial*, 113
*Appalachia: The Voices of Sleeping Birds*, 157
Appalachian Jack (character), 11
Apple, Michael, xvii
Archambault, John, 3, 45, 48, 62, 94. 181
*Arrow to the Sun*, 10, 43, 89, 165, 129, 172, 180, 181

Art and multicultural education, 89-91
Art, 3
*Arthur's Thanksgiving*, 180
Artist notes, 48
Artist visits, 136-40
Artistic style, 30
Artists and authors, 126
*Arts, Human Development and Education, The*, 29
*Ashanti to Zulu*, 50. 72, 77, 165, 167
Aspen Institute, 2
Author notes, 48
Author visits, 136-40
Authors and artists, 126
Awards for illustration, 98-100

Babbit, Natalie, 124
*Baboushka and the Three Kings*, 168
Bader, Barbara, 87
Baker, Betty, 180, 182
Baker, Jeannie, 94
*Banana Bird and the Snake Man*, 90
Bang, Molly, 118
Banks, Lynne Reid, 178
Barnett, Ivan, 182
Base, Graeme, 79, 98
Basic Education Plan. Communication Skills, xv
Bassett, Richard, xix
Baylor, Bird, 166, 180, 181
*Bear and Fly, The*, 62
*Beauty Myth, The*, 153
Begay, Shonto, 182
*Behind the Back of the Mountain*, 90
Bell, Terrel, 21
Belting, Natalia, 166
Bemelmans, Ludwig, 130, 169
Benchley, Nathaniel, 180
Bernhard, Durga, 150
Bernhard, Emery, 150
Beshlie, 110
*Best Times Ever*, 180
*Best Word Book Ever*, 179
*Bevery Hillbillies, The*, 157
Bewick, Thomas, 88
Biases, 164-66
Bierhorst, John, 180
*Big Creatures from the Past*, 113
*Biggest Bear*, 173
*Bill Peet: An Autobiography*, 179, 180
Binch, Caroline, 150

197

# Index

Birch, Carol, 46
*Birdsong*, 49, 50, 52, 66, 72
Birkinshaw, Linda, 113
Birney, Betty, 114
*Black and White*, 3, 51, 98, 116, 117, 173
*Blades*, 182
Blegvad, Brig, 9
Bleshie, 110
Blood, Charles L., 182
Body language (in picture books), 62
Book buyers, 13
Book. *See also* Picture Books
    chains, 13
        designs, 44
        shape, 50-51
*Booklist*, 86
*Books Without Bias*, 178, 179
Booksellers, 13
Borders, 77-79
*Borreguita and the Coyote*, 46
Boston Globe-Horn Book Award, 98
*Boy of the Three Year Nap, The*, 70
*Boy Who Held Back the Sea, The*, 14, 49, 87
Boyer, Ernest, 7
Briggs, Raymond, 118
*Bright Fawn and Me*, 181
Brodsky-McDermott, Beverly, 29
Brooks, Ron, 98
*Brother Anansi and the Cattle Ranch*, 149, 150
*Brother Eagle, Sister Moon*, 48
*Brother Eagle, Sister Sky*, 150, 181
Brown, Marc, 180
Brown, Marcia, 45, 50, 51, 59, 76, 79, 85, 87, 89, 90, 93, 95, 124, 126, 136, 145, 165, 167, 169, 171
Bruchac, Joseph, 45, 150
Brueghel, Pieter, 88
Bryan, Ashley, 89, 98
Bryson, Bernarda, 166
*Buffalo Woman*, 181
Butler, Francelia, 8, 155
Byard, Carol, 150

Caduto, Michael J., 150
Caldecott Award Winners, , 99, 166-75
Caldecott medal, xviii, 98
*Call of the Wolves, The*, 160
*Calvin and Hobbes*, 7
Cameron, Ann, 164
Campbell, Edward, 157
Campbell, Joseph, 10
Campbell, Rod, 114
*Candle for Christmas*, 182
Caravaggio, 86
Carey, Valerie Scho, 182
Caricatures, 161
Carle, Eric, 107, 115
Carter, David, 113

Cartoons (editorial), 24
*Castles*, 113
Cazet, Denys, 75
*Celebrating Children's Books*, 117
*Celluloid South, The*, 157
Center for Media and Values, 2
*Channel One*, 26
*Chanticleer and the Fox*, 170
Charlip, Remy, 116
Chase, Richard, 157
Chauvinism, 161
Cherry, Lynne, 9
*Children's Book Council Calendar*, 109
Children's book industry
Children's Book Press, 150
Children's Choice Awards, 99
Children's literature, 8
    cause of behavior in children, 10
    role in learning, 8
*Children's Literature Association Quarterly*, 43
*Children's Literature in Education*, 10, 85
Children's reading, 13
China—stories from, 168
Christiansen, C.B., 9
*Cinderella*, 169
Classism, 161
*Claypot Boy, The*, 59
Clinton, Hillary, 153
Coal miners (stereotype), 157-59
*Coal Miner's Daughter*, 157
Coalson, Glo, 181, 182
Coerr, Eleanor, 180
Cognitive economy, 26
Cohen, Caron Lee, 182
Collaboration (between author and artist), 126
Collage, 94
Color—preferences, 28
*Color Farm*, 115
*Color Purple, The*, 165
*Color Zoo*, 115
Commission on Achieving Necessary Skills, 23
Communication—human, 14
Communication Skills (Basic Education Plan), xv
Comparing, 43
Composition, 30, 59-83
Concerns Based Adoption Model, 22
*Concise History of Russian Art, A*, 65
Considine, David, 33, 147
Content—selection criteria for, 110-11
Contrasting, 43
Cooney, Barbara, 95, 170
Cooper, Susan, 133, 134
Coretta Scott King Award, 98
Coulthard, Cliff, 90
Coulthard, Terrance, 90
Council on Interracial Books for Children, 10, 148, 175

Cover (of the book), 45
*Cowper's Diverting History of John Gilpin*, 112
Crane, Walter, 77
*Creating Jack and the Bean Tree*, 33
*Creative Classroom*, 154
Crews, Donald, 118
*Critical Thinking Handbook K-3rd Grades, The*, 41
Critical thinking skills, 25, 41-45
Critical viewing skills, 2, 3, 8, 31, 59
*Crocodile Dundee*, 148
*Crow and Weasel*, 180
Crowther, Robert, 113
Cueing, 26
Cues (motion), 33
Cultural racism, 161
Culture bias, 29
Cummings, Pat, 98
Czernecki, Stefan, 46, 77, 78

*Daddy's Roommate*, 9
Dali, Salvador, 118
*Dances with Wolves*, 175
*Dancing Teepees*, 182
d'Aulaire, Edgar Parin, 179
Davie, Helen K., 181
Daynell, Elphinstone, 51, 150
Dead zone (lower right of frame), 66
Dean and Sons, 112
*Dear Zoo*, 114
*Death of the Iron Horse*, 182
Debes, John, 5
Degen, Bruce, 180
*Deliverance*, 157
dePaola, Tomie, 48, 72, 118, 130, 164, 166, 180, 181
DeSauza, James, 149, 150
Design, 30, 59-83
*Dial M for Murder*, 72
Differences—judgment of, 10
Dillon, Diane, 4, 14, 45, 46, 48, 49, 50, 51, 72, 77, 87, 90, 150, 165, 167
Dillon, Leo, 4, 14, 45, 46, 48, 49, 50, 51, 72, 77, 87, 90, 150, 165, 167
Dimensions (of books), 111-12
*Dinner with Fox*, 113
*Dinosaurs: A Lost World*, 113
Disabilities, 156
*Doctor Coyote*, 180
*Doll's House, The*, 112
Dorros, Arthur, 150
*Dream Peddler*, 46, 47, 48, 51, 52, 69, 71, 72, 73, 76, 88, 135
*Dream Wolf*, 179
*Dreamcatcher*, 150, 181
*Duffy and the Devil*, 170
Dust jacket, 45

*East of the Sun and West of the Moon*, 64
Eastern Europe—stories from, 168-69
Egielski, Richard, 45, 49, 63, 72, 79, 94, 95, 127
Ehlert, Lois, 95, 115
Eisner, Elliot, 7, 29
Electronic storytellers, 12
*Elfwyn's Saga*, 3, 45, 48, 79, 95
Elitism, 161
Elkind, David, 6
Emberley, Ed, 115
*Emperor and the Kite*, 168
*Encounter*, 46, 48, 50, 62, 73, 181
Endpapers, 46-48
*Errata*, 8
Esbensen, Barbara Juster, 181
Escher, M.C., 87
*Essentials of Children's Literature, The*, 30
Establishing shot, 48
Estes, Clarissa Pinkola, 9
Ethnocentrism, 161
Ethnogenesis, xvii
Ets, Marie Hall, 172
Eurocentrism, 161
Europe—stories from, 168-69
Evans, Walker, 157
Everett, Gwen, 87
*Everyone Knows What a Dragon Looks Like*, 51, 77
*Experiences in Visual Thinking*, 25

*Fables*, 50, 79, 95
Facial expressions (in picture books), 63
Fairy tales, 10
Federal Office Systems Exposition, 23
Feelings, Muriel, 95, 98
Feelings, Tom, 95, 98
Film theory, 59
*Find Your ABCs*, 180
*Fish Eyes*, 95
Fishbeck, Linda Ellis, 112
5P Approach, 61
*Follow the Drinking Gourd*, 76
*Fool of the World and the Flying Ship, The*, 43, 79, 168
Form—as a selection criteria, 111
*Fortune*, 150
*Fortune Tellers, The*, 75, 127, 151, 152
Fox, Mem, 136
*Fox's Dream*, 48, 51
France—stories of, 169-70
*Free Fall*, 52, 68, 72, 76, 118, 119
Free rider effect, 41
*Freight Train*, 118
French, Fiona, 46, 79, 98
*Friendly Wolf*, 179
Fritz, Jean, 180
*Frog Went A-Courtin'*, 170

## 200 Index

From Reverence to Rape, 153
Front matter, 48
*Funny Hats*, 114
*Funny Little Woman*, 171

Gammell, Stephen, 51, 62, 95, 126, 173, 181, 182
*Garden of Abdul Gasazi, The*, 28, 76, 87, 95
Gay, Tanner Otley, 113
Gender fair (in literature), 153-56
*George and Martha Encore*, 180
Gerbner, George, 12
Gestures (in picture books), 61
Giannetti, Louis, 59
*Girl Who Loved Wild Horses, The*, 72, 79, 86, 172, 181
*Glorious Flight, The*, 51, 169
*Go Away, Big Green Monster*, 115
*Go Away, Stay Away*, 50, 76, 93, 95, 147
*Goat in the Rug*, 182
Goble, Paul, 45, 72, 79, 86, 89, 150, 172, 181, 182
*Golden Age, The*, 87
*Golden Deer, The*, 48, 51, 75
Golden Kite Award, 98
*Goldilocks and the Three Bears*, 43
*Golem, The*, 29
*Good Giants and the Bad Puckwudgies*, 180
*Good Morning, Maxine*, 75
Goode, Diane, 134, 157
*Graceland*, 165
Grahame, Kenneth, 87
*Grandfather's Journey*, xviii, 166, 171
*Grandmother's Album*, 110
Graves, Sharol, 182
*Great Big Schoolhouse*, 180
Great Britain—stories of, 170-71
*Great Kapok Tree, The*, 9, 46
*Great Race, The*, 182
*Green Man, The*, 3, 49, 50, 65, 72, 73, 74, 88, 125, 126, 129, 130
*Grey Lady and the Strawberry Snatcher*, 118
Grossman, Virginia, 45, 46, 150, 180
*Grouchy Lady Bug*, 115
*Growing Up in Prime Time*, 153
*Guess Who's Coming to Dinner*, 150
Guided imagery, 24
Gutter (of the book), 51-52

Hader, Berta, 179, 180
Hader, Elmer, 179, 180
Haginikitas, Mary, 90
*Hailstones and Halibut Bones*, 180
Haining, Peter, 112
Haley, Gail E., 2, 3, 4, 9, 10, 30, 31, 32, 33, 34, 42, 43, 45, 46, 47, 48, 49, 50, 51, 52, 63, 65, 66, 67, 68, 69, 71, 72, 73, 74, 75, 76, 88, 90, 93, 94, 95, 96, 97, 98, 124, 125, 126, 127, 129, 130, 131, 132, 134, 135, 147, 150, 155, 159, 165, 167
Hall, Donald, 95
Hamilton, Virginia, 151
Handford, Martin, 8,
Handforth, Thomas, 168
Handicapism, 161
Hans Christian Andersen Medal, 85, 99
*Hansel and Gretel*, 42, 77, 87
*Harlequinades*, 112
Harris, Louis, xvii
Haskell, Molly, 153
*Haunted House*, 107, 108
*Hawk, I'm Your Brother*, 181
Hawkins, Colin, 114
Hawkins, Jacqui, 114
Hearne, Betsy, 117
Heath, Mini, 90
*Heather Has Two Mommies*, 9
*Heckedy Peg*, 48, 49, 51, 52, 63, 76, 88
Heins, Ethel, 13
*Her Seven Brothers*, 182
*Hero with a Thousand Faces, The*, 10
Hero-quest, 43
*Hershel and the Hanukkah Goblins*, 79
*Hey Al*, 45, 49, 63, 72, 79, 94, 95, 127
Heyer, Marilee, 51, 52, 68, 150
*Hi Mom, I'm Home*, 115
Hicks, Ray, 158
Hill, Eric, 180
Hillbillies (stereotype), 157-59
Hirschfelder, Arlene, 178, 179, 182
Hispanic stereotypes, 172
Hitchcock, Alfred, 60
Hodges, Margaret, 46, 48, 51, 66, 69, 75, 77, 86, 98, 126, 130, 155, 170
Hoffman, Mary, 46, 150
Hogarth famous painter look up first name, 88-89
Hogrogian, Nonny, 168, 170
Hom, Nancy, 150
*Honeybee and the Robber, The*, 107
Horizontal book shape, 51
*Horn Book*, 8, 14, 70, 85, 90, 146
Hortin, John, 25
*How a Picture Book Is Made*, 44
*How Schools Shortchange Girls*, 154
*How the Ox Star Fell from Heaven*, 150
Hughes, Shirley, 9, 33
*Human Body*, 107, 108
Human communication, 14
Human emotion (in picture books), 62
Hunt, Peter, 9
*Hurricane*, 46, 51, 52, 63, 68, 76, 128, 129
Hyman, Trina Schart, 46, 49, 66, 69, 75, 77, 79, 85, 86, 98, 126, 127, 130, 133, 151, 152, 155, 168, 170

*I Spy: The Lift-the-Flap ABC Book*, 114
*If It Weren't for You*, 180
*Iktomi and the Buffalo Skull*, 117, 181
*Iktomi* series, 117
*Illiterate America*, 7
Illustration, 85-106
Image-based technologies, 21
Imagery, 5-8, 21-22, 23
    guided, 24
    in instruction, 24
*In a Dark, Dark Wood*, 113
*In the Night Kitchen*, 75, 87
*Inch Boy, The*, 51, 61
India—stories from, 171
*Indian in the Cupboard*, 178
Ingmells, Rex, 90
Ingram, Jerry, 180
*Instructional Innovator*, 26
Instructional technology, 22
*Interaction of Media, Cognition and Learning, The*, 27
International Visual Literacy Association, xiii
*Is This a Baby Dinosaur?*, 115
Isms, 160-62
*It Was a Dark and Stormy Night: Mystery Whodunit*, 113

*Jack and the Bean Tree*, 3, 10, 30, 32, 42, 43, 7591, 93, 130, 147, 158
*Jack and the Fire Dragon*, 10, 33, 43, 45, 67, 68, 76, 95, 126, 158
*Jack Jouett's Ride*, 50, 88
Jack tales, 157
Jameson, Cynthia, 59
Japan—stories from, 171-72
Jeffers, Susan, 48, 150, 180, 181
*John Rose and the Midnight Cat*, 98
*Johnny Guitar*, 65
Johnson, William H., 87
Jones, Hettie, 181
*Josephina Story Quilt*, 180
*Joshua's Massai Mask*, 150
Joslin, Sesyle, 180
*Journey to the Center of the Earth*, 43
Joyner, Jerry, 116
*Jumanji*, 28, 68, 76, 124, 128, 173

Kate Greenaway Medal, 98
Kaye, Marilyn, 117
Keats, Ezra Jack, 91, 151, 166, 173
*Keepers of the Earth*, 150
Kellogg, Steven, 44, 91, 123
Kerr, Judith, 114
Kimmel, Eric, 79
*King Bidgood's in the Bathtub*, 51, 76
Kirstein, Lincoln, 4
Kleven, Elisa, 150

*Knots on a Counting Rope*, 3, 45, 48, 62, 94, 181
*Koala Lou*, 136
Kozol, Johnathan, 7-8
Kramer, Stanley, 150
Kuipers, Barbara J., 178
Kusugak, Michael, 182

*L'il Abner*, 157
Lacapa, Michael, 89
Lacy, Lyn, 145
*Ladder to the Sky*, 181
LaMarche, Jim, 67
*Langstaff, John*, 170
Laura Ingalls Wilder Award, 85
Lawson, Robert, 179
Learning from visuals, 25-28
Lecapa, Michael, 29
Lee, Jeanne, 150
Leech, Jay, 181
*Legend*, 43, 65
*Legend of the Bluebonnet, The*, 72, 79, 130, 181
*Legend of the Indian Paintbrush*, 164
Lent, Blair, 5, 51, 150, 171, 182
Leodhas, Sorche Nic, 170
Lesser, Rika, 77, 87
*Let Us Now Praise Famous Men*, 157
Librarians, 41
Lift-the-flap books, 109, 114
*Li'l Sis and Uncle Willie*, 87
Link, Martin, 182
Linoleum cut, 95
*Lion and the Unicorn, The*, 85
Literacy, 6
Literature-based learning, 14
*Little Hiawatha*, 180
*Little Leo*, 180
*Little Nemo in Slumberland*, 87
*Little Red Riding Hood*, 46, 49, 77, 168
*Little Runner of the Longhouse*, 180
Lobel, Arnold, 50, 59, 79, 86, 95, 180
Locker, Thomas, 14, 45, 49, 87, 150
*Lon Po Po*, 45, 48, 70, 75, 87, 150, 159, 168
London, Jonathan, 45, 150
Long, Sylvia, 45, 46, 150, 180
Long-term recall, 25
*Look Out*, 114
Lopez, Barry, 180
*Lost Lake, The*, 48, 51
*Love Flute*, 45, 150
Lucas, George, 109
Lynch, Nancy, 110

Macaulay, David, 3, 4, 51, 98, 116, 173
*Madeline*, 130
*Madeline's Rescue*, 169
*Magic Windows*, 112
Maher, Ramona, 181

## 202 Index

*Making Tracks*, 115
Malotki, Ekkehart, 29, 89
*Mandarin Ducks, The*, 150
*Manners and Morals: Hogarth and British Painting 1700-1760*, 88
Marantz, Kenneth, 5
Marcellino, Fred, xiv, 32, 45, 49, 51, 62, 68, 77
Marshall, James, 180
Martin Jr., Bill, 3, 45, 48, 62, 94, 181
*Marushka's Egg*, 77
Mass media and reading, 12
Mathers, Petra, 46
Mayer, Mercer, 51, 74, 77
McCay, William, 113
McCay, Winsor, 87
McCloskey, Robert, 3, 173
McCully, Emily Arnold, 46, 86, 87, 125, 169
McDermott, Gerald, 10, 29, 43, 89, 129, 151, 155, 165, 172, 180, 181
MCGFDAAW, 162
McGowan, Alan, 107
McKenzie, Buck, 90
McKillip, Patricia, 134
McKim, Robert, 25
McKissak, Patricia, 76, 127
Mechanical books, 112-13
Media, 91-94
  literacy, xvi, 2, 25, 31
Media center, 41
Mediacracy, 1
Meeks, Raymond, 90
Meggendorfer, Lothar, 112
*Mei Li*, 168
Melmed, Laura Krauss, 67
Memory, 27
Messages, xv
Messenger, Norman, 114
Mexico—stories about, 172
*Mighty Hunter*, 180
Mikolaycak, Charles, 2, 48, 86, 125
*Mildred Pierce*, 65
Miller, Jonathan, 107, 108
Minneapolis Public Schools, xv
Minorities, 164-66
*Mirandi and Brother Wind*, 76, 127
*Mirette on the High Wire*, 46, 67, 86, 87, 125, 154, 169
Moerbeek, Kees, 113, 115
*Moja Means One*, 95
Molan, Chris, 180
Montage, 60
*Moon in my Room*, 125
*Moon Lady*, 150
*Moon Man*, 90
Moonshiners (stereotype), 157-59
Moore, Robert, 179
Morimoto, Junko, 51, 67, 98
Mosely, Keith, 180
Moser, Barry, 135, 157

*Most Amazing Hide-and-Seek Alphabet Book*, 113
*Most Amazing Pop-Up Book of Machines*, 113
*Mother Goose Favorites*, 112
Motion (cues of), 33
*Mountain Jack Tales*, 4, 49, 96, 159
*Mouse Couple, The*, 29, 89
Movable books, 112
Movement (of books), 111-12
*Mud Pony*, 182
*Mufaro's Beautiful Daughters: An African Tale*, 50-51, 52, 63, 72, 90, 135
Multicultural education, xvii, xviii, 14, 156-57
  and art, 89-91
Munsch, Robert, 182
Murphy, Jim, 160
Musgrove, Margaret, 50, 72, 77, 165, 167

Naisbitt, John, 6
*Napping House, The*, 48, 76
*Nation at Risk, A*, 146
National Catholic Education Association, 2
National Education Association, 146
National Leadership Conference on Media Literacy, 2
Native Americans, 150, 176, 178-81
  stories of, 172-73
Native North America—stories of, 172-73
Ness, Evaline, 173
*Never Cry Wolf*, 160
*New Advocate, The*, 85, 145
*New at the Zoo*, 113
*New York Times* Best Illustrated Children's Book of the Year, 98
Newman, Leslie, 9
Nielsen, Kay, 64, 77
*Nine Days to Christmas*, 172
*Nine-In-One*, 150
Nister, Ernest, 112
*Noah's Ark*, 9, 45, 50, 51, 75, 118
Nodelman, Perry, 123
Nonlinear books, 109
Nonlinear storytelling, 116-18
Noonuccal, Kabul, 90
Noonuccal, Ooderoo, 90
Norman, Howard, 182
North Carolina Department of Public Instruction, xv
*Nude Descending a Staircase*, 33
Number three (3), The (in stories), 43

O'Neill, Mary, 180
*Old-Fashioned Garden*, 110
*On Market Street*, 79
*On Mother's Lap*, 182

*On the Horizon*, 93
*Once a Mouse*, 50, 51, 93, 95, 165, 168, 171
*Open Eye in Learning*, xix
Opening sequence, 48
*Ordinary People*, 72
Oregon, xv
*Orpheus*, 48, 86
Ortiz, Simon, 182
Osband, Gillan, 113
Osofsky, Audrey, 150, 181
*Outside Over There*, 4
*Outwitting the Devil*, 157
*Owl Moon*, 14, 49, 50, 51, 68, 79, 94, 126, 128, 135, 173
*Ox-Cart Man*, 95

Pages, 74-76
Painting, 95
*Pancakes for Breakfast*, 118
Panels, 74-76
Panoramas (books), 109, 115
*Papa, Please Get the Moon for Me*, 115
Paper performance, 111
Papercut, 95
Parent's Choice Award Book for Illustration, 98
Parker, Nancy Winslow, 182
Parker, Robert Andrew, 181
Parnall, Peter, 166, 181
Parrish, Maxfield, 86
Partial pages (book shape), 115
Patriarchy, 161
Patrick, Denise Lewis, 150
Patterson, Katherine, 124, 150
Peet, Bill, 179, 180
Pelham, David, 107, 108
Pencil, 95
*People Shall Continue*, 182
Perdue, Charles, 157
Perspectives, multiple, 2
*Peter Pan*, 180
Photographs—preferences, 28
*Picture Book Animated, The*, 90
Picture Book of the Year award (Australia), 98
Picture books, xvi, xvii, 1-4, 31, 125
    format and features, 44-52
    language of, 2
    publication of, 13
    selection criteria, 110-11
Pictures
    analysis of, 61
    as an instructional tool, 26
    nontraditional picture books, 107-22
    preferences and processes, 28-33
    research, 28-33
    and words, 123-42
Piehl, Kathy, 110
Pienkowski, Jan, 107, 108
Pinkney, Brian, 45, 96, 97,
Pinkney, Jerry, 48, 51, 76, 98, 127, 128, 135
Pinkney, Robert, 48
*Pish, Posh, Said Hieronymous Bosch*, 45, 48, 49, 77, 87
*Platypus and Kookaburra*, 90
Pluralism, 148-52
Pohrt, Tom, 180
Point of view, 2, 3, 65-66
*Polar Express, The*, 29, 45, 51, 76, 128, 173
Politi, Leo, 166, 173, 180
*Pop-Up Book of Firefighters*, 113
Pop-up books, 109, 111
*Pop-Up, Pull-Tab, Playtime House That Jack Built*, 113
*Popcorn Venus*, 153
Popping-out, 111-12
Popular culture, 8
Position, 69-70
*Possum Magic*, 136
*Post Office Cat, The*, 50, 63, 88, 91, 98
Posture, 61-64
*Power On!: New Tools for Teaching and Learning*, 21
Prejudice, 161
Price, Leontyne, 4, 14, 46, 77
Print bias, 24
Print culture, 14
*Promise Is a Promise, A*, 182
Propaganda, 161
Proportion, 70-71
Props, 72-74
Prose learning, 28
Provensen, Alice, 51, 94, 169
Provensen, Martin P., 51, 94, 169
*Psycho*, 60
Puppets, 24
*Puss in Boots*, 4, 32, 45, 46, 49, 50, 51, 52, 62, 67, 68, 77, 124, 131, 132, 135
PWADs, 162-63
PWANDs, 162-63

*Quail Song*, 182
Questions (development of), 42

Racism, 161
Rael, Elsa, 77
*Rainbabies, The*, 67
*Rainbow Serpent, The*, 90, 98
Rand, Ted, 3, 45, 48, 62, 94, 181
Ransome, Arthur, 43, 73, 150
*Raven*, 151
Read and Company, 112
Reading and mass media, 12
Realism (preferences of children for), 28
*Rebel Without a Cause*, 65
Rebuses, 24
Recall of story, 26

*Red Dancing Shoes*, 150
*Red Fox and His Canoe*, 180
*Relatives Came, The*, 95
Religious defamation, 161
Representation (picture books as), 145-96
Retail stores, 13
Retrieval operations, 26
Review process, 4
Reviewers, 4
Reviews, 4, 5
*Revolving Pictures*, 112
Rhodes, Timothy, 46, 77, 78
*Riddle Flap Book*, 114
Ringgold, Faith, 48, 76, 79, 94, 150, 154
*Rising Voices*, 182
Robbins, Ruth 168
Robinson, Charles, 118
Rohmer, Harriet, 149, 150
*Rojankovsky*, 170
Rooster Crows, 179
Rosen, Marjorie, 153
Roughsey, Dick, 90, 98
*Rumpelstiltskin*, 46, 48, 50, 52, 63, 77, 95
*Running Owl the Hunter*, 180
Rylant, Cynthia, 4, 95, 133, 134, 157

*Sacred Paw, The*, 160
*Sailing Ships*, 107
*Saint George and the Dragon*, 46, 66, 69, 77, 86, 98, 126, 130, 155, 170
*Sam, Bangs & Moonshine*, 173
Sanders, Barry, 160
SanSouci, Robert, 45, 48, 51, 75, 76, 96, 97, 128, 135
SanSousi, Daniel, 48
Savage, Stephen, 115
Sawyer, Robert, 112
Say, Allen, xviii, 51, 62, 70, 76, 77, 150, 166, 171
Say, Donald, 48
Scapegoatism, 161
Scarry, Richard, 179, 180
Schields, Gretchen, 150
Schoenherr, John, 14, 49, 50, 68, 79, 94, 126, 128, 135, 173
*School Library Journal*, 44, 86
Scieska, John, 2, 48, 159, 134
Scott, Ann Herbert, 182
Scratchboard, 96
*Sea Tale*, 31, 32, 33, 34, 46, 49, 50, 51, 66, 72, 75, 93, 95, 135
Seale, Doris, 179
Seattle, Chief, 48, 150, 181
Seeing (ways of), 3
*Seeing With the Mind's Eye*, xv
*Self Portrait*, 133
Selsam, Millicent, 115
Sendak, Maurice, 4, 49, 59, 63, 69, 70, 75, 85, 87, 91, 118, 129, 173, 180

Separate-scene covers, 46
Sequence (of a story), 27
Seurat, Georges, 94
*7 Blind Mice*, 94
Sexism, 153. 161
*Sexism in Children's Books*, 154
Seymour, Peter, 109, 113
*Shadow*, 45, 51, 76, 79, 89, 90, 93, 95, 145, 146, 167
Shadow puppets, 24
Shallow processing, 26
Shannon, David, 46, 48, 50, 62, 73, 181
Shannon, George, 59
Shape, 50-51
Shared inquiry, 42
Shepard, Paul, 160
Short-term recall, 25
Shulevitz, Uri, 43, 51, 79, 118, 125, 168
Sidjakov, Nicholas, 168
*Sign of the Seahorse, The*, 79
*Silent Lotus*, 150
*Silver Pony*, 118
Similarities—judgment of, 10
Singer, Beverly R., 182
Singer, Marilyn, 134
Single-image covers, 46
Sisniewski, David, 3
Sizer, Theodore, xvi
*Sky Dogs*, 135
Slapin, Beverly, 179
Sleator, William, 182
*Sleeping Bread, The*, 46, 77, 78
Smith, Lane, 2, 48, 134, 160
*Smokey and the Bandit*, 157
Sneve, Virginia Driving Hawk, 182
*Snow White in New York*, 98
*Snowman*, 118
*Snowy Day, The*, 151, 166, 173
Snyder, Diane, 70
Social construction
  case studies in, 175-81
  picture books as, 145-96
Society of Children's Book Writers, 98
*Something About the Author, Autobiography Series*, 86, 134
*Song and Dance Man*, 51, 62, 126, 173
*Song of the Swallows*, 166, 173
*South Pacific*, 14
Souza, Diana, 9
Spagnoli, Cathy, 150
Speare, Elizabeth, 182
Spencer, Zane, 181
Sperry, Roger, 5
Spier, Peter, 44, 45, 51, 75, 118
Sports mascots, 176-78
*Spot Goes to School*, 180
*Spotted Eagle and Black Crow*, 150
Spreads, 74-76
Square book shape, 51

Stanley, Diane, 150
*Star Boy*, 182
*Star Maiden*, 181
*Star Wars*, 43
Steenland, Sally, 153
Steptoe, John, 29, 51, 52, 63, 72, 90, 95, 135, 165, 182
Stereotypes, xvii, 157-60, 161, 176-78
    unlearning, 178-81
Stewig, John, 41
*Stinky Cheese Man, The*, 44, 48
*Stonecutter, The*, 29
Stories
    differences between, 43
    sequence of, 27
*Story, A Story, A*, 3, 4, 10, 27, 31, 42, 45, 49, 50, 51, 90, 97, 127, 147, 150, 155, 165, 167
Storytelling—nonlinear, 116-18
*Strega Nona*, 48, 75, 166
Strickland, Rennard, 175
*Stupids Step Out*, 180
Styles (of art), 91-94
*Sukey and the Mermaid*, 45, 48, 96, 97, 135
*Sun Is a Golden Earring, The*, 166
*Sunday in the Park with Georges*, 94
*Sundiata: Lion King of Mali*, 92, 127, 135
*Superman 2*, 66
*Surprise, Surprise*, 112
Sussman, Vic, 12
Sutherland, Zena, 10

*Taking Advantage of Media*, 27
*Talking Eggs, The*, 51, 76, 128, 135
Tan, Amy, 150
*Tar Beach*, 48, 76, 79, 94, 150, 154
Taxel, Joel, 145
Teacher training, 26
Teaching methods, 8
Techniques (of art), 91-94
Technological revolution, 21
Technologies, 23
*Teenage Mutant Ninja Turtles*, 12
*Teenage Mutant Ninja Turtles: The Final Battle*, 12
*Teenage Mutant Ninja Turtles: The Final Lesson*, 12
Tejima, 48, 51
Television, xvi, 31
Television versions (of stories), 27
Television viewers, 27
*Ten Little Rabbits*, 45, 46, 150, 180
*Tenth Good Thing About Barney, The*, 9
*There's a Nightmare in My Closet*, 74
*They Put on Masks*, 180
*They Were Strong and Good*, 179, 180
Thinking
    higher levels of, 29
    skills, 3, 8

*Thirteen*, 116
*Thirteen Moons on Turtle's Back*, 45, 150
Thomas, Clarance, 153
Three (3)—the number, 43
*Three Feathers, The*, 43
*Three Little Pigs, The*, 43
Tick, Raphael, 112
Tilt down (point of view), 65-68
Tilt up (point of view), 65-68
*Time of Wonder*, 173
Tokenism, 161
*Tom Thumb*, 67, 79
Tomblin, Gill, 110
*Tracing a Legend: The Story of the Green Man*, 88
*Tradition and Technique Creating Jack and the Bean Tree*, 147
*Training and Development*, 23
*Treasure*, 51
*Tree of Cranes*, 62, 76, 77, 150
*Trees Stand Shining*, 181
Tresize, Percy, 90, 98
Troy, Lily, 150
*Truck*, 118
*True Story of the Three Little Pigs, The*, 2, 134, 159
*Tuesday*, 46, 51, 60, 63, 76, 118, 119
Type, 49
Typeface, 49

*Understanding Movies*, 59
University of Minnesota, 21
*Unlearning "Indian" Stereotypes*, 175, 179
*Uses of Enchantment, The*, 9

Vaes, Alan, 4
Van Allsburg, Chris, 28-29, 45, 51, 52, 68, 76, 86, 91, 95, 124, 125, 128, 173
van der Meer, Atie, 114
van der Meer, Ron, 107, 114
Verbal messages, 28
Versions (of stories), 2
Vertical book shape, 51
*Very Hungry Caterpillar*, 115
*Very Last First Time*, 182
*Very Long Tail, The*, 115
*Very Long Train*, 115
Viewing skills, 10
VIEWs, xv
Vignettes, 74-76
Viorst, Judith, 9
*Visible and Viable: The Role of Images in Instruction and Communication*, xiii
Visual analysis, 32
Visual communication, xvi
Visual culture, 23

# 206 Index

Visual Information Education Workshops (VIEWs), xv
Visual language, 59-83
Visual literacy, 4, 6, 23-24
*Visual Literacy: Connections to Thinking, Reading and Writing*, 24
Visual literacy movement, 5
Visual messages—analysis of, 60
Visualization, xv
Visuals—learning from, 25-28
Vocabulary, 27
VonMason, Stephen, 150

Wagner, Jenny, 98
Wallace, Ian, 182
*Waltons, The*, 157
Ward, Lynd, 118, 173
*Warrior and the Wise Man, The*, 73, 90, 95
Watson, Clare, 79, 180
Watterson, Bill, 7
*Way to Start a Day*, 166
*We Visit the Seashore*, 112
*Weather Pop-Up Book*, 113
Weatherby, Mark Alan, 160
*Weaving of a Dream, The*, 51, 52, 68, 150
Weisgard, Leonard, 180
Weitzman, Lenore, 178
Westcott, Nadine, 113
Wezyk, Goenni, 77
*What Do You Say, Dear?*, 180
*What's In?* (series), 114
*When I Was Young in the Mountains*, 134, 157
*Where the Buffaloes Begin*, 182
*Where the Forest Meets the Sea*, 94
*Where the Wild Things Are*, 49, 59, 63, 69, 70, 118, 129, 173
*Where's Waldo?*, 8,
*Who's in Rabbit's House?*, 77, 90
*Who-Paddled-Backward-With-Trout*, 182
*Why Mosquitoes Buzz in People's Ears*, 51, 77, 90, 167
*Why the Chicken Crossed the Road*, 116
*Why the Sun and the Moon Live in the Sky*, 51, 150
*Widow's Broom, The*, 28, 45, 51
Wiesner, David, 3, 46, 51, 52, 60, 63, 68, 72, 76, 118, 119, 128, 129
*Wilfred Gordon McDonald Partridge*, 136

Willard, Nancy, 45, 48, 87
Willhoite, Michael, 9
Williams, Cratis, 158
Williams, Jay, 51, 77
Williams, Sherely Anne, 150
Wilson, Francis, 113
*Winter People*, 157
Winter, Jeannette, 76
Winter, Paula, 62
Wisniewski, David, 45, 48, 73, 79, 90, 91, 95, 127, 135
*Wizard of Oz, The*, 10
Wolf, Naomi, 153
*Wolves and Men*, 159
*Women Who Run with the Wolves*, 9
*Wood and Linoleum Illustration*, 93
Wood engraving, 96-97
Wood, Audrey, 48, 49, 51, 52, 63, 76, 88
Wood, Don, 2, 48, 49, 51, 52, 63, 76, 88, 125
Woodcuts, 95
Wordless picture books, 62, 109, 118-19
*Words About Pictures*, 123
Words and pictures, 123-42
*Working Cotton*, 150
Wraparound covers (on books), 45
*Wretched Stone, The*, 29, 128
Writing, 133-36
*Writing with Pictures*, 118
Written expression, 24
Wyllie, Stephen, 113

Xiong, Blia, 150

Yeh, Phoebe, 151
Yolen, Jane, 14, 46, 48, 49, 50, 62, 68, 73, 79, 94, 124, 126, 128, 135, 136, 168, 173, 181
Yorinks, Arthur, 45, 49, 63, 72, 79, 94, 95, 127
Young Author Conferences, 133
Young Author Program, 136
Young, Ed, 45, 48, 70, 75, 87, 94, 150, 159, 168, 180, 181, 182
*Yulu's Coal*, 90

Zelinsky, Paul, 46, 48, 550, 52, 63, 77, 87, 95
Zemach, Margot, 170
Zolotow, Charlotte, 180

# About the Authors

**Dr. David Considine** is a professor of Media Studies/Instructional Technology at Appalachian State University in Boone, North Carolina. He served for several years on the Board of Directors of the International Visual Literacy Association and currently is on the board of the National Telemedia Council. His writings have appeared in numerous academic publications including *School Library Journal, School Library Media Quarterly, Educational Technology,* and others.

He is the recipient of the 1994 Jessie McCanse award for individual contributions to media literacy. A frequent keynote speaker at professional conferences throughout the United States, Dr. Considine also conducts Visual Information Education Workshops (VIEW) as part of an extensive program of in-service teacher education at the national level.

**Gail E. Haley** is one of the counrty's most distinguished authors and illustrators of children's books. She has the distinction of being the only person to have won best children's book awards in the United States and England—the Cadecott Medal and the Kate Greenaway Medal. In her Caldecott medal acceptance speech she warned of television's impact on children, and she has become increasingly involved in creative applications of imagery in instruction, including puppets as teaching tools.

She teaches writing and illustrating for Children and Puppetry in Education in the Reich College of Education at Appalachian State University. Ms. Haley is a frequent visitor to classrooms and libraries throughout the United States and overseas as part of her extensive Author/Artist school programs. Working with children and in-service teacher education, she stresses the creative process involved in the development of children's books, and strategies teachers can use to stimulate creative writing among children.

**Lyn Ellen Lacy** has been an elementary media specialist in Minneapolis Public Schools for 20 years and is the author of the District's manual for teachers, *Visual Education: An Interdisciplinary Approach for Students K-12 Using Visuals of all Kinds*. Her articles and book reviews have appeared in magazines nation-wide.

She is a scriptwriter of filmstrip and video biographies. Her book of criticism, *Art and Design in Children's Picture Books: An Analysis of Caldecott Award-Winning Illustrations* was published by the American Library Association in 1986 and is used as a text in children's literature courses around the country. In 1992-1993 she received a grant from the American Council of Learned Societies to study folklore and storytelling. She is writing a book about creative planning for teachers, a history of Minnehaha Falls, a biography of Clement Clark Moore, and a video with Robert DesJarlait about Ojibway pow wow dancing.